Creating an Excellent School:

Hedley Beare, Brian J. Caldwell
and Ross H. Millikan

ROUTLEDGE
London and New York

First published 1989
by Routledge
11 New Fetter Lane, London EC4P 4EE
29 West 35th Street, New York, NY 10001

© 1989 Hedley Beare, Brian J. Caldwell and Ross H. Millikan
Printed in Great Britain

British Library Cataloguing in Publication Data

Beare, Hedley, *1932*
    Creating an excellent school: some new management
    techniques –
    (Educational management series)
    1. Schools. Management
    I. Title.   II. Caldwell, Brian J., *1941–*   III. Millikan, Ross H.,
    1938–   IV. Series
    371.2
    ISBN 0–415–00584–1

Library of Congress Cataloging in Publication Data

Available on request.

Contents

Contents

Contents

Figures

Tables

Foreword

There is much talk these days, in both educational and political circles, about the pursuit of excellence in schools; and a great deal of this talk is unproductive, seeking scapegoats, or looking for instant panaceas. Excellent schools are, as this book demonstrates, the product of good management. Good management, in its turn, depends on a clear understanding of valid management theory and, even more important, the ability to translate that theory into practice.

This volume offers profound insights, in a refreshingly readable manner, into those crucial areas of leadership, culture, structure and public accountability. At the same time there is a sense of vision in the writing, an essential antidote to the gloom and doom widely prevalent in education in many developed countries. It may be that we are so preoccupied with the immediate effects of change that we have lost the ability to visualise long-term benefits. One of the most striking passages in the book looks at the changes that the exponential growth of information technology - home microcomputer and interactive video - may well bring about in our concept of schooling in little more than a decade. Another chapter, **Re-conceptualising the school**, looks at the many innovations that are already experimentally current - flexitime, the vertical curriculum, mastery learning, community support - and depicts ways in which these can be knit together into a total educational experience.

The authors have an extensive knowledge and experience of educational practice in Australia, North America and Europe, linked with a sound grasp of educational theory. They also write well, an attribute not necessarily allied to knowledge. This is a book which a wide range of readers in many countries will find of value: school teachers and school leaders, administrators, lay members of governing bodies and educational committees, lecturers and consultants in education management. **Creating an Excellent School** is a worthy addition to the Routledge (formerly Croom Helm) education management series.

Cyril Poster

Preface:
Why this Book is Necessary

This book is addressed to those who are involved in the running of schools, especially to principals and their senior staffs, but also to those parents and administrators who participate in policy-making about schools. We have tried to make the book not only readable and informative but also of practical value in the day-to-day management of schools.

There are two fundamental reasons why this book has become a necessity. The first is that school administration now takes place in an increasingly turbulent, politically charged environment; bluntly, running schools has become a tough job which involves very much more knowledge and skill than it did even a decade ago. And secondly, there has been almost a revolution in the writings and theories about educational administration since about 1975, largely as a result of the same environmental forces which have so complicated the life of school managers. In consequence, it is essential that those who are running schools or deciding policies about them should be up-to-date in their concepts about management and should not be trying to operate with outmoded concepts. In this book, therefore, we explain why some of the new ideas developed when they did; and then we have tried to put many of these ideas into a form which will make them readily usable by managers and policy makers.

We can demonstrate these changes in several ways, and we amplify our views in the chapters which follow. But to illustrate:

• Since the early 1970s, when so much was written about innovation and change, there has been enormous development in the way we conceive of the change process and change strategies. For example, it is likely that people will now talk of entrepreneurship and intrapreneurship rather than about innovation, and when that term is used it usually is in such contexts as product innovation, or innovation in technology.

• Since the early 1980s, there has been a stream of new ideas about leadership which go far beyond the 'traits' approaches of a decade ago. The 'great man administrator' theories (they developed well before the feminist movement appeared) have now been thoroughly superseded, largely because organisations can no longer afford to function on such strictly hierarchical and centralist lines.

• There is a profound shift occurring in the way we conceive of school systems, especially public school systems. Put simply, the focus has moved away from system administration and towards viewing schools as the essential units in the delivery of learning programmes. System control is giving way to system co-ordination, schools are becoming much more independent and self-determining, school governance has taken over from the central administration many of the functions which were once carried out systemically, and the systems (or governments) have become much more concerned with setting priorities and laying down adequate accountability patterns.

In short, the landscape of school management has changed; we believe it will change even more as the post-industrial economy arrives. There will be more emphasis placed upon the way individual schools operate and are managed because education is so centrally located in the service and information sectors - the expanding parts of the new international economic order. Those who are running schools are expected to be quite sophisticated in their management techniques; and they also are expected to be expert in the theories about management.

Because of the point we have made above about the shift in the way people are now conceiving of public education, with an emphasis upon the school as the prime unit for the delivery of an education service, we have chosen in this book to concentrate on the management of schools per se rather than of school systems or of clusters of schools, though we are aware that many of the concepts we discuss are applicable in educational administration wherever it is practised.

In recent years those connected to education have grown used to the words efficiency, effectiveness, excellence and equity (or equality) - as though the four Es have now replaced the three Rs. Even so, the vocabulary signals a profound shift, for it means that the contributions which education makes to the country's productivity, its competitiveness in international trade, its social stability and its political competence has at last been recognised. Unless education performs, the country cannot prosper. Schools which do not measure up to the high (and sometimes unrealistic) expectations held by parents, politicians and the community will come under very intense pressure, and may well lose money, resources and students. We are aware, then, that those involved in the management of schools need access to the newest ideas and to the techniques which embody them.

The book draws on material which has already been field-tested in dozens of seminars and workshops which we have run, and from our use of these ideas with literally thousands of teachers. Much of the content of this book has already appeared in the articles which we have written and which we know have been widely photocopied and quoted. So we are confident not only about the acceptability but also about the practicality of what we have included here. The book attempts to bring these materials together into one place so that they are more easily accessible to those involved in school management; the ideas do cohere, and they now constitute a reliable base upon which deliberate planning and action can be built.

We are grateful to many people who have supported the production of this book; not the least are our spouses who have not only given us continuous encouragement but have also had to adopt the project as an intrusive member of our families. Typing and production of the script have been expertly handled by Mrs Dorothy Rowlands (now Clarke) and the final typing, re-typing and computer setting by Ms Trudy Lingwood, with significant computer typesetting assistance given by Ailsa Mackenzie and Ross Millward; without their skill, perceptiveness, good humour and unwavering commitment, the book quite literally could never have come into existence.

1

The Movement to Create
Excellent Schools

There are two strong trends which since the mid-1970s have substantially changed the way we now regard and manage schools. The first has been called 'the effective schools movement'; it was in fact a concerted attempt in several countries to rediscover ways of creating really excellent schools. The movement has produced an impressive literature which school managers cannot afford now to overlook.

The second movement was a profound change in the field of study called educational management in Great Britain, and educational administration in North America and Australia, and which has tended to make many of the ideas inherited from before 1975 obsolescent. In this chapter, then, we deal both with the issue of effective schools and with why the matter became so prominent in the early 1980s. In the next chapter we address the advent of new ideas about educational administration and school management.

But this book is not merely an excursion into ideas. We want also to discover what can be done with the notions produced by these developments. In precise terms how can we change the ways schools are run and administered by capitalising on these developments of recent years? In Chapter 4, therefore, we return to the outcomes of these recent movements and endeavour to suggest patterns of operation which might embody the new ideas about school management.

From School Effects to Effective Schools:
the movement from Coleman to Edmonds

One of the most influential scholars connected with the effective schools movement, Ronald Edmonds, wrote in December 1982,

'Educators have become increasingly convinced that the characteristics of schools are important determinants of academic achievement' (Edmonds, 1982: 4). This view is the antithesis of the one widely held in the late 1960s and early 1970s, namely that schools do not make much difference. As Shoemaker and Fraser (1981: 179) point out, disbelief in the efficacy of schools crystallised in 1966 with the publication of the Coleman Report in the USA, which had demonstrated that:

> home environment variables were the most important in explaining the variance in achievement levels for all racial and regional groups, and school facilities and curriculum were the least important variables.

So what caused the change in attitude in the period between Coleman and Edmonds?

From the early 1960s investigation after investigation came up with the same result, that a student's progress at school, his or her success in academic study, is overwhelmingly more dependent on home background than on what the school does for the students. As far back as 1959, the UK Crowther Report had shown the close association between a father's occupation and the educational achievement of his children.

The Robbins Report in 1962, an investigation into the need for places in higher education in Great Britain, took the group of men and women who turned 21 in 1962 and classified them according to characteristics of their parents. Of those whose fathers left school before they turned 16, only 5 per cent went on to higher education; of those whose fathers studied beyond the age of 18, 57 per cent went on to higher education. Put another way, if that cohort is divided according to the occupation of their fathers, 45 per cent of those with fathers in the well-paid professions (doctors, lawyers, senior civil servants) went on to higher education, whereas of those whose fathers were in semi-skilled or unskilled jobs, only 2 per cent went on to higher education (Robbins Report, 1963: 49-54). On the basis of the socio-economic status of the parents, you can predict what the student's school record will be like.

But the most impressive documentation of this thesis resulted from the American study headed by Professor James Coleman, and conducted in the USA in the mid-1960s. It was one of the most comprehensive student surveys ever attempted, covering thousands of children from every part of the nation. The Coleman Report (entitled *Equality of Educational Opportunity*) caused immediate argument around the world when it was published in 1966, for its most controversial finding was 'that schools bring little influence to bear upon a child's achievement that is independent of his background and general social context' (Coleman, 1966: 325).

The follow-up study by Christopher Jencks (1972) reaffirmed the same result and sparked off a similar public debate. The two reports, to quote Kerensky's summary, seemed to prove that:

> the school is a much smaller part of a child's total education than most teachers and parents have assumed . . . What the child brings to school is more important than what happens in the classroom in determining the kind of person he will become (Kerensky, 1975: 44).

Australian evidence made the same kind of point. For example, in the 1960s and 1970s a team of researchers from the Centre for Research in Measurement and Evaluation in New South Wales followed a generation of students through their secondary schooling. From interviews with students and their parents, the researchers created an index to give a reading on 'opinion of schooling'. In only 3 per cent of cases did father and mother have strongly different views about the school and in only 6 per cent of the cases did the student's opinion vary strongly from the father's and mother's; in short, in most homes, mother, father and child all hold the same opinion about the child's school. About one home in four, across all classes of society, was dissatisfied with schooling. The report stated that 'the survival patterns of students from satisfied homes are strikingly different from the survival patterns of the dissatisfied students' (Moore, 1974: 8).

Three-quarters of the students from satisfied homes survived beyond year 10 (age 15/16), yet from the dissatisfied homes, only one half survived to year 10 and only one in six went beyond that level. Thus the parent's satisfaction with the school appears to be an accurate gauge of how well the student is performing. The Generation Study data could be considered from a second perspective. Define the parents' satisfaction with their child's schooling, their socio-economic level, their occupation and so on, feed this in to the computer, and one can predict fairly accurately what does in

3

fact happen to the child, at what year she will drop out of schooling, what her achievement patterns will be up to that point, and what occupation she is likely to pursue.

So The Generation Study researchers concluded:

> When home-based educational objectives clash with school-based objectives, the student normally resolves the conflict by rejecting school. The key figures in this whole dynamic social complex are the parents. It is the parents who can accept or reject aims projected into the home from the surrounding environment; it is parents who evolve the family system of values about education; and it is parents who reject or accept school values . . . It is a most curious paradox that the whole enterprise appears to stand or fall according to the support or opposition of parents - most of whom rarely, if ever, make an appearance on school premises or show any concern or interest in school happenings and affairs. (*ibid.*: 25)

If it is so demonstrable that home and family backgrounds have such an enormous impact on how well a student performs at school, why have not educators invented more efficient models of teaching and learning which link the two prime movers - the home and the school - in some clearly articulated, reinforcing way?

In fact, there were developments along these lines. The most obvious one to gather impetus from these studies was the movement to create boards or councils which involved parents (or parent representatives) in making the decisions about the school in which their children were enrolled. Across the Western world the powers and membership of school governing bodies were revised and where such bodies did not previously exist there were moves to set them up.

In several of the federal programmes instituted in the United States of America, it was a condition of receiving the grants that a school-site council be set up to help administer the funds. In several of the Australian States and Territories, school councils came into existence or else had their powers extended. And in Great Britain, the Taylor Report (1977) recommended important changes to the composition of Boards of Governors and Boards of Managers. In short, education authorities tried to invent formal mechanisms to link school and home in the management of the school.

There was also a concerted attempt to involve parents more fully in the learning programmes for their children. There was a variety of 'open education' techniques tried, and a proliferation of open-plan classrooms in which it was relatively easy for parent aides to be used as assistants to the teachers. A new range of assessment and reporting techniques came into play, and more adequate methods for the school to use to advise parents about the educational progress of their children were invented. In the process, of course, the management of schools became so much the more complicated.

Even so, it remains true that the children of the rich tend to go to richly endowed schools, that children whose parents are educated continue to win almost any educational race against those whose parents are uneducated, that children who have fathers in professional occupations crowd the others out of the available university places, that money spent on upper secondary and higher education continues to subsidise the children of the well-to-do and the middle class and that the school which deliberately sets out to serve the children of the uneducated and the poor is *not* looked upon as an excellent school until it can demonstrate that the children who attend it have made demonstrable gains on normal test scores or in examinations and can compete with students from the more privileged suburbs.

If we needed more evidence, one has only to study some of the effects of the programmes initiated by the Australian Schools Commission since 1972, or to read a book like Connell's *Making the Difference* (1982). In short, the Coleman findings have not only stood scrutiny but also constitute a threat to the existing social order, as well as to the schools which serve that society.

But the social order itself was under attack from other quarters too. The period when the efficacy of conventional schooling was being questioned coincided with developments like the war on poverty; the emancipation of women and the feminist movement; civil rights and in particular the rights of minority groups; the so-called new international economic order, and the emergence politically, economically and ideologically of Third World countries; the conservation ('green') movement; and, importantly for our purposes, the alternative schools movement, acceptance of lifelong learning in a variety of locations, learning networks, alternative and new curricula and learning programmes, and the rise in influence of people like Paulo Freire and Ivan Illich.

People began to understand that conventional schools may unwittingly - or quite wittingly - reaffirm an unjust social order and notions of class distinctions and privilege, that they can be a means of cultural reproduction and that left to their own devices they will probably produce more of the same. To invent alternatives to the current models for schools can therefore be profoundly disturbing to those who now occupy positions of influence and authority, and threatening to those whom the present system has given preferential treatment, status and improved life chances. So it was almost inevitable that there would be some kind of counter-revolution.

The movement to re-establish the reputation of conventional schooling gathered momentum in the late 1970s. In an article published in the Winter of 1973, Klitgaard and Hall asked whether it was possible to identify 'unusually effective schools', for there appeared to be evidence of 'schools and districts that consistently produced outstanding students, even after socio-economic factors were controlled for' (Klitgaard and Hall, 1973: 90).

Of particular interest in this study is that neither researcher was an educator; Klitgaard was an economist with the Rand Corporation and Hall was a Deputy Assistant Secretary in the Department of Defence. Yet even to them it was obvious that something was wrong with the research which consistently failed to show that what goes on in schools influences both how and what children learn. They stated what educators know from experience:

Considering the enormous diversity among the nation's public schools, it would surely be incredible if some were not much better than others. Furthermore, parents and children, administrators and teachers, journalists and taxpayers seem to act as if some schools were unusually effective. (*ibid.*: 91)

And, of course, it is demonstrable that schools do differ on important points.

Some schools consistently have higher achievement scores, lower dropout rates, more college-bound graduates, wealthier alumni and so forth. But these results cannot be entirely attributed to the schools themselves. Pupils bring different amounts of intellectual capital [hear the economists speaking!] to their educational experiences (*ibid.*: 91).

Schools can hardly pride themselves on making higher profits than their competitors if they have much more capital to work with in the first place. But of course they do pride themselves on that; everyone wants to be a millionaire, and envies those who are. That is the insistent problem concerning which schools are labelled effective.

Klitgaard and Hall made an important contribution to the debate by stating that researchers should be looking at the exceptions rather than the averages.

> Surprisingly little research [they observed] has addressed the question of unusually effective schools. Scholarly analysis has concentrated on the average effects of all school policies on educational outcomes (*ibid*.: 92-93).

Although stories about successes existed, the analyses dwelt on programmes rather than schools, on averages across the student population rather than on pockets of 'outliers' - the students or schools where the unusual, unexpected, extraordinary seemed to be occurring. Might there not be more profit in following up the differences rather than the commonalities? So their article is indicative of the change in attitudes which was occurring in the mid-1970s. More importantly, it is a harbinger for a change in methodology, away from large-scale statistical reviews and towards case studies, towards analyses of exemplars.

Another provocative finding emerged too, for they raised the point that the school may not be the best unit of analysis. Might there not be unusually effective year-levels or individual classes? Might there not be unusually effective teachers? And are there unusually effective regions / districts / areas (or school systems)?

Rutter study

So the late 1970s produced some significant studies aimed at showing that schools do make a difference to pupil achievement and at pin-pointing what characteristics were common to those schools which were shown to be effective. One of the most important of these studies was that conducted in twelve inner London schools over an eight-year period by Michael Rutter and a team from the University of London; the findings were published in 1979 as a book entitled *Fifteen Thousand Hours*. In a very useful introductory chapter dealing with previous research, Rutter

(1979: 1) concluded that:

> it does matter which school a child attends. Moreover, the
> results provide strong indications of what are the particular
> features of school organisation and functioning which make
> for success.

The Rutter study was unusual in that it was longitudinal over
eight years from 1970 onwards, dealt with secondary rather than
primary schools and subjected its data to careful statistical and
objective analysis. It concentrated on changes - increments - in
pupil achievement to demonstrate the school's quality (Rutter,
1979: 5). The school effects which the study team looked for
were high attendance (that is, less truancy), observed good
behaviour in school, the proportion of delinquent students at the
school and the school's results in public examinations. The team
found that some characteristics - like the age of the school buildings - had no effect on the outcome measures. The following
seemed to characterise the good schools (Maughan and Ouston,
1979: 18-24):

• Their lessons were work-oriented with time focused on subject
matter rather than on behaviour or administration
• Teachers worked and planned together, and there was strong
supervision and coordination by senior teachers
• Formal reward systems, public commendation, and immediate
feedback to students on good performance existed in the good
schools
• Students were expected to take responsibility for day-to-day
matters in their school - like looking after their own books and
facilities
• Homework was set and followed up. The good schools openly
emphasised academic performance and students were expected to
work hard and to succeed
• The good schools had a good atmosphere and ethos.

American studies

On the other side of the Atlantic, studies carried out in the USA
in the late 1970s were also developing an inventory of the characteristics which seemed to be common to those schools judged to
be excellent or effective. D'Amico (1982: 61) has commented that

four studies laid the groundwork for most school improvement efforts, namely those by Brookover and Lezotte (1979), Edmonds and Frederickson (1979), Rutter (1979) and Phi Delta Kappa (1980), but one could also include Weber's of 1971 and Austin's Maryland study (1978). These studies seem to be among the most frequently cited.

Weber, 1971

The study by George Weber was conducted in 1971, and was principally concerned with how well inner-city children could be taught to read; effectiveness was therefore measured by a reading achievement test. The study concerned four city schools (two in New York, one in Kansas City and one in Los Angeles). The common factors he observed in the four schools making up his case studies were strong leadership, high teacher expectations of the students, an orderly purposeful school climate and (not surprisingly) strong stress on reading.

Austin, 1978

The study by Gilbert Austin (1978) in Maryland identified eighteen high-achieving and twelve low-achieving schools, found to be 'outliers' from the states' 'accountability data'; so his were 'case studies of exceptional schools' (Austin, 1979: 12). The factors which accounted for differences among schools were strong principals who participated in the instructional programme; high expectations held by those principals about themselves, the teachers and the students; and a school programme which emphasised intellectual rather than affective goals.

Brookover and Lezotte, 1979

The Brookover and Lezotte (1979) study was carried out on six 'improving' primary schools and two 'declining' schools in Michigan, using a case study method which allowed the researchers to conclude that the improving schools were likely to have principals who were curriculum leaders, who asserted themselves in that role, who maintained tough discipline and who assumed responsibility for evaluating pupil achievements.

Phi Delta Kappa, 1980

The Phi Delta Kappa study included case studies of eight exceptional primary schools as well as material from 59 other cases and about 40 research or evaluation studies; it also used eleven experts. Effective leaders, it claimed, were those who set goals and performance standards, and maintained a good working environment. They were 'enablers', giving teachers room to get on with their teaching, and marshalling political, parental and financial support for the school (Shoemaker and Fraser, 1981: 180).

Edmonds and Frederickson, 1979

Ronald Edmonds devoted more than a decade to school improvement. As senior assistant for instruction in the New York City public schools he developed one of the first formal School Improvement Projects in the USA. His research on effective schools began in 1974 with case studies of schools which were 'academically effective with the full range of their pupil population, including poor and minority children' (Willie, 1983: 4). He continued the research when he was a faculty member at Harvard from 1978 to 1981 and thereafter when he moved to Michigan State University. Willie concludes:

> Ron Edmonds' belief that pupil performance depends more on the character of the school than on the nature of the pupil's family captured the imagination of educators . . . [He] did not deny the significance of family background in the adaptation of children, but he gave greater weight to the school's response to the family background of children as the determining factor in pupil performance (*ibid.*).

Edmonds argued that there were five characteristics which seem to be 'the most tangible and indispensable' (Edmonds, 1979: 22) in those effective schools which have been the subject of detailed research. He described those features as follows:

• 'They have strong administrative leadership' (*ibid.*). Later he added the principal's 'attention to the quality of instruction' (Edmonds, 1982: 4)
• They have 'a climate of expectation in which no children are permitted to fall below minimum but efficacious levels of

achievement' (Edmonds, 1979: 4)
- 'The school's atmosphere is orderly without being rigid, quiet without being oppressive, and generally conducive to the instructional business at hand' (*ibid.*). Elsewhere he calls it an 'orderly, safe climate' (1982: 4)
- The school has 'a pervasive and broadly understood instructional focus' (*ibid.*), and he comments that the effective school is prepared to divert its energy and resources away from other areas in order to further that instructional objective (1979: *loc. cit.*). Indeed, he is quite precise about that instructional focus. 'Pupil acquisition of basic school skills takes precedence over all other school activities' (*ibid.*)
- Finally, effective schools ensure that 'pupil progress can be frequently monitored'. They have the means whereby 'the principal and the teachers remain constantly aware of pupil progress in relationship to instructional objectives' (*ibid.*).

We will return to a consideration of these essential characteristics to be found in a good school. First, however, we need to be aware of some of the factors which shaped the effective schools movement and which led it to take the approaches it did. There are four aspects deserving of comment.

Measuring effectiveness

First 'effectiveness' has always been an elusive term, and it must be clarified before we can understand the significance of what is meant by 'effective schools'. Chester Barnard's definition has been a robust one since he invoked it during the 1930s in his classic work *The Functions of the Executive*. 'An action is effective', he said, 'if it accomplishes its specific objective aim' (Barnard, 1938: 20). 'To effect' means 'to bring about, to accomplish'; thus to be effective, an action or an institution or an individual must bring something about, must accomplish something. Indeed, the term implies that the action is deliberate. You are effective if you set yourself a target and then hit it. Definition of a target is a prior requirement before it is possible to be effective.

There is a distinct difference between 'effectiveness' and 'efficiency'. Both derive from the same Latin roots, and both involve accomplishment, but the word 'efficient' also implies productivity, accomplishing an end without waste of effort or resources; it implies getting value for money.

So a school can be effective but also inefficient; it achieves its objectives but at too great a cost. A school can be efficient (that is, sparing in its use of resources) but not necessarily effective (that is, good at achieving results). A school which is efficient and effective, may not necessarily be excellent - in the sense of being the best among its peers. But most important of all, a school cannot be either efficient or effective unless it has objectives, targets to achievement. So there need to be at least some outcome measures which can be used to separate effective schools from the middling or ineffective ones.

How is one to demonstrate effectiveness, achievement of a sought outcome? The American studies used as performance indicators the national standardised achievement tests. Rutter, on the other hand, used absenteeism, behaviour in school, officially recorded delinquency and public examination results. Thus in the USA 'effectiveness' meant raising the average scores in the school in mathematics and reading. Put bluntly, school effectiveness usually meant literacy and numeracy. Judging the effectiveness of a school by this criterion should cause disquiet to educators.

As we well know, one way to raise the average scores is to exclude from the sample those students whose scores will fall below the average and will therefore pull the average down. This can be done by the simple device of advising the underachieving student to go elsewhere for his or her education; and it is sad to note that some schools have used this device over the years and have been judged excellent accordingly. Suppose we judged the effectiveness of a hospital on the proportion of its patients which it can discharge in good health; the way for a hospital to stay on top of the list would be for it to admit only those patients who were already reasonably healthy or who had a high probability of recovery. To retain its reputation for effectiveness, it would refuse to admit any patient who was terminally ill or whose illness presented the doctors with difficulties, and it would certainly not involve itself in the risky business of experimentation and medical research.

It was so easy to use this effectiveness measure in the late 1970s, when there was so much discussion on school achievement testing, on levels of literacy and numeracy, and so vigorous a campaign about getting back to the basics. 'Mastery learning' also grew up in this period. In the USA, state legislatures were mandating the basic competencies which every student must acquire before graduating from general education. It was in this context that a new enthusiasm for a core curriculum arose.

But if educators want recognition of effective and excellent schools, they must define more precisely what their objectives are, win concurrence - at least among their parent population - for those objectives, teach to the objectives and then regularly apply indicators or measures which quite clearly demonstrate whether progress is being made towards those objectives. You simply cannot have an 'effective' school unless it has specific aims and unless progress is monitored in some way.

Second, there is a dangerous and also deliberate coincidence about the fact that 'school effectiveness' became such a lively fascination at the same time as questions about efficiency were being raised, particularly by politicians and legislatures. The economic downturn from about 1975 onwards turned off the stream of money for education and with it, so it seems, the public's thirst for innovation, compensatory programmes, educational expansion, improvement in teacher qualifications, smaller class sizes, better building designs and so on.

From the mid-1970s educators were confronted with demands for accountability, for productivity, for a return to basic learnings, for contraction of the curriculum to a core of essential skills and concepts, for better use of personnel and so on. Many educators took a long time to get over the cornucopia mentality, the view that diagnosing a deficiency was strong enough argument for more resources; they simply did not comprehend the climate in which administrators were being told, 'If you want something more, then you must give up something as a trade-off.' Better use of existing resources, not more resources, became the prevailing rhetoric.

It was in this context that educators began to talk about effective schools. The public climate which encouraged that kind of concentration implied several axioms. Being effective as a school does not mean seeking more resources; it assumes achieving better outcomes with the resources you already have. Being effective assumes a re-concentration on what is basic to schooling; it means getting rid of frills and homing in on what is the school's essential task - teaching children and improving scholastic performances. Being effective often means literally improving student performances in reading and mathematics.

13

Case studies

A substantial proportion of the effective schools research is based upon case studies, not on statistical analyses; it resulted from what is called naturalistic research methods. It should come as no surprise that a case-study approach has been popular with the effective schools movement. The mid-1970s saw a revulsion within the social sciences to the heavily statistical kind of research which seemed to drain all the vitality and meaning out of the objects being studied.

So naturalistic research - ethnographies and case studies in particular - were increasingly being used. But case studies have important limitations. They are clinical studies of a phenomenon or phenomena; they reveal the dynamic of the case, but as a result limit what generalisations you are able to make. They encourage you to observe and record - 'thick descriptions' they are called in ethnographies. But no one can record everything, and so there must be omissions and selectivity not only in what you record but also in what you see and observe. Thus observer bias is always a problem in case studies. More important, the observer may draw conclusions - even about the single case - which are the result of his or her own tunnel-vision.

Finally, case studies are minefields for the person trying to attribute causes. Because two observed phenomena occur together, you cannot infer what relationship, causal or otherwise, there might exist between them. For example, most of the studies draw judgements about the principal in the effective school, but we do not know whether the principal causes the effective school or whether the school creates the effective principal. It is what Beare (1985) has called the 'Canute principle'. If King Canute had really wanted to impress his followers about his effectiveness to rule by divine right he would have planned to be carried down to the seashore when the tide was about to turn. Then his command to the waves to recede would have created a myth about him as a king who could work miracles.

In consequence, Ralph and Fennessey say that 'the effective schools perspective' is more a 'rhetoric for reform' than a 'scientific model for evaluation'. Of course, there is nothing wrong with that; a reform does not have to start with findings from research, and it may be driven quite legitimately by a political or a professional imperative. But it is important not to claim more from the research studies than the data and methodologies warrant.

The characteristics of good schools

From the studies, educators have endeavoured to draw up an inventory of the qualities which we should seek to develop in a school in order to make it effective. D'Amico (1982: 61) refers to this list as a 'recipe'; Lezotte (1982: 63) retorted that it was a 'framework', not a recipe. Elsewhere, Ron Brandt (1982: 3) refers to the 'new catechism for urban school improvement'.

We should be sceptical about a 'recipe' approach as though there is one best way of doing things; indeed educators who talk seriously about 'diversity' and 'individual differences' should not adopt practices which lead to new conformities and standardised treatments. Thus several writers have expressed disquiet that 'effectiveness' depends so heavily on test scores (see Brandt, 1982: 3 and Cohen, 1981: 59). Indeed Edmonds' five factor formulation was based on standardised tests in basic skills. Brandt (*ibid.*) warns that 'this basis for effectiveness could lead to practices many educators think unwise: uniform state-wide curriculum; fixed promotion standards; a required college-preparation programme for every student'.

Cuban (1983: 695-696) adds the same warning. He is agitated about 'the notion of a single, best curriculum, echoing the pre-1900 years of public schooling' reasserting itself and leading towards a 'more uniform track for all students'. He also worries about the emergence of a 'single best way of teaching'. In the pursuit of effectiveness based on test scores, he warns, declining attention might be given to 'music, art, speaking skills, personal growth, and self-esteem'.

Conservatism about schooling

So while we are by no means opposed to attempts to improve school effectiveness, it is important to be wary of the context which produced the school effectiveness movement. Thus:

• School effectiveness is about schools. It often implies a continuation of schools and schooling in their current form and in their present institutional frameworks
• School effectiveness implies the existence of outcome measures, often the standard achievement scores in reading and mathematics. It has therefore been associated with the 'back to basics' and 'literacy and numeracy' lobbies, and assumes a conservative way

of looking at the curriculum
• School effectiveness concerns have grown up alongside concerns about productivity, efficiency and accountability. In consequence it could easily become another 'cult of efficiency' movement, based upon economic rather than educational imperatives
• Coming as it did as a kind of reaction to programmes aimed at redressing social inequities and the influence of social class on educational outcomes, and to the thrust towards alternatives to conventional schooling, school effectiveness could well reconfirm a pecking order in schools based upon social class
• School effectiveness usually involves some kind of evaluation and review. The school effectiveness movement runs the risk of allowing the reimposition of controls, especially management and political imperatives, which could confirm or reinstate the existing forms of domination and power distributions. It could also encourage a return to a prescribed common curriculum for all children
• Finally, school effectiveness may perpetuate current practices rather than address the shock of rapid social change and the arrival of the post-industrial economy.

The notion of culture

Quite clearly, much of the work on effective schools adopts a traits approach, somewhat similar to the way leadership behaviour was researched in the 1960s. Two important recent developments have muted this tendency however. The first concerns the new methods of analysis. We referred earlier in this chapter to the fact that the social sciences have, in recent years, adopted more naturalistic methods for research, in particular case studies and ethnographies. As we show in the next chapter, Greenfield (1975) argued that educational administration theory was being built up by means of the wrong kind of generalisations. A phenomenon has unique features determined by time, place, history and so on, and we frequently miss the really significant aspects of the phenomenon by imposing upon it a preconceived, ideologically biased, theoretically foreign framework for observation and commentary.

Critical theory in sociology goes further and argues that theory usually is ideology, and that we automatically impose conformity, control and domination when we apply theory; theory usually embodies the current hegemony, and to use its constructs is to imprison and not to liberate.

Not surprisingly, then, those who take this point of view favour methods which carefully observe and describe, but stop short of interpretation and generalisation. They reject quasi-scientific methods using hypotheses and sophisticated statistics, the so-called scientific positivism. They reject the structural/ functional approach as being only half-truth, logical only in so far as it suits the user's logic, in practical terms a necessary evil but malevolent nonetheless largely because it is so mechanistic about human beings.

It was almost inevitable that an emphasis upon ethnographic methods (derived from anthropology) would raise the important consideration of how far other anthropological concepts can be applied to educational organisations. The same has been the case elsewhere in the social sciences. So there has now developed a very strong, new interest in the micro-culture of organisations. Indeed Jelinek, Smircich and Hirsch (1983: 331-338) maintain that the study of 'organisational cultures' has added a third powerful strand of thinking into administrative science, so long dominated by the two extended metaphors of the organisation as a machine and the organisation as a living organism. They say:

> Our ways of looking at things become solidified into commonly accepted paradigms limiting what we pay attention to; new ideas in and of themselves can be valuable. Culture as a root metaphor for organisation studies is one such idea (*ibid*.: 331).

Before one can comprehend the writing about cultures, school cultures in particular, we need to understand what is meant by the term 'paradigm' and how it influences our language, thinking, and organisational activity. The word was made popular by Thomas Kuhn in his now famous *The Structure of Scientific Revolutions* (1962). A paradigm is simply a 'view of reality', the framework one uses to systematise the perceptions one has of what appears to be happening around one.

Each paradigm, it is important to realise, is an approximation to reality. None of us comprehends reality in all its fullness, and we all observe selectively. We then proceed to develop meanings by drawing similarities and generalisations. A paradigm is therefore built up and expressed through analogies; in verbal terms, then, it is revealed in metaphors, recurrent imagery, patterned language, favourite similes. From observing these, one can unravel what are the core assumptions upon which our paradigm or view of the world is based.

Thus you are certain to have a paradigm which represents to you what a school, schooling and your particular school are. Indeed it is wise to make that paradigm explicit, at least to yourself, for it will provide the key to explaining why you do what you do as an educator. There is some vision about education, a set of core assumptions, which drives your whole professional life forward. Those who are associated with your school also have their own paradigms about the school. Do you know what they are? How do the parents, your teachers, and the students typically depict the school, to themselves and to others?

When a group of people share the same world view, when their paradigms are consistent with each other or are sufficiently homogeneous in their core assumptions, then a common 'culture' emerges. That group of people begin to manifest parallel behaviours, similar speech patterns, common ways of explaining their particular universe; in short, the group becomes tribal. Thus the principal, if he or she wishes to develop a strongly cohesive culture for his or her school, must address those elements which handle the school's environment for learning. There are always some common ideas which do emerge when you listen carefully to what people say about schools and when you observe what is done in particular schools. There are, in short, common paradigms which will give us clues for action and planning.

In summary, then, what seems to be emerging as a much more powerful factor about the acknowledged 'best' schools is that they have developed a culture, milieu, environment, atmosphere, a *cultus corporis*, which in a myriad of ways influences how well children learn. For example, the single feature emerging from Edmonds' five-factor model of an effective school is that it is focused on instruction and learning. It has its act together. The principal is an instructional leader, first and foremost. The teachers see their prime role as teachers and instructors. There is a known instructional programme. The students are expected to perform well in it. The school climate is built around an expectation about learning. Progress in learning is constantly assessed.

The effective school, even in Edmonds' framework, is a concentrated culture, based upon a core assumption about its prime function, instruction and learning. Coherence like this within subjects, across subjects, across year groups, among classroom approaches, does not emerge by chance. It is driven by a common vision about education, about the school and about what the school's programmes are for. It comes from a collectivity of people who have derived a collective vision or picture together.

There is now a rich literature on corporate cultures and on ways in which the corporate leaders can act positively in order to build the kind of organisation they want by taking note of the aspects of culture which, anthropologists have discovered, are the most influential in establishing cultural norms. They include subjects like values; cultural heroes; the place of saga, myths and legends; the cultural priests; rites, rituals, ceremonies; cultural networks; tribal activities and patterns of social interaction; symbols, icons, and sacred sites; and so on. All of these are applicable to schools.

More constructively still, the best principals embody a paradigm that is consistent with their school, which ennobles it and points to what is, could or should be, and which he or she helps to manifest in concrete ways within the school. It begins to show in the way the school is run, its furnishings, its rewards and punishments, the way its members are organised or controlled, who has power and influence, which members are honoured, which behaviours are remarked upon and so on. All of these things create the climate within which children learn and which is powerfully pervasive in those learnings.

Towards excellence in organisations

It is not surprising that writers on organisations have rediscovered an interest in excellence, for considerations of culture force us to ask what combinations of factors produce the climate in which some organisations either win pre-eminence in their field, or emerge as the companies to be copied and emulated, or begin to amass enviable profits. Some companies also seem to maintain market leadership over many years because the chemistry of their activities appears to be right.

The popular interest in excellent companies is usually attributed to four widely-read books. *The Art of Japanese Management* by Pascale and Athos (1981) came to terms with a growing concern among American businesses that Japanese firms were beating them at their own game and were stealing from them the niches in the markets which the Americans had occupied for several decades. How did it come about, for example, that

Japanese car manufacturers could effectively crowd out of the market some of the long-established Detroit firms? Or that Japanese motorcycles had virtually destroyed Britain's share of that market?

Pascale and Athos argued that it was something in the Japanese character, the way managers thought about their employees, the way the workers regarded the company in which they were employed, the approach to training and worker development and the Japanese disregard of some artificial western categorisations which had made the difference. In short, there was a cultural factor at work here which was giving the Japanese the market advantage. Could other countries learn from, indeed copy, the Japanese examples?

Theory Z by William Ouchi (1981) concentrates on those differences between American and Japanese firms, and its title is an obvious attempt to jolt Americans out of the Theory X and Theory Y paradigm developed by Douglas McGregor (1960). American business has been successful, Ouchi argues, because their management styles suited the conditions in the first three-quarters of the century; but that success had led to what he calls 'superstitious learning', lessons based upon dogma and unexamined beliefs. The new kind of organisation resulting from a belief in Theory Z is significantly called by Ouchi 'the industrial clan' (Ouchi, 1981: 188-189).

The most famous of the four books is *In Search of Excellence* by Peters and Waterman (1982). The book reports the findings of a project funded by the management consultancy firm McKinsey into the 62 American companies which had maintained a reputation for excellence for more than a quarter of a century. The authors discovered that these firms had eight common attributes, but they do not treat these in the same way as a traits approach would suggest. Rather, they conclude:

> The excellent companies seem to have developed cultures that have incorporated the values and practices of the great leaders and thus those shared values can be seen to survive for decades after the passing of the original guru. (*ibid.*: 26)

Peters and Waterman are unequivocal about the leadership of those firms. In the excellent American companies, the managing director's most important function is to embody the organisation's culture and to be custodian of the business's values. Most of the excellent companies had, somewhere early in their history, a leader who became a folk hero, about whom legends and stories gathered and who in the company's later years is looked back on as the one who epitomised what the company stood for.

The fourth book, Deal and Kennedy's *Corporate Cultures* (1982), analyses the excellent companies in terms of the components of culture like values, heroes, legends, rites and rituals, the place of ceremony and so on. They conclude by suggesting that the organisation of the future will become 'atomized', broken up into autonomous units, a kind of 'no-boss business'. For it to work, however, they argue that 'strong cultural ties and a new kind of symbolic management will be required' (Deal and Kennedy, 1982: 177).

There has followed a spate of writings on excellence since these books appeared. But it is important not to lose sight of the international economic context in which the issue of excellence emerged. Just as effective schools grew out of a concern about basic competencies and rested upon the conclusions which can be drawn from standardised test scores, so excellence in companies grew up in a period of financial uncertainties and the onset of the post-industrial economy; excellence therefore came to denote market competitiveness, the ability to hold a place among those companies which were unusually productive and which were seen as the market leaders.

When schools took up the issues of excellence, then, it was in the context of ideas about market forces, and it is not surprising that the rest of the imagery about markets was also applied to education in the same context - such as serving the clients, increasing productivity, resource management, programme budgets, corporate management styles, market niches, accountability to the stakeholders, education seen as an export commodity, education's contribution to the national economy, and being responsive to market forces. Notwithstanding that context, schools and principals have much that they can make use of from the work on organisational excellence.

In the chapters which follow, then, we show how these new organisational notions - particularly school effectiveness, leadership behaviours, organisational cultures, and excellence - can be exploited positively by school managers in ways that will obviously benefit those for whom the school really exists, the learning students. We take up these ideas in Chapter 4 and the subsequent chapters. Before we can do so, however, it is necessary first to look at the way the field of educational administration underwent a major metamorphosis after 1975 and how that change has also contributed to our awareness of how to build a truly admirable school.

2

Educational Administration Theory
Since 1975

In the previous chapter we traced the rise of interest both in school effectiveness and excellent schools, showing that the movements are in large part explained by the political context within which they grew. In this chapter we turn our attention to the scholarly field of educational administration (as it is known in North America) or educational management (to use the term employed in Great Britain). There has been a similar metamorphosis occurring since the mid-1970s which has not only transformed the field but has also rendered obsolescent much that was written prior to that time.

In April 1975 a conference was held at the Ohio State University in Columbus, Ohio, to honour the retirement of Roald Campbell, for forty years an influential figure in educational administration. It was no ordinary conference, for it brought together most of the people who had made an impact during the twenty years (1955-75) of the 'theory movement' in educational administration in the USA. In his conference summary, Cunningham wrote:

> During the late 1970s, the field of educational administration is in some intellectual disarray and is seeking either affirmations of the directions taken in recent years or indications of appropriate alternative futures (Cunningham *et al.*, 1977: vii).

A year or so later, Culbertson who, as Director of the University Council for Educational Administration (UCEA), had played such a seminal role during those two decades of the theory movement, commented that 'our intense romance with theory, as defined in the 1950s, has notably cooled', that the movement 'has largely

23

spent itself' and that a re-evaluation of its basic assumptions was under way (Culbertson, 1980: 326-329). By 1979, Griffiths identified 'intellectual turmoil' and 'an awakening of criticism' in educational administration which, he admitted, seemed to be 'challenging all the premises that I have accepted during my career'. He spoke of 'the quite painful process of trying to think oneself out of a paradigm one has lived with, even contributed to' (Griffiths, 1979: 43-44). It appears, then, that the field of educational administration took a sharp plunge into uncertainty, at least in the USA, from 1975 onwards, and that by 1979 it was a field characterised by creative confusion.

In consequence there are many new ideas that have come into currency since 1975 and which ought to be finding their way into the management of schools. It is not that the ideas before 1975 are unimportant or are necessarily unsound; the danger is that many people who are in charge of schools know only about the pre-1975 ideas and may not be aware how to adapt, change or even replace the structures and procedures which have derived their legitimacy from ideas which may be now severely dated. For example, in her book outlining her research into the nature of the primary school principal, Judith Chapman (1987: ch.6) discovered that the managers of schools in the State of Victoria comprehend the change process largely in traditional terms, in the way it was described and practised in the 1970s when it usually went under the name of 'innovation'. The principals seemed less certain about entrepreneurship and intrapreneurship, about structures that are simultaneously loose and tight, about the cultural components of change. There are other resources and ideas available to them, some of which we endeavour here to make available to them.

Even so, it has to be admitted that the theory movement and the field prior to 1975 had been very productive; in fact, it established educational administration as a serious academic field. It was helped by the fact that a dam-burst of new models and ideas had emerged from the allied areas of Business and Public Administration, Sociology, Social Psychology and Political Science. For example, the Blake and Mouton Managerial Grid, the matrix organisational structure, systems theory, PERT (Program Evaluation and Review Technique) and PPBS (Program Planning Budget System), most of the change theories and many of the other materials which constitute the content of educational administration theory and practice were generated elsewhere and borrowed by educators. Even so, educational administration studies *per se* did produce several significant advances (Halpin and Hayes, 1977: 268-270).

The Leadership Behaviour Description Questionnaire (LBDQ) came out of Halpin and Hemphill's leadership studies; the Guba-Getzels model showing the nomothetic and ideographic dimensions in role behaviour provided a framework for a spate of studies and research; Griffiths and his colleague led in the analysis of the role of the principal; Carlson's studies of superintendent succession and the adoption of innovations brought new perspectives to the field; Halpin and Croft developed the Organisational Climate Description Questionnaire (OCDQ); and Willower brought attention to Pupil Control Ideology. It was a fertile period, and its outcomes were stimulating, useful and indeed usable.

Since the theory movement acted as such a stimulus for the field of educational administration, it is illuminating to note how the movement started. The genesis is usually considered to have occurred at a landmark meeting held in Denver, Colorado, in 1954 under the auspices of the National Conference of Professors of Educational Administration. The NCPEA had come into existence many years before 1954, and consisted largely of people who themselves had come through the practice of school administration.

As Halpin and Hayes, (1977: 265) describe it, the 1954 NCPEA Conference invited as keynote speakers three behavioural scientists who were not members of that club of professors of educational administration and former administrators. As it happened, the three - Coladarci, Getzels and Halpin - were all psychologists and they criticised 'the shortcomings in research methodology that were rampant in the then CPEA endeavours'. So there exploded on the educational administration area a new set of theoretical ideas, new metaphors to illuminate current thinking, the possibility of new applications from allied fields and, perhaps most important of all, a conceptual frame both to guide and to synthesise research efforts (see Getzels, 1977: 9-16).

Sometimes a gathering like that of 1954 can have an influence and significance well beyond what could have been imagined at the time. It was Getzels, in fact, who voiced such a notion at the 1975 Columbus conference. Some meetings of scholars, he maintained, become watersheds for later developments or can be viewed as historical landmarks, separating the past from the future. He cites several examples drawn from the sciences (Getzels, 1975: 3-4). The period 1974/75 was obviously another such watershed, symbolised by two conferences, namely the International Intervisitation Program (IIP) in Great Britain (1974) and the Columbus Conference (1975).

Not surprisingly, then, a spate of papers surveying the state of the art of educational administration appeared from the mid-1970s (Halpin, 1973, 1977; Iannaccone, 1973; Taylor, 1975; Greenfield, 1975; Walker, 1975; Roald Campbell, 1977; Getzels, 1977; Erickson, 1977; Griffiths, 1975; Culbertson, 1980; Harman, 1980; Friesen *et al.*, 1980; Willower, 1981). What emerged is a picture of a field in ferment, ready for new conceptual departures, new systematisers and some new methodology.

We need to know about these developments and be capable of applying them in the operation of schools; but, in order to do so, we here attempt to delineate some of those significant strands which since 1975 have combined to change the face of educational administration.

A new diversity of approaches

The first and most obvious factor causing the boil-over after 1975 was that many of the practitioners and scholars associated with the early development of educational administration as a discrete field were being succeeded by a new group. In addition, the field had expanded enormously and there were now many more people working in it. Furthermore, there was now a set of managers in educational positions with considerable sophistication about the research and writings in educational administration. The exploding number of studies, courses and topics between the 1950s and the 1970s had been highlighted by Getzels (1977: 10-11, 14-16) in the mid-70s, but there was a remarkable escalation in the late 1970s. By 1980, Culbertson noted, 375 universities and colleges throughout the United States were offering courses or programmes for educational administrators; there were no fewer than 55 such institutions in Great Britain, 30 in Canada and 37 in Australia (Culbertson, 1980: 322-323).

A consequence of this proliferation in courses, scholarship and practices is diversity, both in ideas and approaches. Further, it has now become harder to keep track of who is doing what and in what location. The problem, then, had not been one of fecundity or productivity, but rather of communication, dissemination and distillation, for one must keep track of current work in order to capitalise on it.

It is also now apparent, especially in retrospect, that the theory movement prior to 1975 had been too narrowly based. In its enthusiasm for structure and logic, it tended to exclude elements which were not amenable to that kind of analytical approach. The mode encouraged in the days of the theory movement is demonstrated in an article by Jerald Hage written in 1965 entitled 'An Axiomatic Theory of Organisations'. Hage describes his approach as follows:

> The major purpose of this paper is to suggest a theory of organisations in an axiomatic format. Eight variables are related to each other in seven simple, two-variable propositions. These seven propositions are then used to derive twenty-one corollaries. An eighth proposition, which sets the limits on these propositions and corollaries, completes the theory. It defines two ideal types of organisations. The propositions and corollaries provide twenty-nine hypotheses, which are used to codify a number of research studies (Hage, 1965: 289).

Given the premises upon which the exercise starts, the argument is conceptually tight, neat in its classifications, disciplined in its purpose. It has a mathematical precision. An axiom is a self-evident truth; from the axioms one can derive theorems consistent with them; combining or developing the theorems produces corollaries, which link together to form a neat mesh called theory. It was an approach adopted by Griffiths, himself a person with mathematical training, in his important book *Administrative Theory* (1959), and one which promised exactitude and the chance to develop a discipline which would be scientifically respectable. It made the field of administration (including educational administration) susceptible to careful, defensible research. The field seemed to be going somewhere.

By 1975, it had become clear that it might be going to some wrong places. It is interesting to see the imagery used at this time. Erickson's article for the Columbus conference was titled 'An Overdue Paradigm Shift in Educational Administration, or, How can we get that Idiot off the Freeway?' (Erickson, 1977: 119-138). The term 'paradigm shift' derives from Kuhn's suggestion (Kuhn, 1970) that the major scientific revolutions have come about because someone is able to take the current universe of knowledge and, by pushing it into one corner of the window of thinking, thereby clear the screen to accommodate a bigger picture of the world. As Erickson's subtitle suggests, the idiot on the motorway is too slow, too narrow in his command of speed, and he piles up the faster traffic in an impatient queue behind him. Halpin and Hayes titled their review article 'The Broken Icon, or, Whatever Happened to Theory?' (Halpin and Hayes, 1977). It was as though a new pantheon was taking over from the ruling deities.

New paradigms

The confrontation between the older Titans and the newer Olympians was neatly encapsulated at the London conference for the International Intervisitation Program in 1974. At that meeting, and in the presence of many of the established scholars and leading administrators identified internationally with the field, Greenfield gave a bravura performance when he delivered his paper on phenomenology, thereby beginning a controversy and heated debate which spanned the next decade (Greenfield, 1975). Why was the phenomenology debate so important? By the late 1970s, it was clear that the real, messy world of the decision-maker and the policy analyst is not easily contained by the theory movement's concepts and often defy scientistic precision. Researching educational organisations is not like studying a cadaver, because their most significant aspects - their dynamism, what constitutes their livingness or soul - are often overlooked if one uses a tight analytical framework.

The phenomenology debate presupposed new methods and a different conceptual framework for inquiry; it concentrates on what is - the uniqueness of time and place - rather than on making the organisational world conform to sets of rules. Greenfield argued that:

theory usually oversimplifies the variety and complexity of human experience within organisations

and that:

organisations are, in Pondy's (1978) term, 'multicephalous', i.e. they have many brains that sustain mind, meaning, values, and culture.

So, he concluded,

> My concern in organisation theory is that we are restricting
> one another's thinking by writing or searching for universal
> truths that fit within a framework that is narrower than the
> reality it is trying to represent (Greenfield, 1979: 97-98, 110).

Greenfield's challenge was a well-intentioned attempt at questioning incomplete models which by their nature will be only partially
satisfactory, and the debate which followed his 1974 paper
demonstrated how difficult it is to develop new paradigms and to
gain acceptance for new modes of thinking.

The new ways of conceiving of organisations were given
their shape from developments in sociology, especially critical
theory being sponsored by Habermas and the Frankfurt School, by
neo-Marxian approaches to the economy and by anthropology,
particularly from a realisation that tribal behaviours are exhibited
by organisations and within western countries no less than they
are among Indians and Pacific Islanders. Among other things,
these new approaches focused attention on language, on metaphor
and on the culture of human groups.

New considerations and new terminology began to emerge
in the field, including reality construction and consciousness,
mobilisation of bias, legitimating functions of education, educative
functions of participation, cultural reproduction, production and
contesting of knowledge, administration as emancipatory or dom-
inating, adult learning, access to and manipulation of knowledge
in schools and privatisation of learning. A shift in values was now
being seen as critically important.

Willower (1981) was obviously concerned that the new
approaches might prove to be too destructive, causing rejection of
ideas that could be quite helpful. He expressed the belief that the
so-called phenomenological critique and the Marxist critique failed
to provide answers to several important questions:

> The first [phenomenological] view implies a study of educa-
> tional administration that rejects system type theories and is
> based on the expressed feelings and experiences of individu-
> als, as well as a critical treatment of the schools' effect on
> individual development. The second (Marxist) view implies
> a rejection of 'abstract' theories, [giving] attention to the
> schools' social, economic and political context, and a focus

29

on school structures that promote the interests of the privileged classes including those that impact on social control and the nature of curriculum.

Willower concluded that 'neither of these views is likely to lead to ideas presented as hypotheses to be tested publicly by their skeptical formulators' (Willower, 1981: 119) and that neither had 'made a distinctive empirical contribution to educational administration' (*ibid.*: 127) - an assertion that may have held in 1981 but is now no longer true.

Education as a loosely coupled system

In that review, Willower also examined the merits of the loose-coupling concept popularised by Weick (1976) and the decoupling/legitimation view of Meyer and Rowan. He found the first to be as 'slippery as it was intriguing' and suggested that:

> it may be time to move toward less relaxed meanings, and greater attention to the objects of coupling whether systems, subsystems, positions, persons, social structures, attitudes, tasks, behaviour, goals or whatever. That kind of list suggests the potential confusions that can arise when related meanings spur multiple applications. After the problem of meaning is dealt with, explanations are needed that provide accounts of how coupling works as a variable in organisations (Willower, 1981: 121).

Although Willower found the formulation of Meyer and Rowan to be 'somewhat clearer along these lines', he suggested that decoupling or loose coupling does occurs in the supervision/instruction connection. He noted the progress made in research on loose coupling and with studies of organisational complexity which examined a number of variables, citing the work of Miskel and his associates, the school effects research and Erickson's view of the importance of placing 'educational administration squarely in the context of student outcomes' (*ibid.*: 124, 126). Mention was also made of studies of administrative roles and pupil-control ideology. Loose coupling has therefore proved to be a useful idea for administrators.

Culture and metaphor

The late 1970s and 1980s also saw the emergence of culture as a new root metaphor for administrative theory (Smircich, 1983), and recognition of the power of organisational language. Everything about an organisation is transacted by means of language, and language by its very nature consists of analogies. The metaphors we customarily use to describe both organisational activity and the institution itself are value-laden, embody a view about culture and society, indeed create the myths by which we live.

Our perception of reality is the result of our own myths and legends revealed in the selection of language we use to describe that reality. Thus, organisational theory is a mixture of 'contending mythologies'. The point has been made lucidly by Bates:

> Any adequate theory or effective practice of educational administration must necessarily . . . be concerned with the nature of the myths that guide the organisational life of the schools and with the characteristics of interpersonal life through which such myths are perpetuated and negotiated (Bates, 1982: 6).

He then proposed that the key aspects of cultural [or organisational] myths are metaphors, rituals and negotiations.

Elsewhere, Morgan argued that 'the logic of metaphor has important implications for the process of theory construction' because metaphor generates 'an image for studying a subject' (Morgan, 1980: 611). Yet any metaphor is only a partial truth; not all the features of one object apply to the second. So when an organisation is described as a machine, or as an organism, or as a system, or as a team, or as theatre, each metaphor carries different value orientations, different conceptions of how the organisation operates, different ideas about its purpose, different ways of viewing its structure and its meanings.

A metaphor consistently used creates a myth, a body of folklore, and rituals based on behaviour which act out that prevailing metaphor. So, Bates argues:

> Education systems are then in a sense a physical working out of the cultural metaphors and myths held by educators and administrators. Many of the metaphors . . . are . . . ritualised in the forms of organisation, ceremony and interaction which

are typical of schools (Bates, 1982: 8).

As Morgan (*ibid.*: 613) points out, the 'orthodox view in organisation theory has been based predominantly on the metaphors of machine and organism' but what would happen if someone invented more richly textured analogies for organisations? Several writers (see, for example, Carper and Snizek, 1980; Mills and Margulies, 1980) have tried to develop organisational typologies based upon the 'ideal types' (that is, pictures or images) which emerge from the literature. Carper and Snizek (1980: 74) observe that the 'management theory jungle' has in part been created by the absence of a 'uniform research vocabulary that can be shared by all investigators'. So Morgan concludes:

> Different paradigms embody world views which favor metaphors that constitute the nature of organisations in fundamentally different ways, and which call for a complete rethinking as to what organisation theory is all about (Morgan, 1980: 620).

Indeed, Burrell and Morgan's book *Sociological Paradigms and Organisational Analysis* (1980) has provided one of the most widely used classifications, based upon a four-cell matrix. Since 1980, then, 'organisational culture' has become a powerful new concept in administration and management.

New tools of analysis

A further factor which brought about changes is that educational administration is a derivative discipline, which has borrowed many of its concepts and models from psychology, sociology and economics and has also leant heavily upon allied fields like business administration and public administration. While this tendency among educators to borrow has been creative, it nevertheless leaves the education field prey to theoretical movements and developing uncertainties in those associated fields.

This vulnerability was highlighted by Iannaccone (1973) while the theory movement was still full-blown. Research activity in educational administration had become problematical, Iannaccone argued, because one needed to be a well-experienced researcher in psychology or in sociology, say, before one could explore the intricacies of administrative behaviour. Thus educational administration was being defined by sociologists and psychologists, not by educators, and because those teaching and practising educational administration tended to bring practical experience, not a background in an academic discipline, to their roles, they were not equipped to carry out much systematic inquiry, at least as it was then described and circumscribed. Iannaccone also warned that those actually doing the job of administration in an increasingly turbulent and political world could find that the research work had little relevance, let alone reality, to it.

By the early 1980s, the economic and political climates within which schools functioned had changed so radically from what it was like in the 1970s that there was a sharply focused need to bring administrative thinking up to date.

Culbertson tried to re-track the studies of educational management by proposing that research ought to be redirected at current practices and at finding a 'theory of practice'. Iannaccone had suggested the same; those working in the field of educational administration ought to be confident enough of themselves to devise their own methodologies, and should not subscribe to the academic equivalent of colonial cringe.

The practice of school and educational administration is sizeable and substantive enough as a field to admit to its own idiosyncrasies and uniqueness and to be capable of calling the shots in its own esoteric area, even while accepting what help it could from other disciplines. It should not be left to csars from other territories to tell us how to govern our own principality.

In simple terms, the scholar and practitioner who understand the world of the educational administrator ought to be confident about devising their own analytical instruments which will stand the scrutiny of anyone from inside or outside of the field, and they should work without intellectual inhibition and without apology or deference to anyone in any other areas of research. Iannaccone was unkind enough to label the theory movement's work as 'pseudo-research' and he said the movement was characterised by 'dubious theory and suspect research' (Iannaccone, 1973: 55, 56).

So Culbertson argued that a major priority for the 1980s was that of evolving a new framework for theory development, and this would involve a 'study of the conditions, events, processes and problems indigenous to management and leadership in educational systems'; we need to be constructively critical about generalisations developed in this field, and we should be sponsoring 'new concepts and modes of inquiry not inherent in the earlier theory movement', he argued (Culbertson, 1980: 339-341). On his broadened list of methods he included:

• field studies and field-based inquiry
• the methods of futurism
• comparative research
• case study materials
• an analysis of 'the form of words, symbols and other rhetorical forms' used
• inductive modes of inquiry
• ethnographic methods
• policy research

Riffel was even bolder; he believed that progress is made 'through the calculated rejection of demonstrably inadequate conceptions, no matter how much power they once might have seemed to possess'; that 'theoretical pluralism' should be fostered; and that we needed 'playfulness', the willingness to 'relax our rules in order to explore the possibility of alternative rules' (Riffel, 1978: 146-148).

Willower also noted the increased use of 'reality oriented' methodologies: 'field studies, case studies, observations of administrative work in the Mintzberg style, research on feelings, attitudes and perceptions or on reality as it is constructed or enacted.' In a tacit acknowledgement of the complex environment in which the work of educational administration is now conducted, he suggested that 'as collective bargaining becomes more important . . . theories of conflict, negotiated order, power and economic self-interest or public choice could be expected to play a larger part in preparation programmes.' He offered his own picture of a proper preparation programme, reflecting his philosophical view which 'blends empiricism, instrumentalism, and naturalism . . . and sees man as part of nature, in a community and in a world' (Willower, 1981: 124, 128-129).

Policy studies

What happened instead, however, was that the management of education became engulfed in the massive business administration tidal wave, driven by economic rationality, economic instrumentalism, a movement to the conservative right in politics and the imperialistic demands of those powerful bureaucrats and politicians who had become obsessed by trading imbalances, by the new international economic order and by the onset of the post-industrial state. The real world of the administrator had become violent territory.

Since school is the community's major device for socialising the next generation, the public rediscovered education with a vengeance. And in much the same way as Sputnik in 1957 focused attention on what the schools had not been doing by being left alone, the heat of public anger threw up questions about standards; about the survival skills of reading, writing and calculating; about young people unprepared for the labour market; about diminishing resources and rising costs; about public attitudes to public institutions; about accountability; about participation; about the quality of teaching; and about the right of private persons to upset the stable state of public life. Schools did not cause these problems or even have power to solve them.

It was simply a predictable turn of events that once again schools would be asked to take the blame for society's uncertainty with its future. The result was that fierce heat turned on to the areas of policy-making, the policy process, the content of particular policies and the uncertainties of educational planning. Educational administration had become enormously taxing, very complicated and enmeshed in a thicket of policy problems.

An educational administrator will simply not survive in the current climate unless he or she has skills in policy analysis. An administrator handles, generates, judges, focuses, implements policy, and policy by its very nature is political. The administrator needs skills in metapolicy, in the politics of participation, and so on. Similarly, organisations are now subject to more frequent and more radical structural change as political pressures, economic stringency, more highly specialised personnel and a turbulent social environment produce the need for procedures and structures which can cope with fluctuating demands.

Corporate planning and programme budgeting

Several strong policy issues emerged during the 1980s as a result of the new economic climate. Perhaps the most insistent was that of accountability, especially the aspect related to programme budgets and outcome measures. Several Australian states, particularly New South Wales, South Australia, Tasmania and Victoria, introduced corporate planning and programme budgeting at all levels, including the school. Operationally defined, corporate planning is a continuous process in administration which links goal-setting, policy-making, short-term and long-term planning, budgeting and evaluation in a manner which spans all levels of the organisation. It aims to secure the appropriate involvement of persons who have responsibility for implementing the plans as well as of persons with an interest or stake in the outcomes of these plans (Caldwell, 1983: 2).

As proposed for education, corporate planning differs from traditional approaches to planning and from earlier attempts at corporate planning. The major characteristics are now those suggested by Russell Ackoff, probably the most articulate and respected advocate of the contemporary approach to corporate planning. Ackoff believes that the essential difference among alternative approaches to planning is their orientation in time:

> The dominant orientation of some planners is to the past, *reactive*; others to the present, *inactive*; and still others to the future, *preactive*. A fourth orientation, *interactive* . . . regards the past, present, and future as different but inseparable . . . ; it focuses on all of them equally. It is based on the belief that unless all three temporal aspects . . . are taken into account, development will be obstructed (Ackoff, 1981: 53).

Ackoff proposed three operating principles of interactive planning: the participative principle, the principle of continuity and the holistic principle. Of particular interest is his participative principle; Ackoff contends that 'in planning, process is the most important product. The principal benefit of it derives from engaging in it.' It is only through participation that the members of an organisation can understand how it works and how they can serve its ends. As well, Ackoff (1981: 65) believes that 'it is better to plan for oneself, no matter how badly, than to be planned for by others, no matter how well.'

Interactive planning forces planning units into a new mode of operating; those 'who are normally planned for' are given the chance to engage in the process, and the professional planner and the executives are in consequence required to provide

> whatever motivation, information, knowledge, understanding, wisdom, and imagination are required by others to plan effectively for themselves (Ackoff, 1981: 65-66).

So it should be a matter of concern for educators that where corporate planning approaches have been initiated, the groundwork has often been laid on the basis of reports from private management consultants.

Allied with the movement towards corporate planning models has been a trend that might on first appearances seem to be a contradictory one, namely the tendency for a substantial degree of responsibility to be located at the school level for goal-setting, policy-making, planning, budgeting and evaluation. In general terms, the approach calls for a systematic and significant shift of management from the central office to the school, a tendency contrary to that which has traditionally prevailed in government schools. What is required, then, is school-based management within a framework of a corporate plan for the system as a whole.

Simpkins, after studying published statements related to school administration in Australia, noted that two distinctive configurations of power and service relationships are projected. He observed a shift from the Traditional Centralist-Unity configuration to an Emergent Devolution-Diversity configuration.

The first implied a 'closely integrated pattern', with a 'highly centralised form of school administration . . . translating central policies into standardised instructional programmes offered on a state-wide basis'. The central government was depicted as democratically responsive, taking official responsibility for all schools and acting sensitively to 'definitions of public need conveyed through formal and electoral avenues of representation'. The public was depicted as 'united, distinguished by a common outlook and shared needs'. Thus, Simpkins argued, the Traditional Centralist-Unity configuration takes the form of 'administrative centralism . . . compatible with the process of translating educational policy into uniform school services for a homogeneous society,' and is frankly a line currently favoured by many governments, both on the left and the right of politics.

Simpkins depicts the Emergent Devolution-Diversity configuration as one embodying both 'decentralisation and delegation . . . with external representation to broaden decision participation at central, intermediate and local levels'. The central government is depicted as 'sensitive to social diversity, and responsible to varied public needs articulated through both formal and informal channels of demand'. The public is recognised in this model as being 'pluralistic in its diversity of interests and politicised in taking initiatives to press sectional claims'. Thus there develops a 'decentralised, open form of system administration . . . [with] the necessary adaptive capacity to cater for varied needs in times of social change and diversity' (Simpkins, 1982: 62-63).

At the time of writing, Simpkins believed that the second mode was replacing the first, but what emerged in the 1980s in several countries was direct confrontation between the two modes and a widening gulf of bitterness and stridency among the contestants.

School councils

Embroiled in this development was the school council movement, with the creation of school boards in the Australian Capital Territory, school councils in South Australia and Victoria, governing bodies in the United Kingdom and revisions to school governance patterns on the continent. The new powers given to school councils took educators into quite new territory, with the line of responsibility no longer department or LEA to principal to staff.

There was widespread misunderstanding of what was occurring in respect to school councils. A general belief prevailed in Australia, for example, that the country was simply following developments in the United States. This, of course, is not true; school councils with these powers are virtually unknown in that country or any other country as far as government schools or public schools are concerned. Jerome Murphy (1980: 15) of Harvard's Graduate School of Education made this observation in a comparative study:

> Australia has been flirting with the idea of parental control of schooling through the creation of parent councils at each and every school. If successful, this would devolve parental control further than has traditionally been the case in America where local boards operate at the school district level.

But the same tendencies also developed in Great Britain under the Thatcher Government.

The development did raise issues relating to power, authority and influence, conflict, decision-making, policy-making and negotiation, the role and influence of teachers, and of who should participate in the process of policy-making and governance.

The role of the head of school

Out of all this context grew an over-riding concern about the skills needed in the person who was called upon to manage the school. In Australia, for example, a major study on perceptions regarding the role of principals was conducted by Duignan (Coordinator), Harrold, Lane, Marshall, Phillips and Thomas (1985). Chapman (1984), of Monash University completed a study related to the training, selection and placement of principals, and the Australian Council for Educational Administration (ACEA) gathered information for the same project on professional development opportunities for principals. Another project, the Effective Resource Allocation in Schools Project, run under the auspices of the Commonwealth Schools Commission, developed materials to assist principals and other school administrators with school-based budgeting, and monitored the developments in corporate planning and programme budgeting (Caldwell and Misko, 1984). Similar schemes can be cited for the USA, Great Britain, Sweden, and Singapore, for example.

The way forward

So we must not denigrate the achievements in educational administration prior to 1975; indeed those associated with the field have left a rich legacy. But since the mid-70s the field has become less certain, more turbulent and less systematically coherent.

We also now acknowledge that there will never be a comprehensive theory about organisations because all human beings carry about with them their own cultural baggage, and because no human being or human enterprise exactly matches the next. Any proclaimed theory has, therefore, to be treated with constructive scepticism. This is not to say that theories are not useful or unnecessary, that they cannot be used as the basis for action or for planning or that generalisations are impossible. Such is quite clearly not the case. But theory can be held so tightly that it becomes dogma, even bigotry - a blind attachment to a belief which is never radically questioned or tested.

In a whimsical article on this point, Hedberg, Nystrom and Starbuck propose that organisations should be looked at as processes; that rigid structures will guarantee only 'lethal tragedies'; that organisations should not live in palaces but should camp in tents; that they must fly, but not fly apart. So in the spirit of playfulness advocated by Riffel, they propose six desirable characteristics in organisations (Hedberg *et al.*, 1976: 41-63).

• Minimal consensus: most organisations ask for more consensus than is useful
• Minimal contentment: excessive contentment incubates crises, but sufficient discontent is an insurance against surprises of crisis proportion
• Minimal affluence: organisations which have too much stagnate
• Minimal faith: an unpredictable environment calls for the ability to jettison, without regret, pet plans and fixed beliefs
• Minimal consistency: perfection itself justifies dissatisfaction
• Minimal rationality: the more explicit and manipulable a model is, the more detail it has omitted.

These prescriptions would cause Weber and F.W. Taylor to turn in their graves but will probably keep many current administrators out of early ones. The scepticism which pervades the principles holds out hope for administrative theory.

The fact, then, that educational administration is now more diffuse has collected a more disparate band of researchers, practitioners and writers and is far less certain about itself can be seen as an advantage. The field's anxieties and self-doubts could well indicate creative torment, the kind of troubled matrix which signals strength rather than despairing, and the sort of questioning which separates the intellectual heroes from those self-satisfied with a world less problematical and less exciting.

We cannot pretend that this book addresses all of these concerns about school and school system administration, although it will explain why we felt compelled to undertake an exercise in synthesis and explanation. We hope this book will be found to be an honest attempt to make some of the new ideas and approaches available in a readable form especially for those who are responsible for running schools or for formulating school policies. If nothing else, we would like to help engender some confidence among those who carry the huge burdens for educational management in the contemporary contexts.

This survey allows us also to draw some conclusions about educational administration at the present time. With respect to *theory* there is now general recognition of the inadequacies of much that went under that name. At the same time, the contributions of the theory movement to describing and explaining the phenomenon of educational administration are acknowledged.

With respect to *research*, a diversity of approaches and in a variety of settings is now being encouraged. With respect to *the needs of practitioners*, the present turbulent context calls for the application of a variety of insights and new approaches. There are now strong differences among those associated with the management of schools, many of whom are not professional educators. Even so, we sense both among educators and among those whom the school serves an impatience to move ahead with a greater sense of certainty, purpose and urgency than has been evident in the early 1980s.

In the previous chapter, we considered the movements which have brought to the fore effectiveness and excellence in schools. This chapter has traced the recent developments in the field of educational administration. We are now in a position to explore how these ideas can be applied in individual schools and educational agencies.

3

Re-conceptualising the School

In view of the facts that there have been so many changes in the theory of educational administration over recent years and that there has also been such strong attention given to ways of improving the operation of schools in order to make them more efficient, more effective and 'excellent', it would be surprising if the way we conceive of schools had not undergone similar kinds of transformation at the same time.

But there is a more important question underlying the issue addressed in this chapter. We showed in Chapter 2 that the effective schools movement was in part a reaction against the radical politics of the late 1960s and the early 1970s; the movement in fact reaffirmed the efficacy both of the conventional school and of the traditional curriculum with its emphasis on basic skills - tests of these competencies were largely the criteria for assessing effectiveness. Subsequently, the rhetoric about excellence tended to re-establish the value of competition and encouraged rewards for the winners, for those who came out on top.

All this occurred in the face of an international economic order which was undermining the verities of the past and casting doubt on practices which simply perpetuated convention. The danger inherent in both the effective schools movement and in the literature on excellence, then, is that they will confirm a view about schools which ought to be revised. Do the new concepts which have come into vogue since the mid-1970s suggest new ways in which we could visualise schools and schooling?

So, in the present social and political contexts, what constitutes an excellent school? What is excellent schooling? And what do parents and students now expect of schools? These questions represent some of the common threads of the current concern about schooling and education. The thesis of this chapter is that comprehensive formal education is being constricted by structural and operational impediments, a narrowness of role perceptions and an unnecessary commitment to traditional kinds of fiscal and structural support and power.

The formal responsibility for schooling rests ultimately with the whole of society, and is not the sole province of Ministries of Education (national or provincial or state); it is a shared responsibility and it includes the corporate sector and local municipalities, among others. In consequence, the present formal structures of and community attitudes to schooling need to be significantly changed if the potential of this important resource is to be realised both in terms of benefit to individuals and also for the nation.

Schools need to become more responsive to a wider community; they should cease to be captive to the traditional 'owners' (specific government departments or ministries, teachers and children) and they should become genuinely available to all who want access to the facilities and services which schools have to offer. But they clearly cannot be open like this while they continue in their present mode. Consider, then, some of the factors which have contributed to the present nature of schooling.

Expectations for schooling

Society's expectations for schools and for teachers are obviously undergoing significant change. Parents are becoming more involved in the decision-making processes of schools through membership of school councils, of principal-selection committees and the like; the costs of schooling continue to increase; teacher unions are demonstrating increasing concern over teaching processes and student supervision; a sound education becomes increasingly a prerequisite for a stable career - or indeed for any type of employment; and the ideologies of several layers of government intrude more obtrusively on school philosophies and on the determination of educational policy.

Schools are becoming very different places on the inside as well, and their roles and practices grow more complex as students, teachers and parents become more articulate in expressing their preferences. The question to be addressed in the face of widespread restructuring of school systems, then, is whether schools have changed enough. How well are they keeping pace with societal expectations? How well do they perform what they claim to be doing? Are schools so fettered by systemic constraints and traditional attitudes that genuinely excellent, student-centred schooling is prevented from occurring?

There has probably not been an equivalent period of such radical change as now, either in terms of structural reform of state educational systems or in curriculum content. However, these reforms may not have gone far enough in that they have been conceived of within the framework of existing structures. For example, the hours of student attendance (that is, the shape of the school day) seems to have missed out on any serious consideration, yet the traditional school day constitutes a major constraint on any serious evaluation or restructuring of the nature and quality of schooling. Timetabling and student groupings continue to be conventionally organised in most schools. And teacher-union stereotyping of the role of the teacher imposes rigidities on the process of schooling.

Consider three additional factors which complicate reforms. First, there is a widespread tendency to treat education and schooling as synonyms, perhaps to simplify the problems and to target political action. Schooling is but one formal component of a child's education, and a great deal of education has always taken place outside of schooling. Secondly, it seems that most people regard the curricular and financial responsibility for public schooling as being predominantly that of a Department or Ministry of Education, or of a public authority. Increasingly, enterprises which accept school leavers are taking a more serious interest in the quality and substance of schooling, and in the final qualifications which constitute entry standards for work or for further study. It may well be time for the corporate sector, statutory authorities and other agencies to make major investments, both of money and influence, in a number of aspects of formal education.

Thirdly, governments continue to assume that the economies of scale associated with larger enterprises, especially businesses, will bear a direct correlation with the unit effectiveness of schools. Because, internationally, increasing emphasis is being placed both on the autonomy and the uniqueness of the individual school, the procedures for the system-wide provision of resources and services must also accommodate a genuine devolution of responsibilities. The proclivity of bureaucracies and unions to retain centrally as much power as possible continues to frustrate and stifle excellence of operation within individual schools.

We have reached a point therefore where we need to think beyond traditional structures, traditional attitudes about schooling and traditional patterns of responsibility and ownership. The quality of schooling - both government and non-government - appears to be under attack from all sides; both sectors are being challenged about academic standards; we are witnessing across several countries vehement and consistent criticisms from the supporters of the government system against the non-government sector; the more broadly-based conception of education as the total development of the child continues to conflict with public, teacher and teacher-union notions about what schooling should be and what constitutes the teacher's role; and the traditional, community-based agencies (like church, the village culture, local clubs and sporting teams) which supplemented the efforts of teachers and schools are a diminishing stable and positive influence for an increasing number of children and young people.

The instability generated by this kind of turbulence has impacted upon both teachers and schools, as well as upon the parents and children who support them, even though many of the government-imposed changes to school systems appear to have had relatively little direct impact on classroom teaching. However, to the extent that low teacher morale has a direct influence on actual teaching practice, the trauma of change is penetrating the class-room and is influencing the quality of instruction.

Parents, largely because they are themselves now better educated, are taking a greater interest than ever before in the nature and quality of the schooling their children receive, yet at the same time many are confused by new technology, new (to them) processes in mathematics and science, and so on. There is also a more immediate awareness among students and parents of the need to gain the type of education which will help with access to preferred tertiary education and/or the career of choice.

Some of the curriculum changes being mandated at system and national levels are causing many within the education profession, as well as within the wider community, to question both the direction and quality of imposed change and to worry about the impact upon the local school. Whilst governments may be applauded for adopting policies which espouse greater effectiveness, relevance and social justice in schooling, the rhetoric does not always match the reality; many of the policies are aimed at the reduction of budgets rather than at providing excellence of school experience.

Parents in several countries have clearly become concerned about the quality and perceived value of the instruction their children receive, or might receive, in a particular school. Many are genuinely fearful of a progressive lowering of academic standards at a time when their country's competitiveness in world trade and technology is being seriously questioned. There is now a greater percentage of children (approximately 30%) attending non-government schools in Australia than at any time since the Education Acts of the 1870s and 1880s, and the drift from the 'free and secular' schools of the government system to the fee-charging, religion-based schools of the independent and catholic systems appears to be continuing. There is also significant movement between schools within each of the sectors.

What is the reason for this restlessness? When questioned about the decision to move their children from one school to another, parents tend to justify their actions by quoting a combination of factors, only some of which are directly 'academic' in the strict sense of the word. Many parents, while acknowledging the importance of academic standards and breadth of offerings, consider that school should offer much more than merely intellectual development. The components which promote personal growth and which they seek, include:

• greater levels of extra-curricular activity
• a more broadly based formal curriculum
• more effective sanctions against disruptive behaviour
• greater stability in staffing
• the provision of psychological and social support structures
• the observance of religious beliefs and an emphasis on moral standards
• evidence of a genuine concern for the individual child, for standards of work, and so on (Millikan, 1986: 39-52).

The extent to which these aspects are observed or achieved varies, of course, and even the schools chosen as alternatives to those which may be geographically nearer do not always deliver in the ways parents expect or might prefer. The fact is that all schools fall somewhat short of parents' and society's expectations and probably of their own, possibly because such expectations are frequently unreasonable or unrealistic and are difficult to achieve within existing structures and operating patterns.

Are we aiming too high?

Most schools clearly cannot 'educate' the 'whole' child, especially across the spectrum of intellectual, social, moral, ethical, aesthetic, cultural, physical, psychological and spiritual criteria, and they never will be able to without major changes to the ways in which we currently conceive of and operate schools.

To an extent, schools and school systems have brought these high expectations upon themselves by presenting to their potential constituencies statements of aims and objectives which are too idealistic. It is not unusual to find school objectives containing statements like 'to educate the child to the maximum of his/her potential', 'to educate the whole person', 'to educate according to individual needs', 'to develop a sense of citizenship, social responsibility and national pride', and so on. How many schools purposefully set out to incorporate into the formal curriculum practices reflecting such aims and objectives, and if they do, how successful are they? How are such things measured? Can schools adequately demonstrate that they are effective in achieving these objectives? Further, many of the existing structures and operating procedures in schools seem to be designed more for administrative expediency and teacher convenience than for the genuinely individual, developmental and educational needs of every single child.

So the quality, nature and role of schooling are appropriately being questioned. But other changes are being imposed without much societal input. Governments in several OECD countries continue to force economic stringencies on to systems and individual schools, to raise concern about retention rates in the post-compulsory years and to question the relevance of curricular content in the senior years for vocations and employment opportunities. The impetus for such questioning appears to be as much political as educational. Specialist training, especially for primary teachers, is being eroded in favour of more generalist teacher training. Specialist courses to produce kindergarten/pre-school teachers are systematically being phased out in both Australia and continental Europe in favour of child-care programmes. Specialist, curriculum development departments and other support services are being dismantled, and schools are now expected to be responsible for providing these services themselves.

The integration of those with recognised disabilities into mainstream schools, while commendable in theory, is creating significant difficulty and anxiety in many school communities where there is an underprovision of appropriate support. Many of these policies result from a concern for greater economic efficiencies and to reduce the percentage of government budgets expended on education.

And there are other pressures. Employers and tertiary institutions are querying the academic standards of exit-students from secondary schools. The moral guardians of society question discipline standards, teenage attitudes, the lack of respect for others and for property, codes of behaviour, the general tone of school and, periodically, aspects of curriculum content.

All user groups are questioning the efficacy of the schooling process in terms of the 'product'. Teacher unions have become more militant over improvements in teaching conditions and salary levels, and in more specifically defining the role of teaching. Teachers are under pressure to take additional school-based responsibility for areas such as curriculum development.

Schools are increasingly having to write proposals for additional funding for programmes many would see as essential for meeting the most basic needs of students. They are also being called upon to provide school-based responses to proposed structural and operational changes, and to establish an increasing number of school-based committees. These increased loads have resulted in rising levels of stress-related absenteeism and in attrition from the teaching service. For many, teaching appears no longer to provide the professional status or the job satisfaction it once did.

The result is that, as governmental and societal pressure for greater accountability at every level of school operation increases, schools are buckling under the pressure to deliver the quality of service their stated aims and objectives suggest and that parents and society at large are coming to demand. As they are presently structured and operated, schools cannot deliver comprehensive 'education' like this. A normal, healthy and balanced life-style comes from a combination of sound schooling, a stable two-parent family, an accessible extended family of grandparents and relatives, a family affiliation with a local church, being a known and respected member of a close-knit and supportive community and so on. For increasing numbers of children this kind of combination no longer exists.

So schools are being asked to shoulder the responsibilities which were hitherto the province of these other bodies, but without any, or at least insufficient, additional resources, and in many instances without the necessary expertise. Being legally *in loco parentis* does not automatically confer the capacity to be a substitute for all of these other support structures. The teaching role itself has become more demanding, but is exacerbated by these additional (and, some teachers would argue, non-teaching) responsibilities.

Many parents are also clearly agitated about societal values and they look to schools to apply some kind of remedy. We witness daily a progressive, subtle acceptance of the permissive society; at almost every level of social communication there is undermining of moral and ethical standards, and an increase in personal gratification and freedom of expression without sufficient responsibility or respect for the rights and freedoms of others. Television, video, stage, music and cinema are shapers of attitudes as powerful as any school or home. Parents feel powerless to control these influences and they tend to call on the school for the additional personal and social guidance. Teachers appropriately claim that they are unqualified, and do not have the time, to provide this kind of support system.

There are many imaginative, and educative things happening in schools, and all schools have dedicated, well-qualified and energetic teachers. But the original question remains. What constitutes an excellent school in the eyes of parents and society? Can schools provide within existing structures and operational patterns what parents and society want? And can the stated charter of schools continue to be the education of the 'whole child'?

Whose responsibility does it then become to ensure that children and young people grow up with a healthy attitude to society and self, treasure the best of the past and work to develop a secure future for the whole of mankind? Since most countries have laws which make school attendance compulsory between certain ages of one's life, it may not be proper that schools, and teachers in particular, walk away from both the professional and moral responsibility to develop the whole child. But it is a question of capability rather than culpability.

Teachers are trained to teach, but most are not trained to be counsellors, child psychologists, social workers or ministers of religion. Many are trained in particular specialisations which have applications beyond the specific development of the intellect or which are an established part of the formal curriculum; these include physical education, the fine arts and aesthetics, arts and crafts, health and human relations, and it is in these broad areas of 'curriculum' and the 'total school environment' that some redefinition of the role of schooling and of teaching needs to be undertaken.

Schools could, in the interests of both children and the future of society, take on the responsibilities which for increasing numbers of children other agencies are progressively neglecting or which are becoming less influential, but it is unreasonable and inappropriate to expect this additional burden to be carried by teachers alone if the existing school structures and progressive economic stringencies are maintained. As another option, responsibility for formally educating children could be shared with the wider community; school systems might continue to be responsible for the provision of qualified teachers for formal classroom instruction, while other agencies take on the responsibility for providing qualified social workers, child psychologists, nurses, counsellors, ministers of religion and any other experts necessary to meet the full educational and developmental needs of children and young people. In either case, schools would have to become more autonomous and diverse, and would have to modify their procedures in a number of ways to meet these new conditions.

Consider, then, how the school components which follow might look if they were reconstituted along the lines we have discussed above:

• mastery learning
• vertical curriculum
• flexible school day/week
• flexible teacher employment and working conditions
• use of community support personnel
• commitment to the total educational development of the child.

Mastery learning

Mastery learning essentially rests upon a philosophy which asserts that anyone can learn anything, provided that the material to be learned is suitably subdivided into manageable, sequentially developmental components, and that enough time is allowed for the learning process. Students must master one component before progressing on to the next.

Two genotypes exist in common practice. The first is group-based and teacher-paced. Students learn both through their own efforts and in dialogue and cooperation with their teachers, and with each other through peer-tutoring. By this method, individuals may progress at their own rate, though the group largely stays together in a developmental sense. The teacher may permit differential subgroupings to develop within the larger group to accommodate optimal progress for each student. Group activity is encouraged, but not at the expense of the fast learners (whose progress might be curtailed) or of the slower learners (who may be left behind). Additional subgroupings are generated as the need arises.

The second type is individual-based and learner-paced. In this instance, each student progresses at his or her own pace without necessary reference to the developmental rate of peers. Teachers work with each student as an individual rather than with the whole group or with subgroups. Students more clearly belong to cross-age 'home' groups rather than to chronological-age, year-level form-groups. Each student, rather than the teacher, takes on the primary responsibility for his or her own progress. Support and encouragement from older and more advanced peers, in addition to the support and guidance of the teacher, is a significant characteristic of this approach. Recent research on mastery learning (Kulik, Kulik and Bangert-Drowns, 1986; Guskey and Gates, 1985, 1986) report extraordinary student achievement with this method.

The most important feature of mastery learning is that it accommodates the natural diversity of ability within any group of students. The fast learners need not be delayed by waiting for the slower students, and the slower students are not 'left behind'. Thus, with careful preparation and greater flexibility in instructional methods, all students can be appropriately accommodated according to their respective levels of understanding and they can progress at their own rate. It works particularly well with hierarchically and sequentially ordered subjects like mathematics, physics and languages, but can also easily accommodate discrete topic subjects such as history.

The role of teacher changes from that of purveyor of all wisdom and becomes more that of facilitator of the learning environment; the teacher ensures the availability of resources at the time they are needed and for the duration they are needed. Actual teaching will be directed to individuals, or to small groups of children dealing with essentially the same problem or learning mode, rather than to the entire class of students. The teacher monitors more closely the progress of each student and ensures that concepts and processes are understood before the student progresses to the next component.

The emphasis in mastery learning is on individualised corrective instruction, on readiness and relevance and on accessibility of material within appropriate time-frames. Students do not 'fail' in mastery learning programmes; rather, the content and time-frames of their learning are differentially paced to accommodate each student's level and rate of understanding. Further, in properly administered programmes, given the required motivation and application, students cannot avoid learning what is set down by the teacher (or the student) to be learned, providing motivation and application are maintained. In traditional teaching-learning patterns, the controlling factor is the predetermined time-block; in mastery learning, the controlling factor is the material to be mastered - time is a flexible vehicle within which the learning takes place. And because progress to the next component requires mastery of the present component, foundations and preliminaries are always established.

Benjamin Bloom of the University of Chicago first articulated the concept of mastery learning in the late 1960s. Many schools have since successfully adopted the method, and it has been incorporated into such programmes as IGE (Individually Guided Education), IPI (Individually Prescribed Instruction), PLAN (Programme for Learning According to Need), LFM (Learning for Mastery), and PSI (Personalised System of Instruction).

However, whilst mastery learning produces an intimate knowledge of each student's progress and areas of competence and difficulty, it is administratively much more complex to operate than the traditional large-group, same-age, horizontally organised modes of instruction. While there has been almost continuous research undertaken since Bloom's initial thesis, there continues to be controversy about the effectiveness of mastery learning methods. However, most researchers are willing to acknowledge that the increased emphasis on individualised instruction does assist students of all levels of ability. But the method does place much greater demands upon teachers, who need to break into units or modules all the subject matter to be learned in every subject area. These units of work vary from between six and twenty weeks' duration depending upon the particular model adopted. Formative assessment procedures must be developed for both teacher and student assessment of the student's work and progress.

An important aspect of the concept is that the student takes greater responsibility for his or her own learning, which in turn builds self-confidence and personal motivation. Where mastery learning has been introduced within the more traditional, horizontal curriculum of year-length courses, the faster students must be provided with extension units or packages, whilst the slower students may need supplementary loops for the set number of units within the year time-frame. It very quickly becomes apparent, then, that the traditional notions of 'classes' and 'grades' become a handicap, indeed self-defeating as, for example, the faster students are continually held back within any year level, even though their knowledge expands through their work in extension units.

Vertical curriculum

A more appropriate way of accommodating the differential rates of student progression through mastery learning techniques is the vertical curriculum, in which all subject areas are subdivided into sequentially developmental units and placed on a vertical grid. In this kind of timetable students may work individually or in small groups and can take advantage of peer-assisted or cross-age tutoring opportunities.

In England the best-known single-subject example of this strategy is the Kent Mathematics Project (KMP) devised by Bertie Banks. There have also been developed in England 'mini-schools' (see *The Countesthorpe Experience*: Watts J. (ed.)) where groups of same-age students work with a number of teachers over a wide range of subjects. Teachers act as both tutors and general counsellors. However, in vertical curriculum, the concept of year-levels is no longer relevant; rather, students at any point in their schooling work within vertically constructed, sequentially developmental, subject areas. (Some schools operate modified vertical curriculums at certain levels only.) Because of innate ability, interest in particular subjects, or greater motivation to study one subject rather than another, students can be at different levels in their various subjects within their own programme of study. If a student grasps mathematical concepts easily and sees this activity as intellectually rewarding, her rate of progress in mathematics may be significantly faster than that in a subject which has less immediate appeal.

This differential rate of progress is perfectly normal, since all students have different interests, abilities and levels of motivation in different topics and subjects. It becomes the teacher's responsibility to ensure that no one subject area is pursued at the expense of all others or that no one area is disregarded, and that a reasonable balance is maintained among the components of the student's study programme.

In practice, then, each student negotiates his/her own programme of study, and takes more personal responsibility for his/her own progress, under the supervision of the classroom teacher. This monitoring can be administratively time-consuming for teachers, but is outweighed by the benefits to students. There is in any study regimen normally a combination of core and elective components, the selection of which is undertaken with teacher advice and guidance. Whilst certain lesson content will continue to need group explanation, teaching becomes much more individualised, because students will be at different levels of progression within the units of work and progressively they will be working on different units. In short, the nature of the teaching task has been substantially reformed.

Flexible school day/week

The conventional structure of the school day and of the school week ignores the contextual reality of individual schools and communities by assuming that the schooling needs of all are exactly the same. Hence many countries have legislation which specifies that schools operate between certain predetermined hours each day and for a defined number of days each year; term dates are also prescribed. Thus the right of the school and the community to cater for the wishes of a particular community is restricted.

In a neighbourhood in which a proportion of the parents are involved in shift-work which does not happen to coincide with the established hours of schooling, it would make sense if one, or some, of that community's schools could open earlier or remain open later, could cater for the care as well as the educational needs of young children, or could accommodate the learning needs of older students, including parents. There seems to be no good reason why school buildings and their equipment should be available for relatively restricted periods of time and to a relatively select group of people - predominantly those between six and eighteen years of age.

A more flexible approach would permit schools, if there was the need and if they so chose, to open significantly earlier and/or to close significantly later than they do at present. The timetable could be blocked in such a way that subjects were offered at various times throughout the day, in much the same way as the vertical curriculum structure makes possible. The duration and timing of daytime attendance would need to vary according to the age and the developmental levels of students, and the degree of flexibility would also vary significantly between primary and secondary levels of schooling (if those terms remain usable). Older secondary students could usefully gain much more through a longer contact-day than is open to them in most schools at present.

The freeing-up of the school day, and therefore of the school week, creates greater opportunities for a much more diverse and creative approach to curriculum design and to school operation. Schools could, with the agreement of their parent body, offer classes both earlier and later than at present, and could accommodate special interests and special needs of both students and parents; a flexible day could generate greater cooperation and less duplication between neighbouring schools in the offering of specialist courses for small groups of students.

The degree of flexibility will, of necessity, be dependent upon the age-range of the children. However, whether the model occurs within a P-12 or K-12 (age 5 to 18 years) setting, within the more common administrative groupings of junior/ middle/ senior or primary/ secondary sub-divisions, or even in only limited contexts within levels, and particularly when it is applied in conjunction with mastery learning and a vertical curriculum, the school's conventional mode of operation will begin to dissipate and undergo a sea change.

There are many interesting examples which can be cited. One approach adopted by the Sutton Centre in Nottinghamshire, England, (see Table 3.1) was to divide each day into three time-blocks (morning, afternoon and evening), 15 in all for the week, of which all students and teachers must attend ten. This provides a great amount of flexibility, yet within regular structures.

Another is the 45/15 term operating in Washington State, USA, in which students and staff are engaged in four, 12-week blocks comprising nine weeks (45 days) on task followed by three weeks (15 days) recess. Each of the four cohorts of students begin their twelve-week cycles three weeks apart, providing staggered entry points and holiday breaks throughout the year. The school plant can thereby be used for 48 weeks in the year - a much higher ratio of use than occurs in most school systems.

Table 3.1 Teacher Flexitime Employment Patterns

	Teacher	A	B	C	D	E	F	G
Monday	☐ am	√	√	–	√	–	√	–
	☐ pm	√	√	√	√	–	–	√
	☐ even	–	√	√	–	–	√	√
Tuesday	☐ am	√	√	√	–	√	√	–
	☐ pm	√	√	√	–	√	–	√
	☐ even	–	√	–	–	√	√	√
Wednesday	☐ am	√	√	√	√	√	√	–
	☐ pm	√	√	√	√	√	–	√
	☐ even	–	√	–	√	√	√	√
Thursday	☐ am	√	√	√	√	√	√	–
	☐ pm	√	–	√	√	√	–	√
	☐ even	–	–	√	√	–	√	√
Friday	☐ am	√	–	√	–	√	√	–
	☐ pm	√	–	–	√	√	–	√
	☐ even	–	–	–	√	–	√	√

Notes: Each teacher is scheduled for 10 half-day sessions.

Teacher A   has a typical week - five days of teaching during the day.

Teacher B   has all Friday and Thursday afternoon free.

Teacher F   teaches mornings and evenings, and has all afternoons free.

Teacher G   has every morning free.

The seven configurations demonstrated indicate some of the possibilities available in flexitime arrangements.

Woodleigh School at Baxter near Melbourne, Australia, developed the 'seven week plan' in which the 7th (middle) week of each 13-week term was devoted to an elective activity such as producing a musical, scuba-diving, ecological research, running a business, canoe expeditions, and many others. They also operated an extended lunch break to cater for the same kinds of activity. Many non-government schools have extended their school days to 4.30 and 5.30 p.m and often to Saturday mornings to accommodate sporting activities, orchestral rehearsals, clubs and societies, and other cross-level activity, although these extension programmes ought to be seen as the norm in all schools, and better utilisation of school plant and teaching expertise ought to be standard practice.

It is sad to recognise, however, that administrative considerations and economic restrictions constitute major impediments to more flexible operational patterns. Homogeneous age-groups of students are much easier to plan for and to teach than are heterogeneous groupings, but such age-level groupings assume fallaciously a sameness of need and ability. It is easier for teachers to group-teach by lecture method, a practice based upon the assumption that students have equivalent understanding, capabilities, and capacities. Yet schools are full of children who daily verify that this is not the case, and whose behaviours reflect their lack of engagement in these formal activities, and thus, the patent inappropriateness of such a learning practice.

The extended and more flexible school day also creates the opportunity to incorporate in the curriculum both cross-level and non-academic offerings, to build additional components into the formal school day, such as religious observances, group discussions and projects, films, visiting speakers, pastoral care and other social support mechanisms, and to include knowledge/skills development in areas which may not normally be covered by the 'formal' academic curriculum (like clubs, societies, hobby and recreational programmes).

The extended school day is not designed necessarily to include more academic study, but may simply offer personal development opportunities within a supervised educational environment. It could be argued that schools would therefore be taking over a parenting role by gainfully engaging young people rather than leaving them to return to empty homes to watch questionable TV programmes, or to fill in time at shopping centres or other venues *en route* from school to home.

Flexitime employment of teachers

A more flexible deployment of teaching staff becomes a necessary part of the notion of a flexible school day; teachers would need to negotiate with the principal the ways in which they would fulfil their teaching contract (see Table 3.1) within the school's new operational arrangements.

Under flexitime arrangements, teachers could undertake their full-time teaching load largely as they do at present, or they may exploit the advantage which flexitime arrangements can provide. For example, some may chose to fulfil their normal full-time contract over four days, or to have late starts or early finishes, or to take half-days off on particular days of the week.

In some community colleges in Leicestershire, England, teachers may 'trade' an evening session for one morning or afternoon session on up to three days per week. It also creates the opportunity for job-sharing, and permanent part-time work. A more flexible approach to the school day also provides increased opportunity for professional development of staff, whether school-based or at tertiary institutions. It permits more opportunity for on-site professional reading and writing. It also has the potential to reduce leave for special purposes, for personal shopping and the like, and to improve significantly teaching practice, working conditions and life-style without loss of full-time employment or jeopardising a full-time salary.

But to accommodate an extended school day or week, a vertical curriculum and mastery learning, and to encourage society to take greater responsibility for the operation of schools may well require that more adults be recruited as a normal part of the school's complement of support personnel. The provision of these extra people clearly could not come from within existing education budgets.

Community support personnel

There is in all school communities a large body of under-utilised expertise which could reasonably be harnessed for the benefit of schools and students. This human resource pool includes active and retired professional and business people, community artisans, parents and grandparents, the unemployed (both youthful and more mature) and so on.

In addition, schools increasingly need the assistance of school chaplains, nurses, psychologists and counsellors, and social workers, and of people like ethnic aides to assist with translating and with understanding the cultures of the diverse range of nationalities which make up a significant proportion of some student populations.

Part of this potentially available pool of adults could be accessible to schools free of cost. Retired professionals and business personnel are covered by superannuation and pension schemes and formal unpaid involvement with schools may well be welcomed by many of them; they are often well qualified (in a formal academic sense) and with significant work experience, and want to keep active involvement in their fields. Other professional expertise would need to be paid for, and would constitute a charge against government or the corporate sector, or possibly the particular community, though in the interests of social justice some subsidies would be necessary.

However, under no circumstance should these potential additional personnel be seen as replacements for qualified teachers. Rather, they would be additional classroom and school resources. Certainly, the cost of these extra personnel ought not come out of Education budgets unless these were to be significantly enlarged. Some of these charges would appropriately be against other ministries such as Social Welfare, Trade, Industry or Health. Merely to itemise these makes our case. Schools are being changed; they no longer fit the conventional mould, and even reasonable innovations like mastery learning, a revised school day with extended hours of operation, and a widening clientele are transforming the way schools are conceived of, and are pushing them into involvement across boundaries no longer impervious. In consequence, it may become necessary to fund a part of the education enterprise in new ways.

The corporate sector, as a major user of educated youth, may be called upon to make a greater direct contribution to the provision of schooling through a device like a per capita tax on the number of employees. Schemes such as 'schools adopting a business organisation', 'or organisations adopting a school' provide opportunities for direct support in various forms - both resource supplementation and work experience.

In any case, most teachers, individually and collectively, do not have the combined training or expertise to supply the quality or volume of moral, psychological, emotional, spiritual and cultural nurture which society is coming to expect of schools. Competent teachers would not feel threatened by the inclusion of other professionals and lay assistants in schools and in classrooms, and most would welcome the support which these persons would bring to the complex and responsible task of educating the young. The benefits of this more comprehensive approach to formal schooling would be enormous.

Thus, it becomes a national question as to what sort of society we wish to have in the future, and whether schools are able to provide the support and up-bringing which society expects for the coming generations. If schools are to be responsible for the total development of the child, there needs to be a re-appraisal of the roles of schools and of teachers.

Total educational development

We have already referred several times to the 'development of the whole child', intellectual, social, psychological, ethical, moral, spiritual, physical, cultural and aesthetic. Most schools concentrate on a few of these elements only, largely ignore others, and give major curricular emphasis to intellectual development.

Increasingly schools are responding to the student's need for social, emotional, and psychological support by providing pastoral care programmes, and within these there may be some intentional reference to moral and ethical responsibility. Many government and most non-government schools in Australia also employ chaplains and counsellors.

In Australia, 'Church' schools — those of the Catholic system, and those affiliated with protestant denominations — give some degree of emphasis to formal religious education and to its public observance like assembly or classroom prayers, masses, hymn singing, bible readings, and so on. However, these aspects are differentially practised and valued even within the different Christian denominational schools.

Others, however, do very little in the way of formal religious observance, and although government schools are by legislation 'free, compulsory and secular', many employ a school chaplain, and some enact religious ceremonies. Clearly there is a differential appreciation of the value of these aspects in both government and non-government schools. The issue becomes one of balance between these various elements of the total curriculum.

Increasing numbers of parents are expressing support not only for a wider range of curricula and other educational components, but also for discipline, religious and moral awareness, respect for the person and property of others, and extended extra-curricular activities. For some parents, there is a belief that pastoral care and personal support programmes will be more effective in schools which have some religious observances. But by whatever criteria one uses as the basis for judgement, it is transparently clear that all schools, no matter what their designation, have failed to educate 'the whole child'. Furthermore, it is unlikely that they will ever be able to do so, and doubtful whether they should even try.

What the various publics are asking of schools and of education agencies are at the least contradictory and at the most unachievable; and many of the demands being placed upon schools, even those which appear reasonable and educationally persuasive (like individualised programmes, mastery learning, the better use of facilities, better timetabling, better use of staff, a more flexible school day) lead to fundamental transformations of what we have come to call 'school'.

Excellence in schooling and excellent schools are therefore elusive terms. They pose enormous problems for those who manage schools chiefly because the societal expectations inherent in the terms are so widely discrepant.

In this chapter we have given consideration to several educational reforms which might be considered mainstream, which almost commend themselves and which if introduced would clearly improve the quality of schooling. But the discussion has also shown that each of these changes would alter the school in substantial ways and, were one to employ them all, commendable though that might be on educational grounds, it would radically transform what we have come to identify as school. That being the case, how then could we recognise excellence at all in such an unconventional landscape?

And this conclusion raises for us a formidable paradox, for as we discovered in Chapter 1, the effective schools movement and the call for excellence both grew out of reaction, a milieu which called for a restoration of some of the conventional patterns of schooling. On face value, it is a no-win situation for educators unless we can construct from this matrix combinations of elements which will both conserve the best from the past and also reify usable techniques from the ideas and expectations which have emerged from the present. Although this may seem a difficult task, it is one worth attempting when survival is the reward for the exercise.

In the next chapter, therefore, we return to what the effective schools research has shown us and to what the literature on excellence has taught us; and we begin the process of building models which a school manager might put into operation in his or her school.

4

Coming to Terms
with Administrative Structures

It would solve many community problems if schools were able to educate the whole person but, as we indicated in the previous chapter they are clearly not geared to do so at present. None the less, different elements in society keep loading schools with expectations which they simply cannot fulfil and then they vilify education for not satisfying those desiderata.

Educators have responded predictably; since schools cannot fill the role of being a 'one-stop social welfare agency', let us define (the educators have said) why schools do exist, what their prime functions are; we can then concentrate on carrying out those functions really well and resist the pressure to dissipate the efforts of school people over too wide a splay of activities. In this respect, the effective schools movement has been very helpful for it has focused attention once again on teaching and learning or, more precisely, on instruction and on learning outcomes. It is possible to observe, monitor and coach teacher performance; and it is possible to measure what students have learnt - or some of it. So while schools may leave many things to chance and many activities undocumented, in these two important, pivotal respects - teaching performance, student learning - they can decide to be explicit, targeted, and ruthlessly systematic.

The essential task of schools - teaching and learning

One of the problems posed by the programmes for school effectiveness, and many of the school improvement programmes which they spawned, is that the school's effectiveness was judged on a narrowly instrumental approach to measuring student learnings, in short on tests of the ability to read, write and calculate; and there is more to good schooling than that alone. It was this kind of instrumentalism which pervaded much of the report of the US National Commission on Excellence in Education entitled *A Nation at Risk: The Imperative for Educational Reform* (1983). It had used as its 'indicators of risk' the results from standardised tests over 25 years, Scholastic Aptitude Test (SAT) scores, science achievement tests, armed services recruitment examinations and literacy test results (*A Nation at Risk*: 8-9).

The Carnegie Task Force's report which appeared three years later was significantly titled *A Nation Prepared* (1986), as though in answer to the National Commission's assertions. Nevertheless, it argued that schooling itself needed rebuilding; repairing is not enough because the existing model is so seriously flawed and limited.

The Coalition of Essential Schools grew out of the same awareness that there were some essential functions which schools must perform, and from which nothing should be allowed to deflect them. The Coalition resulted from the findings of 'A study of High Schools' headed by Theodore Sizer, formerly Dean of Harvard's Graduate School of Education and later Headmaster of Phillips Academy; the study was sponsored by the National Association of Secondary School Principals (NASSP) and by the National Association of Independent Schools (NAIS). The Coalition consists of approximately forty schools, with ten making up a core group to work with Brown University to produce a charter for the reconstruction of secondary education. In its simplest form, the Coalition's view is that 'less is more', that schools have taken on too many chores and their health will be restored only if they shed the peripheral duties and concentrate on achieving their essential mission.

In consequence, the Coalition developed nine principles which encapsulate the essence of what schools stand for and which might well be taken as a manifesto for any school. The nine principles are as follows (Sizer, 1986: 41):

• *Schools have an intellectual focus*
Schools cannot be all things to all people; essentially they exist to help people develop their minds

• *The school's goals should be simple*
The school's prime purpose is to ensure that every student masters a set of essential skills or areas of knowledge. It emphasises

mastery learning of a clearly defined syllabus

● *The school goals apply to all*
The school's goals apply to the entire student group, not just to a
subset of it. The school needs to tailor-make its courses so that
every student has the opportunity to learn well

● *The governing metaphor is the student-as-worker*
The school's activities are based upon the student-as-a-learner, not
on the teacher as the worker delivering an educational programme.
So the school emphasises that the students themselves are responsible for their own learning

● *'Student exhibitions' are required*
The school requires that the students demonstrate that they have
mastered the course. So a certificate, or a qualification, or gradua-
tion means no more than that the students can present evidence
that they have learnt and can perform well

● *Attitudes are important*
The tone of the school depends upon good attitudes. The school
will therefore embody the values of 'unanxious expectation', trust
and decency, and parents will be treated as 'essential collabora-
tors' in developing these values

● *The staff are generalists first and specialists second*
Each staff member is expected to have a commitment to the whole
school and what it stands for. These generalist responsibilities
overarch the teacher's specialisation in particular subjects in the
curriculum

● *Education is personalised learning*
Both teaching and learning need to be personalised. For this reason, no teacher should be given so many students that she cannot
identify with each one personally; so she should have fewer than
80 students under her tutelage. And the teachers should
unreservedly have responsibility for choosing the pedagogies
which ensure that each student has a suitable course of study

● *The budget demonstrates priorities*
The school's resources, especially its budget, should feed what is
of highest priority; the school may have to curtail or eliminate

some services in order to preserve the quality of its essential services.

Our discussion has therefore led us to one of the basic building blocks for creating an effective and excellent school. The school must focus on essential tasks, and it ought to be structured around those essentials. Interestingly, this is one of the planning principles enunciated by Peters and Waterman (1982), based upon their findings from a survey of America's most successful companies. 'Stick to the knitting', they advise; the excellent organisations are those which know what they do best, which have expert skills in a certain area, and which pour their attention into that area rather than allowing their strength to be dissipated or spread too thinly. The Coalition for Essential Schools has made the educational application of this point simply and in telling fashion. School, in short, is a learning place which focuses on the learner.

This is exactly the conclusion which has also emerged out of the effective schools research. In Chapter 2 we cited the five points about effective schools which had been developed by Edmonds. Other criteria have been added since the early 1980s, other factors have been isolated and other techniques developed. Mellor and Chapman (1984) and Mulford (1986) have each tried to recreate the list of qualities to be found from the studies of effective schools, for example. But one dominant thread runs through them all, namely, that the instructional programme is the school's *raison d'être*.

By the early 1980s, therefore, there emerged substantial agreement about the characteristics common to the schools which people admired. Edmonds' simple five factor formula is a convenient basis for some commentary about the implications for individual schools.

Effective schools have a clearly articulated instructional focus.

It is interesting to note how frequently the term 'instruction' appears in the effective schools literature. The best principals are not so much school organisers or managers, but rather are instructional leaders. The best teachers are those who have high educational expectations about their students and who are not coy about formal instruction. The best schools have clearly defined instructional tasks, that is, programmes of formal teaching. Some of the literature argues that the most effective classrooms are characterised by more time spent on task, by periods of formal instruction and by an ordered, systematic approach to teaching and learning.

Perhaps it is just as well for schools to be recalled from the disparate functions and scattered activities loaded upon them. Schools will continue to be concerned about children's social welfare, of course, but it becomes mainly a question of orientation and focus. Schools exist to sponsor learning and that prime purpose should infuse everything that the school attempts to do.

Effective schools use systematic evaluation and assessment.

No organisation can be effective unless it has goals to be accomplished. Effectiveness *means* goal accomplishment. It is not surprising, then, that good schools have a curriculum which is constantly evaluated and that pupil progress is regularly assessed. Shoemaker and Fraser (1981: 181) write:

> The belief in the need for well defined instructional objectives and a comprehensive evaluation system has become so common as to be almost meaningless. Nevertheless, student achievement is related to students' and teachers' knowing where they are heading and finding out how far they have progressed . . . In the high achieving schools instructional objectives guide the programs, and testing and evaluation are given serious and deliberate attention.

There is an expectation in effective schools that all students will learn well.

Shoemaker and Fraser (*ibid.*) report that the 'most consistent finding' in the school effectiveness studies is 'the crucial connection between expectations and achievement'. Quite simply, the students live up to the expectations the school has for them. They are expected to achieve; they do achieve.

The Coleman Report (1966) listed 'destiny control' as a factor powerful in determining a student's performance in school. The term means the degree to which students considered that they themselves are in charge of their own lives. Interestingly enough, one means of increasing the students' level of 'destiny control' is through having their parents involved in the life, work and programme of the school. If the parents show they can change the *status quo* by their actions, the children will also believe it about themselves. Carol Lopate (1969: 143-144) has shown the ramifications well when she wrote:

> When parents are involved in the decision-making process of education, their children are likely to do better in school. This increased achievement may be due to the lessening of distance between the goals of the home and the goals of the school and to the changes in teachers' attitudes resulting from their greater sense of accountability when the parents of the child are visible in the schools. It may also be related to the increased sense of control the child feels over his own destiny when he sees his parents actively engaged in decision-making in his school.

Wilbur Brookover, who has featured prominently in the effective schools research, reported in 1978 on a study he and a team from Michigan conducted to trace the way in which a school's climate or sub-culture affected learning. They found that a 'student's sense of academic futility clearly contributes more than any of the other climate variables' (Brookover *et al.*, 1978: 312). What improved student performance, apparently, were the teachers' commitment to improvement, high academic expectations about the students revealed both in overt evaluation and in telling the students what was expected of them and deliberate effort by the principal. Students apparently need to be given repeated assurances that they can learn and that the system can be mastered. Thus Brookover discovered (*ibid.*: 315, 316):

• 'That teachers in higher achieving schools spend a larger proportion of class time in instruction'
• That lower achieving schools tend to write off a larger proportion of their students
• That the higher achieving schools tend to create 'activities in which groups of students are competing as teams rather than individually'
• That teachers in the higher achieving schools 'make immediate corrections and provide re-instruction when students failed to give correct responses'. Positive reinforcement was given to students who gave correct answers.

An effective school has an orderly and safe climate which encourages learning and teaching.

Because school climate is a subject which has been given fairly extensive treatment in the literature on educational administration, it is apposite here to ask what management structures one tends to find in an effective school. Scholars have for several years been fascinated by the question of whether the organisational frameworks of the school and of the school system have any influence on how well children learn. We all suspect that they do, but how does one demonstrate the effects, and which factors are the critical ones?

In 1979, Cecil Miskel reported on a Kansas study which attempted to document some of those organisational factors which help a school to be effective. Miskel argues that an effective organisation will be characterised by productivity, adaptability, loyalty and job satisfaction. At least it is demonstrable that teachers will perform their teaching tasks better if they are satisfied with their jobs, if they are able to make quick adjustments to changing circumstances and if they have 'faith and trust in the leader'. Miskel was able to conclude from his study (1979: 114) that:

> more effective schools, as perceived by teachers, are charac-
> terised by (1) more participative organisational processes (2)
> less centralised decision-making structures (3) more formal-
> ised general rules and (4) . . . high professional activity.

This is a useful finding, though one has to admit that the Rutter study does not agree with (1) and (2).

If generalisation is possible, then, we could judge from the previous four axioms that the effective school concentrates on its prime professional task of teaching and learning. It gains its eminence because it does not allow trivialities or distractions to deviate it from that task. In addition, it believes that good teaching, not sloppy practice, is expected of every teacher; and it believes that every student can learn, wants to learn and should be overtly expected to learn. All of which leads to the fifth point, the school's leadership.

Effective schools have strong educators as their principals.

The principal usually features in any litany about effective schools, but it is interesting that no clear portrait emerges, at least concerning the way he or she organises the school or concerning managerial style. Apparently the effective principal can be collaborative or dictatorial, humane or stern, but the one common characteristic which emerges is that the effective principal must be an educator - a person who is quite clearly an instructional leader.

Hough (1984) has pointed out that many aspects of school (and school system) administration appear to be rather tenuously linked with the school's main tasks of teaching and learning and it may be seductive to consider whether an educator is needed to carry them out. But it is in the area of culture manager, the one who maintains ultimate aims, that the educator quality is so vital. Hough therefore proposes that when any one of the numerous considerations, questions or policy issues confront the administrator, the most important 'referent question' in deciding on an answer is to ask, 'Which option would most appropriately support the selected curriculum purpose of the school?' (Hough, 1984: 60, 61). In short, the leader or principal must understand about curriculum.

New organisational structures: corporate management

If schools are to be focused upon their essential mission rather than being sidetracked into peripheral (although commendable) purposes, and if the instructional programme is to dominate the thinking and functioning of everyone associated with the school, especially the principal who is 'the instructional leader', the teachers (who have high expectations about learning and the learner) and the students (the 'student-as-worker'), then in quite practical terms what will the organisation of the school look like? How will it be structured? The short answer is, 'in several ways'. Not in one way only, and not according to 'one best way'. Not bureaucratically either, at least not pervasively so. In fact, it is likely that several structural formats will be operating concurrently in the school. So those who manage schools need to become quite sophisticated about organisational structures and about some of the recent thinking which has produced concepts like 'corporate management'. Structures exist primarily for educational purposes.

Bureaucracy was the pervasive, almost universal, organisational form which resulted from the industrial revolution; and it has affected the way schools are organised because the introduction of universal schooling coincided with industrialisation in the western world. Bureaucracy was especially suited for large-scale organisations which coordinate the work of hundreds of employees performing defined, predictable tasks in a rationally configured operation conducted within a fairly stable working environment. The inflexible, unchanging nature of the bureaucratic organisation has been one of its strengths; it was reliable, both for those working in it and for those being served by it. In consequence, the nature of its service was unwavering, and all those who contributed to its outputs could depend upon each of its carefully defined parts to fulfil the function assigned to it. In theory at least, bureaucracy removes personal whimsy and idiosyncracy from the organisation's delivered service, and puts each person and each operation into a proper slot which ensures a fully functioning and satisfying whole. Bureaucracy is good for ensuring stability; it is ideally suited for stable conditions; and it usually delivers a stable, predictable product or service.

Bureaucracy, the 'ideal form' usually attributed to Max Weber, has six essential characteristics. First, as the word itself suggests, it operates by division of functions; the total operation is divided logically into component parts and these are assigned to specialist units. Secondly, those units and the people in them develop technical expertise in carrying out their specialist tasks. So it is possible to draw up duty statements for each position in the organisation, which spell out the special competencies expected of the persons who fill each position. Thirdly, each of the tasks and the operating units are coordinated into a coherent whole by uniform procedures and lines of communication; so rules and regulations standardise work practices and allow each unit to interlock with every other unit.

Fourthly, to ensure that the activities of each part, each operation and each officer are regulated in a way that harmonises with the whole, each position is assigned a status which defines the degree of responsibility attached to that position. Fifthly, each position is supervised by having all the parts logically coordinated into a hierarchy, with the more senior members supervising the work of those below them and the person at the head of the pyramid ultimately responsible for the integrity of the whole organisation. And all this ensures the sixth quality, impersonality;

the service is delivered logically, predictably and in the same form regardless of who the customer is and regardless of what persons are filling the organisational roles. All these characteristics are evident in schools; indeed, schools have sometimes been described as archetypes of bureaucracy.

One of the most obvious consequences of the onset of the post-industrial economy, the information society and the recent developments in educational management techniques and theory is that a single and simple bureaucratic structure can no longer cope with the complexities of management. By now, this point should be self-evident, but in practice - especially in government departments, large institutions, some big corporations and many school systems - the classic, one-dimensional bureaucracy is depressingly alive and well, even though the style is under heavy assault.

In most western countries, two apparently contradictory developments seem to have been occurring over schools. There has been a tendency to push more and more responsibility on to the local schools; to encourage people to establish new, independent schools to serve the expressed wishes of a client group; and to legislate so that all schools, public and private, have governing boards which make explicit as well as legitimate the formal participation of parents, students and the community in educational decision-making. This tendency has carried labels like decentralisation and devolution, privatisation, and participation. It is a movement away from the centre and towards diversified control.

The second development is recentralisation; governments and ministers have tried to reassert control in several key areas like resource management, measuring outcomes, programme budgeting, teacher appraisal and setting global priorities. This second transition has been accompanied by formal restructuring of education systems so that the lines of control are simplified and made more direct; by the imposition of a number of efficiency disciplines, both financial and managerial; by abolition of many advisory and consultative bodies (such as councils, boards, commissions and quangos) and their replacement by units, both inside and outside of the bureaucracy, with clearly specified purposes.

The two movements - a simultaneous decentralising and recentralising - are implied in Peters and Waterman's term 'loose/tight structures', a common characteristic of their identified excellent companies. It is as though in areas of central importance to the health of the whole organisation there is firm central control; and where creativity, entrepreneurship and local initiative are needed, there is wider freedom given to the member units. So there are new, post-bureaucratic modes of operation from which schools could now copy or learn.

In his provocative book *Gods of Management* (1978), Charles Handy tries to diagnose the characteristics which will be found in those organisations able to flourish in the 'new order', a reorganised society in which work becomes more professionalised, where management by consent or by contract becomes more common, where the notions about 'work' change, in which 'money is paid for work done rather than for time spent', where technologies are harnessed to replace people-work as much as possible, where work hours become more flexible, where people belong to small self-contained units rather than to huge organisations, where 'organisation villages' replace the megalopolis. It is worth analysing these developments to see what light the new corporate structures can throw upon educational organisations.

Handy's view (1985: 388-397) is that several of the basic assumptions which underlie organisations, especially bureaucratic ones, are not only being questioned but are also about to be superseded. He suggests four ideas that will have to be discarded. The first is that 'concentration plus specialisation equals efficiency'. This formula, he says, has been at the heart of organisation for at least two hundred years; it is after all a bureaucratic construct. The idea is that if work is divided up into its parts, then people can develop specialised skills and concentrate them on those component parts of the operation; hence the process becomes highly skilled and efficiency results.

The problems in this idea have now been well documented. For example, specialists, whether they are professionals or unionists, become protective of their territory and allow no one else to intrude on to it; at the same time they become indispensable - indeed, able to impede the whole process by withdrawing their goodwill when it suits them. Further, goal displacement occurs; the narrow objectives of the unit or specialist become more important than the overall objectives of the organisation. Hence there is now a developing tendency to recruit generalists and then to train them in a specialisation; and for multi-skilling, so that anyone in the organisation can lend his or her hand in several places within the organisation when the need arises. Beware Parkinson's Law and the Peter Principle!

The second assumption to be questioned is that hierarchy is natural. The ideas that everyone needs positional authority to get the work done or that workers need supervision because they will slack if it is absent are being displaced by a collegial work environment and by ideas such as that status can be fluid and depends on the task at hand ('situational leadership'), that authority comes more from peer recognition and respect than from position, that those affected by decisions should participate in making them and that responsibility for the organisation, for its tone and its productivity are shared by everyone in it. Collegiality is tending to replace hierarchy.

Thirdly, the idea that labour is a cost is being challenged. People are not commodities like machines or buildings and ought not to be treated as property; rather, people are assets with variable skills, able to be developed and used, and to which the organisation makes a commitment once they become part of it.

Finally, the organisation itself is not property; it is in a real sense owned by everyone in it, not by a proprietor. So those who manage the organisation are not to think they are running a machine which puts profits in its owners' pockets; for the profitability of the company affects the life of everyone who works in it. Rather, the manager manages lives as much as he or she does profits. As Handy states:

> Is it not more sensible . . . to regard shareholders only as the providers of finance, with financial privileges proportionate to the risk they run, rather than owners? Who then are the owners? Or does ownership no longer have any real meaning? Is stakeholding the new concept, implying that there are a number of interested parties each with rights and duties appropriate to their interest? (Handy, 1985: 395)

Thus, what emerges if these assumptions are discarded are new ways of imaging organisations. Handy suggests that the idea of 'salaries' would give way to paying people for a service rendered ('fees, not wages'); that we might view equipment not as independent of people but as the means of extending people's capacities ('tools, not machines'); and that people will clearly pay for value added to a product (an intangible characteristic) as much as they will for the product itself (a tangible object), all of which Handy calls the 'economics of quality'.

The new kind of organisation which develops from these premises, then, is 'federal', a combination of many autonomous units or individuals who are prepared to work together (literally, to cooperate) to achieve common goals. They are all stakeholders or 'owners'; they expect to be rewarded for what they contribute and how well they contribute; they may be simultaneously involved with several such federations ('spliced careers'); and they do not necessarily regard themselves as 'employees' or 'employers'. Handy's views are shared by many other writers.

In his analysis of how the giant American firm AT&T should restructure to ensure productivity, Alvin Toffler (1985) developed a model for the 'adaptive corporation' which would replace what he called the 'corporate dinosaurs' - huge organisations incapable of adapting to the new environment of the 1980s and 1990s. He made a distinction between the functions which could be contracted out and those which could be performed only by the parent company; the former he called 'modular functions' and the latter 'framework functions'. By this means he developed an organisational structure which he called a constellation.

> The framework functions are concerned primarily with coordination, the definition and maintenance of standards, and the provision of specialised services and resources . . . to companies and organisations that are part of the constellation as a whole (Toffler, 1985: 141).

Were we to apply this idea to educational contexts, we discover that there are some functions which it is beyond the capacity of any one school - government or non-government - to perform, and these framework functions (such as implementing national or provincial priorities) usually fall to some governmental or systemic instrumentality or they may be carried out by some hub organisation acting on behalf of the schools which affiliate with it. In addition, the school itself as an organisation in its own right will have some essential framework functions and some modular functions which could be handled in ways quite different from the way they are performed at present.

There develops in Toffler's adaptive corporation, therefore, a centre or core which retains 'tight control over technical quality, research and development, major investment decisions, planning, training, and coordinative activities' and which becomes 'the intelligence center of a large constellation of companies and organisations'. Indeed, the corporation need now employ only a core staff which is smaller in number, more highly qualified, and more synoptic in its roles than the management staff used to be, a group 'whose essential product is leadership' (*ibid.*: 128).

The 'modular functions' provide fascinating possibilities for educators and schools. Toffler rightly insists that it is not necessary for an organisation to own all the units which provide it with services or which perform some of its functions. And schools know this. For example, schools have for years hired on a part-time basis the services of musicians to teach components of the music courses, without ever feeling the pressure to employ that person as a full-time staff member; and schools have leased out tuck-shop and cafeteria management rather than employ their own staff to operate this part of the school's services. In some countries, and in some schools, cleaning and grounds maintenance are also contracted to a local firm.

But Toffler proposes a much more extensive shedding of functions to subsidiaries. He argues that functions that are repetitive (cleaning), capital intensive (purchase of expensive machinery or equipment), socially or politically controversial (media relations, counselling or social welfare) or which can 'piggy-back on someone else's capability' (for schools these would include the production of some curriculum materials, or evaluations, research and development projects, and even some of its teaching functions) could well be discharged by 'spinning off subsidiaries and contracting out' (*ibid.*: 139).

In short, it would be possible for teachers to function as providers of services rather than as employees, to supply schools with expertise of various kinds without having to be subject to the complicated fabric of governmental or systemic career structures. School management could become the activity of a core staff which recruits instructional service from subsidiaries, professional companies of teachers. Or school systems could also change, with an operating core to coordinate activities and with schools functioning virtually as autonomous units providing education to a client area or community for a contract price paid from the centre. Schools themselves could then become the spin-off companies, or the operating but relatively independent subsidiaries. In addition, the advisory and professional services units could also become free-standing, spin-off companies.

In discussing their 'organisation of the future', Deal and Kennedy (1982: 182-196) propose a similar structure which they call 'atomized organisation'. It has four major characteristics:

• *Smallness*

The units or atoms are small, consisting of no more than one hundred people. Cohesion and vitality are generated because the members feel in control; they know each other, indeed usually on a first-name basis; they can develop genuine teamwork; they can interconnect with other units by means of telecommunications and are therefore freed from the overburden of middle management; and they can build strong cultures

• *Member ownership*

The atomised organisation develops 'affiliations of convenience'. Rather than trying to provide all the organisation's service units in-house, it is prepared to franchise out those operations which can be handled by entrepreneurial enterprises working in association with the company. It is even willing to let its own members form spin-off enterprises, and allow them to separate from the parent company in order to run these ancillary enterprises. Franchising, say Deal and Kennedy, epitomises the mode of operation of the atomised structure

• *Lean middle management*

The middle manager was in the past largely a communication channel, a link between the work units and top management. But in so acting, the middle manager became 'a filter of enthusiasm, ideas, and initiative from below'. The atomised organisation has a very much reduced role for the middle managers, there are fewer people at this level and the communication function is now carried much more effectively by technology, usually in the form of interactive computer links. Since the atoms are relatively autonomous, there is less need for the supervision which middle management once provided; instead the units survive or flourish according to whether they can deliver a quality service. They are 'supervised' according to acceptability of their product or their service

• *Culture*

The glue which welds together this kind of 'radically decentralised atomised organisation' operating in a 'dispersed, helter-skelter world' is the corporate culture, which we discuss at length in a subsequent chapter. The key role for senior personnel, therefore, and especially for the chief executive, is to manage the organisation's beliefs and values, its purposes and its conceptions of self - in short, its culture.

This structure is entirely consistent with trends now appearing in school systems across several OECD countries. The atom, of course, is the school - the basic operating unit for the system. Schools are being given, and are willingly accepting, greater autonomy, more responsibility across a wider range of functions, and are displaying an obvious willingness to justify their product to their immediate constituency by means of negotiated performance indicators.

Many of the systemic services - like advice on and maintenance of audio-visual, computer, and gym equipment - are being replaced by self-help coalitions among schools or by using local businesses. Many educators have set up and then moved into their own small businesses servicing schools with professional advice. Curriculum development, evaluation and even the business areas like fund raising are now being assisted either by private consultancies, or by a group of schools pooling their collective resources, or by teachers forming their own out-of-school teams or coalitions. Finally, school systems are tending to disband their centralised agencies, to break them up into smaller entities and to locate them physically closer to schools. It is a trend which managers of schools could well capitalise upon, by deliberately forming local networks of franchised services.

Finally, Naisbitt and Aburdene (1986: 45-78), in their list of ten features of the reinvented corporation, show remarkable consistency with these new modes of restructuring organisations. Their list is as follows:

• The best companies are those that foster personal growth; people are assets to be developed and nurtured, not merely 'employees'
• The manager's new role requires him or her to be a 'coach, teacher and mentor' to the people in the company
• Employees are stockholders, or more precisely stakeholders, in the company; people expect to be rewarded for their productivity, not merely 'for just showing up in the morning'
• A variety of services will be contracted out; and some people will be leased in to perform certain tasks
• The 'top-down authoritarian management style' is being replaced by networking; everyone is a resource for everyone else

- The company is often a 'confederation of entrepreneurs', where creativity and intuition are encouraged
- 'Quality is paramount'. 'Quality first, cost second'
- The 'holistic, intuitive thinker' who can act on hunches will solve problems ahead of the number-crunching, rational analyst. So intuition and judgement are valuable assets in people
- Large companies, to be competitive and adaptable, have to behave like or adopt the values of small businesses
- Quality of life - a nourishing environment for people - is one of the factors valued in a successful company.

Corporate management structures in education

Many education systems are now trying to adopt these new 'corporate management' structures. Many schools could do so too, although it is surprising how experienced some schools are already; it is as though, because schools deal daily with a great number of people in a service-oriented industry, they have already discovered how to practise these techniques now being discovered by other industries.

The term 'corporate management' has obviously been derived from the way in which large, multi-national corporations are now being structured. These organisations clearly cannot function like bureaucracies because, if they did, the firm would be too unwieldy and slow-moving to survive in the intensely competitive environment of international financing and trading. Speed, initiative, local entrepreneurship and creative management are needed in order to keep the competitive edge in an intensely dynamic, fluid and sometimes volatile market context.

In matters of overall importance to the organisation, the top managers keep tight control. So the nature of the firm, its style and culture, the areas in which it will operate, its major developmental thrusts and the markets it will target upon are aspects kept under surveillance by the managing board and its chief executives. For these purposes there is a Management Information System (MIS), a constantly upgraded, computer-based repository of strategic information about the organisation and its current trading practices, so that any line manager can gain almost instantaneous access to the vital data about the firm. The headquarters are geared for speed and accuracy in tactical movements.

But apart from these areas which govern the essential nature of the organisation, a great amount of discretion and freedom is vested in its local branches. The managers are expected to act without much reference to the Head Office, and with the speed, local knowledge and acumen which closeness to the local context breeds in them. Thus the local branches operate like semi-autonomous units, as firms within the firm, as 'quasifirms', to use Schumacher's term.

This kind of structure explains why educational organisations can appear to be travelling in two directions at once, decentralising and recentralising concurrently, laying down strong control from the centre for some parts of the enterprise's operations but at the same time trying to encourage local autonomy (school-based decision-making) and devolving an increasing number of functions to local units like the school or regional office. Corporate management is post-bureaucratic, for it requires managers who are canny enough to know how to balance local enterprise against corporate cohesiveness.

Corporate management structures develop some familiar characteristics. The top management is usually collegial, with the key decisions being made in a cabinet-style setting. Usually, the chief executive and the divisional heads meet regularly over the crucial business confronting the organisation. There is good reason why collective decision-making is necessary, for organisations are now so large, cover such a wide array of matters, operate in so many areas and imply such a range of background and specialist knowledge that no one person could be expected to command all the data. Many managers do become very skilled at learning details, but it is not prudent to assume that they must. In consequence, it needs a chief executive - 'a collective head' - to decide on most matters, especially ones that are of concern to the life and death of the organisation. Thus, the use of the term 'corporate'. The organisation behaves like a body, consisting of several limbs and members. The chief executive coordinates the activities of the several parts, but does not presume to be able to do the work of all the members and is prepared to let the mind and vital spirit within the body prevail.

But how is such an organisation controlled? Usually in two ways. First, it builds a culture which pervades all the organisation's functioning. Secondly, it tends to exercise control through resource management, by such devices as programme budgets, productivity audits and resource agreements whereby finance and goods are given against a planned audit of usage and outcomes. Such a device has the advantage that the feedback can come by means of the MIS and is accessible through the computer file; thus the checking can be unobtrusive and need not disrupt the ongoing activity of the local unit.

Corporate management structures, like any other management device, can be subject to abuse and can bring unintended consequences, although many of these can be avoided if the organisation has a strong culture. Further, any structure is only an approximation to what is really happening inside the organisation and is based upon a metaphor which is only partly true of the organisation. No enterprise involving people can be adequately described or depicted in mechanistic, structural or architectural terms, and wise managers or school principals will be constantly reminding themselves about the half-truth behind the metaphor.

The functional design

In schools and school systems - or in 'multi-site schools' where there are several campuses involved - there are some practical outcomes from applying the corporate management techniques. One of the first is an administrative structure (and 'organisation chart') which frees the school or the units inside the school from unwarranted centralised control.

Any change in administrative structure can be viewed as cynical if the central administrations retain tight, hard-fisted control over the policy areas which are the chief domains of schools. In the central administrations of Australian states, a very important trend is now emerging in the form of a new structural shape. The divisions of pre-primary, primary, secondary, technical and teacher education are being done away with, and the division of duties has been derived by cutting the cake the other way, into functional areas. Thus, there is now likely to be a curriculum division handling teaching and learning programmes throughout the years of formal education; a personnel division concerned with staffing across all schools - preprimary, primary and postprimary; a planning division; a research and development division; a resources division; and so on. These functions cut across all schools and all grade/year levels (see Figure 4.1).

A change to a functional design has profound implications for schools upon which they should capitalise, for it deliberately weakens the control which any one branch or division can have over a particular school or category of schools. A secondary school division, for example, can virtually own the high schools,

Figure 4.1 The Divisional and Functional Structures.

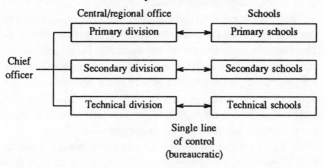

By divisional structure

Central/regional office   Schools

Chief officer

Primary division ⟷ Primary schools

Secondary division ⟷ Secondary schools

Technical division ⟷ Technical schools

Single line
of control
(bureaucratic)

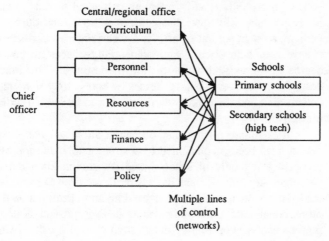

By functional structure

Central/regional office

Chief officer

Curriculum

Personnel

Resources

Finance

Policy

Schools

Primary schools

Secondary schools
(high tech)

Multiple lines
of control
(networks)

since it controls for the schools within its ambit, staffing, staff development and promotion, curriculum, resource levels, financing and so on. A division of responsibility by levels of schooling has the effect of hermetically sealing a group of schools within the control of one branch of headquarters. It is a structure built for paternalism and tight, comprehensive control.

When, however, the system's structure is functional in design, each school must go to separate divisions for resources, for staff, for curriculum advice and materials; no one Head Office division can exercise tight and total control over any one school. The functional design therefore casts the Head Office in the role of a supplier of resources; the emporium from which the school requisitions its supplies. The Head Office becomes the coordinator rather than the controller, the agency which draws boundaries and establishes frameworks. But the design also liberates the schools, the principals and teachers in important ways.

The new design forces the central administration into a servicing (rather than a controlling) mode; it emphasises collegiality (cooperation among professional equals) rather than hierarchy (obeying what your superior tells you); it effectively replaces paternalism (where a superior does all the work and thinking for you) with diversity (that is, allowing individual schools to take initiatives which will make them different from each other); and - perhaps most important of all - it forces principals and schools to behave autonomously and entrepreneurially (that is, to take a fair degree of responsibility for their own destinies). The functional design by its very nature forces schools to be more self-determining and the central administration to be less custodial and protective.

It is not surprising that decentralisation and the functional design have been accompanied by a strong public and professional acceptance not only of school-based decision-making, but of the fact that the formal councils where those decisions are locally made should include the school's public and clients, as well as its professional staff. Governing bodies in England and Wales, their powers and responsibilities much strengthened by the 1986 Act, (Sallis, 1988), school boards in the USA, and school councils in a number of Australian states, have gained new prominence as devices to provide a formal and legitimate arena in which the school's staff (the teachers), its clients (parents and students), its shareholders (the public) and its trustees (taxpayers, local representatives and politicians) can confer and make determinations relating to each local school.

In short, then, the functional design introduces for schools a better balance between central control and local initiative and, if it is implemented honestly, this kind of structure gives a great deal more responsibility to schools and their local managers.

Structural overlays

A second interesting characteristic emerges when schools are given more responsibility for their own affairs, when a wider range of functions relating to education are bequeathed to them and when they become more resilient, more professional, more locally responsive. Organisationally, they become multidimensional. Put another way, there is not one structure which adequately explains what they do, and they have to be geared to change their style of operation according to the business at hand.

There are at least four administrative domains which are fairly distinct in educational organisations, and educators must learn not only how to operate in each domain but also how to switch gears adroitly - by adopting different roles, modes of operating and tactics. Each domain has its own typical structures. Educational administrators may find themselves like actors playing several bit-parts in several plays; they need to learn their lines and enter the stages in the appropriate scenes, on the appropriate cues and garbed appropriately for the part.

Each administrative domain has its own norms and unifying visions, each functions by its own set of governing principles, each warrants its own technologies, each confers its own identities on the actors and - perhaps most important of all - each domain can be at odds with the others. This plurality within the one enterprise has not been adequately acknowledged. Kouzes and Mico (1979: 460) warn:

> Since independent decisions made in each domain impact upon the others, each struggles to maintain its integrity and seeks to balance the power in the system . . . The domains often find themselves in a struggle for control of the [organisation].

What then are the four domains? The typically bureaucratic structure is ready-made for those ongoing tasks principally related to resource management and routine operations. But the bureaucratic format is ill-equipped to accommodate rapid and constant change, and for long-range planning it becomes quite inefficient. Thus, for developmental activities within the organisation - the kind of exercise which requires multidisciplinary skills, close teamwork, varieties of perspectives, and in which no one person or unit can command all the answers - a 'temporary systems' task-force structure is needed similar to the mode used in research and development (R & D) organisations. Thus, at one and the same time, there may be the two organisational modes or structures in existence, one overlaying the other. The bureaucratic is concerned with the routine, maintenance functions; the temporary systems, ad hoc, organic structure deals with the planning, the developmental and many of the policy generation functions.

The matrix organisation is, of course, the formal outcome. In this kind of structure, any officer may have a line function which makes him or her responsible for a part of the normal, routine operations of the organisation. At the same time, that person could be drafted into a cross-sectional team to handle a specific project, planning task, or policy exploration.

Professional activity tends to be different from either of these two domains. Professionals tend to act according to a collegial structure and with a client-orientation. Because professional activity is a servicing activity, it assumes that you are giving help to particular clients. It will not tolerate the piecemeal approach of the bureaucracy since it is people oriented. So professionals work best in a team setting where common and specialist knowledge is shared, where leadership is by consensus rather than by conferral and where team members operate as though they are among equals. So when matters which are overtly educational are under consideration - at school, regional, or system level, and in areas like curriculum - professional educators tend to behave as though they are members of a clinical team of experts.

Finally, the most inefficient way to manage an organisation is to put it in the hands of committees. Committees are for policy generation, not for decisive management. Committees are - in the literal sense of the word - political; they are parliamentary in the way they operate. On the other hand, the bureaucratic pyramid of power is unquestionably feudal; it was simply not designed to be democratic. To be precise, bureaucracy is feudal, not democratic. Many of the problems organisations have in coping with political actions - both internal politics and the external claims of their stakeholders - derive from wrong structures and inappropriate administrative design, and those problems will not be met or solved until the need for an appropriate structure for political activity is recognised.

In consequence, the policy-making or the political domain requires not a bureaucratic but a parliamentary mode. We have apparently recognised this fact because of the number of school councils, advisory boards and education commissions which have been set up. But to play the politician in that setting demands a particular set of behaviours, whereas to act like a bureaucrat will bring coals of fire on your head, for the parliamentary mode assumes quasi-legal actions, building up sets of by-laws, an executive officer role, papers which lay out policy options, working with power coalitions and so on.

We have identified four domains for organisational activity. There is the routine operational management domain, usually with a bureaucratic structure; there is the planning and developmental domain, usually with a 'temporary systems' mode of functioning; the professional domain operates collegially, like a team of clinicians; and the political domain uses a parliamentary mode with all that is implied in the term. Given the nature of the functions in each domain, the principal actors cannot use the same behaviours in the same way in the different domains, nor are the same managerial structures appropriate in each domain, nor can the same decision-making tactics and control devices be used in all domains. Further, some people are required to participate in more than one domain and often in all of them. Those actors, in short, must learn to play several, quite different, roles.

Let us therefore consider in more detail some of the organisational implications for the educational manager.

The operational domain

For decades bureaucratic structures have enjoyed almost universal acceptance for the operational domain, because the tasks can be defined logically and the operations rationally coordinated, the decision-making areas are clear-cut and the bureaucratic mode provides obvious audit controls like supervision, accountability, checking and double-checking.

Generally speaking, we do not have much trouble comprehending the bureaucratic and the operational; we have been living with them for years. The trouble is that we know almost nothing else, we try to apply bureaucratic remedies everywhere, and we try to make all functions operational in the sense of standard, not subject to change, and predictable - in fact homeostatic. Because, to keep a complicated organisation intact, there are too many activities for everyone to master them all, we are apparently willing to trust each other enough to let some build up an expertise in one area, some in other areas and then to throw ourselves on each others' goodwill and efficiency.

Bureaucracy, therefore, is a mechanism for the logical coordination of human endeavours. Because the person at the top of the organisation chart focuses that endeavour, bureaucracy implies top-down management, an authoritarian structure which puts everyone under the supervision of someone else. So when the school is dealing with standard areas - like paying its accounts and keeping its books, the regular payment of salaries, leave of one kind or another, supervision and maintenance of the buildings, equipment and grounds, timetables, record keeping and official correspondence, public information, personnel services, to name some obvious ones - then the school needs a reliable delivery system which routinises each person's contribution to the total operation. In short, it is in everyone's interest that some parts of the school's operation be efficiently bureaucratic.

Thus, in some areas of a school's functioning, bureaucratic structures will remain the best option we have available, but they are likely to become increasingly amenable to the use of computers, electronic mail, paging and cueing devices, and to demand that we have increasingly more skilled technical operators.

The projects and planning domain

For developmental activities or for special projects within the organisation, a 'temporary systems' structure is needed similar to that used in R & D organisations. In short, we create task forces or project teams. In an organic, temporary systems mode, leadership and roles are task-specific and change according to the task in hand. In these cases, the organisation gathers together from wherever they are available in the enterprise a group of people who collectively have all the skills and knowledge to do the job in hand.

A team leader is usually appointed to chair the group and to ensure its cohesion. Status and roles are assigned to the team members; any mode of operation is legitimate providing the task is tackled competently and then completed within the timetable

86

set. Team members may serve full-time or part-time; some may leave the team when their contributions have been made, and others may join. It is a fluid, ad hoc, dynamic structure. The team remains in existence only until the task is accomplished and then it disbands.

The task force mode is constantly in use in schools, and for a variety of purposes - to plan and then manage a sports day or a theatrical production; to plan extensions to a building or a new curriculum policy; to run a project in conjunction with a town festival, and so on. In many of the task forces, a member with positional status in the school can be an ordinary team member and people can assume leadership on a temporary basis in the project. So for planning, developments and projects, the organisation shifts into another gear, albeit temporarily, and concurrent with other operational activities.

There has, of course, been criticism of the matrix organisation, but largely for the wrong reasons. Most people who complain about it want a return to the simple days when you had one boss and an orderly quiet life. However, the new mode is now well established. The task force format is in evidence whenever there is set up a commission of inquiry, or a special investigation, or a special project, or a planning authority. Organisations use the temporary systems mode continually, often without realising that they are doing so.

The professional service domain

Neither of the tactical structures so far mentioned is adequate when a professional service has to be delivered to a client or set of clients. The essential reason is that such a service must be client oriented, not organisation oriented. A mode of operating is required which literally takes the client's part. Professional activity will not tolerate the universal approach to problems or clients adopted by bureaucracy. Professionals at their best behave like a cooperating, clinical team of experts.

The term 'clinical' can be misunderstood. It implies that, in the interests of the patient, the client, or in this case the student, the professionals will pool their insights and skills to ensure that the best diagnosis is made, the best collective wisdom is accumulated for the person receiving the service and the most competent operation is carried out. Teachers are very adept at working in the professional domain; they confer about the progress of individual students, share their impressions and discuss pedagogic strategies; they plan curricula collectively; they devise policies cooperatively. In matters affecting teaching and learning, teachers almost automatically drop into the typical professional-collegial mode.

The political domain

But neither bureaucratic nor temporary systems, nor clinical team processes are adequate for activity in the political domain; political activity is any action concerned with the polity, the body of citizens associated with the enterprise. Political activity obviously requires a different paradigm, and it is usually a parliamentary one where decisions are made by a committee or council of representatives.

Those who have to play political roles in such a setting (and the school principal is usually one) must recognise that the parliamentary mode imposes on them the function of chief adviser and executive officer, the writing of policy papers, working with power coalitions and lobby groups and so on. It is this domain in particular which is becoming rapidly more demanding for school principals. For example, Naisbitt (1982) warned that representative democracy is being superseded; that people are more frequently acting for themselves, not content to leave their cause to someone else to represent their interests.

Since government is becoming more decentralised, policy-making takes place in a network of arenas involving local, district, regional, state, national and sometimes international bodies and jurisdictions. People are also more inclined now to distrust institutions; either bypassing them or undermining them or setting up rivals to them are commonly used ploys. In addition, people are inclined to attack entrenched power structures, especially hierarchies which take the final decisions far from the point of implementation and effect. Legal authorities are likely now to be under constant challenge. While the political domain assumes more importance, then, at the same time it is becoming more perplexing, more problematical and less tidy as an area within which to work.

In summary, a single-dimensioned organisational structure is no longer sufficient for an educational enterprise, and the key operators, including the school principal, will need to be adept at changing administrative tactics and structures according to the task in hand. In particular:

• for routine, managerial tasks, a bureaucratic mode is likely to be appropriate

• for tasks requiring professional expertise, the participants need to be skilled in working as a team of clinicians sharing interlocking skills, and as colleagues or peers where skill and expertise take precedence over positional status

• for planning and developmental tasks, a problem-oriented, project-based task force or working party mode is appropriate, in which leadership depends on the task and is situational, and where the task force disbands at the completion of the task

• and for political activity, a parliamentary format is appropriate, in which the key operator is acting as an expert policy analyst, an adviser and the executive who translates policy decisions into appropriate operational outcomes.

These kinds of composite skills will need to be learnt by all those who occupy key administrative roles within the organisation. School managers will need to be sensitive to what mode is appropriate in any one setting, and must within the course of their daily activities develop the ability to change (and to do so quickly) from one mode to another as required. These different styles of operating are depicted in Figure 4.2.

Education as a loosely coupled system

One of the important facets which must be addressed in any structural arrangements is the endemic disconnectedness within schools and education systems. They are not tight organisational units and they cannot be. One of the first to show the extent of the disengagement of the parts of a school system was Hanson (1976) who argued in a perceptive article that to use a bureaucratic model to explain what was happening inside an education system, or, even worse, to assume that a bureaucratic structure will ensure adequate controls inside the system, is fallacy. His article (entitled significantly 'Beyond the Bureaucratic Model: A Study of Power and Autonomy in Educational Decision-making') quotes Lortie:

Figure 4.2 Operating Modes and Multiple Structures

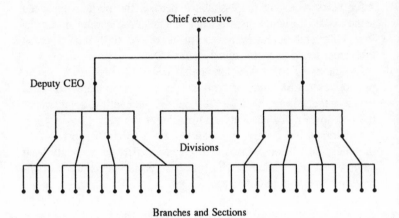

Mode 1: The bureaucratic mode

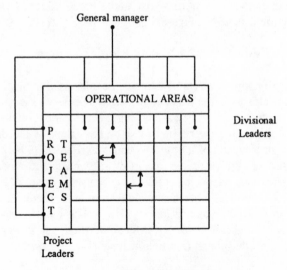

Mode 2: The project/temporary
systems mode (matrix)

Figure 4.2 Operating Modes and Multiple Structures

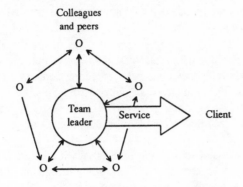

Mode 3: The clinical/collegial team mode

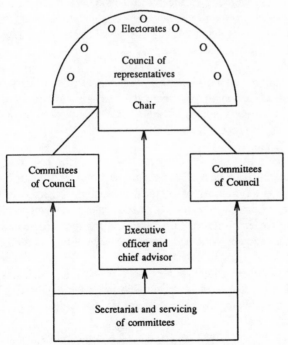

Mode 4: The parliamentary mode

> The bureaucratic model . . . does not prepare us for many of
> the events that actually occur in public schools . . . In this in-
> stance, the several strands of hierarchical control, collegial
> control, and [educator] autonomy become tangled and com-
> plex (Hanson, 1976: 27).

Much of the tangle, as Hanson rightly points out, derives from the
fundamental contradictions between professionality and bureaucracy. He therefore suggests an 'Inter-acting Spheres Model (ISM)'
to explain how a school system in fact works, a suggestion which
anticipated the theory about loose coupling in organisational systems.

As Hanson sees it, the bureaucratic model projects an image
of the leader systematically controlling events in the school by
pulling the levers of authority and enforcing rules of behaviour.
Yet a shrewd observer will recognise that teachers make many of
the decisions relating to the real function of the school and they
do so without reference to anyone else, including their own colleagues or the principal. 'They are the ultimate authorities in the
teaching-learning process', he says.

> The rational network of impersonal school rules tends to stop
> at the classroom door, where the teachers begin making up
> their own personalised, flexible rules to aid them in the in-
> structional process (*ibid.*: 29).

Inside the classroom and with her own class, the teacher controls
an educational process which cannot be monitored by an outsider,
so great is the number of personal interactions engaged in by the
teacher. Learning seems to need 'an unencumbered, non-
prescriptive environment' whereas efficient resource management
needs 'a rationally oriented, prescriptive environment' (*ibid.*: 30).
So the principal acts as a buffer or as a gatekeeper. The system,
district or school administrators make policies and decisions about
procedures, yet it is the teachers who make the day-by-day operational decisions inside the classroom. Hanson concludes (*ibid.*:33):

> Hence the intensive concern among administrators and teach-
> ers with providing enough freedom from constraints to enable
> teachers to perform unique acts of creation in the classroom,
> but not so much freedom as to allow fomentation of uncoor-
> dinated and unsystematic efforts.

In consequence, it is as though administrators and supervisors work consistently inside one sphere, that of managerial activities, and the teachers act autonomously inside another sphere, that of instructional activities. The two spheres interact but are not concentric, and some office-holders - like the principal - act as the gatekeepers at the intersection. While Hanson would argue that this is a desirable situation since it preserves from debilitating outside interference the 'semi-sacred teacher-student relationship' (*ibid.*: 34), it means that the real process of education is never completely supervised and can never be externally controlled. And control is the motive of political activity.

Meyer, Scott and Deal (1979) have taken up this point, arguing that if 'organisations succeed by developing effective structures that coordinate and control work process and regulate environmental demands', then schools (and school systems) are 'peculiarly ineffective organisations'. Thus, the writers claim (1979: 5-6):

> they do not control their work processes very well, particularly those most closely related to their central educational purpose: instruction. Instructional activities go on behind closed doors of isolated classrooms. Collegially based professional controls are known to be weak, there are only minimal efforts to coordinate institutional activities . . . The schools seem to be . . . classic examples of organisational ineptitude.

They are inept, however, only when one views them from the standpoint of political controls and of traditional approaches to organisation. From another perspective, schools and school systems have a remarkable record; they have remained stable and identifiable over time and they have enjoyed public support when they 'conform to institutional rules defining what a school is' (*ibid.*: 13). The rules may have little to do with how well its children learn or are taught. Yet:

> a school is a successful school if everyone agrees that it is a school; it is not a successful school if no one believes that it is a school, regardless of its success in instruction or socialisation.

They go on:

If there is no objective or 'market' definition of success, the consensus of those most involved is obviously crucial. For this reason, school organisations are highly sensitive to dissidence and dissatisfaction, and attempt to moderate, coopt, and conceal it. By and large they succeed (*ibid.*: 14,15).

What emerges, therefore, is an interesting picture. The instructional process goes on, more or less successfully but largely unmonitored and uncontrolled. The structural framework supporting the operation is often inappropriate for the operation since it appears to be predicated on wrong assumptions about the operation. Yet the inept structure and the instructional process have retained public acceptability because they conform with institutional norms and behaviours which, in a sense, wall off the real educational process from external invigilation.

We owe a great deal in the management sciences to creative analogies drawn from the biological sciences. In particular, systems theory grew from biological systems; the analogy was applied from organisms to organisations, and a fresh way of looking at behaviours inside organisations was invented. The concept of open and closed systems was a further extension of the same analogy; from that analogy grew the notion of 'open education', education which uses community resources, which interacts with its community and is in active symbiosis with it. It is not surprising, then, that in time the coupling of biological cells, a part of the theory base about living systems, should also be applied to organisations.

The first person to make the application appears to have been Glassman in an article written in 1973. He was searching for 'unifying concepts' or 'isomorphisms' which provided a simple overarching abstraction of particular actions or behaviours. He happened on the notion of loosely coupled systems. Organisms usually seem to survive if there is 'coordination among parts of [the] living systems', with the 'degree of coupling, or interaction, between two systems [depending] on the activity of the variables they share' (Glassman, 1973: 83,84). The organism tries to maintain a healthy, stable state. But health may be dependent upon how well certain maladies or dysfunctions can be isolated within the cell where they occur. So, Glassman points out:

The stability of systems may be due . . . to *lack* of communication [our emphasis] . . . In the fully joined system . . . a

perturbation in any one variable would require readjustment
of all the other variables of the system ... A system whose
parts are less richly interconnected ... forms local stabilities
which ignore limited perturbations elsewhere in the system.

Thus a local sickness or upheaval in one of the cells does not require a complete reorganisation of the entire system (*ibid.*: 84,86).
At the end of his article, Glassman makes the extrapolation to
bureaucracies. Even when the larger system breaks down in full
or in part, he says, some components can carry on as though nothing untoward has happened.

Glassman's thesis was taken up later by Karl Weick (1976),
who applied the concept of loosely coupled systems to educational
organisations. The prevailing ideas on organisations, Weick con-
tended, do not throw much light on how 'loose assemblages (like
schools and school systems) retain sufficient similarity and per-
manence across time that they can be recognised, labelled, and
dealt with', for they exist inside what he calls 'soft' structures.
Weick, with characteristic whimsy, puts it this way:

> To develop a language for use in analysing complex organi-
> sations ... is a reversal of the common assertion, 'I'll be-
> lieve it when I see it' and presumes an epistomology that as-
> serts 'I'll see it when I believe it'. Organisations as loosely
> coupled systems may not have been seen before because no-
> body believed in them or could afford to believe in them. It
> is conceivable that preoccupation with rationalised, tidy, effi-
> cient, coordinated structures has blinded many ... to some
> of the attractive and unexpected properties of less rationalised
> and less tightly related clusters of events (Weick, 1976: 2,3).

Weick proposed that educational organisations do not conform
with the conventional theories about organisations, and that it may
well be their very diffuseness which has kept them alive. If the
educational organisation was really made to conform with the
theory, the action could 'promote its decay' as a useful organisation.

Indeed Meyer, Scott and Deal (1979) showed that schools
have tended to be least specific in the areas closest to their mission, namely what is actually taught to the students in individual
learning locations and the methods of instruction used by the
teacher. Educational systems have plenty of clearly enunciated,

job-specific policies in areas like teacher credentials, certification and accreditation of programmes, titles for courses, categories and levels of students and so on, but these are all peripheral to the teaching task, and, when it comes to the actual task of instructing, the interchange between teacher and taught is idiosyncratic, un-policed and usually unobserved.

Actual and direct control over instruction, they argue, would kill the process of teaching through standardisation. Thus the edu-cational organisation is a buffer against interference in the uncer-tainties of instruction which 'can be assigned to the trusted care of particular teachers who operate backstage, behind closed doors'. The organisation, in other words, is a loose linkage between actors who are relatively autonomous (Meyer *et al.*, 1979: 14). It turns out, then, that schools are really the forerunners of the kind of or-ganisations being described in corporate management terms!

What then should the principal or the educational manager do? A loosely coupled system like a school is, by its very nature, its own best friend and worst enemy. It is an organism whose cells are so shielded from the other cells in the body that an ail-ment in one set of cells is not necessarily transferred to any other set of cells. The organism can tolerate many diseases or relative failures in parts of its network and yet still continue to operate, still show abundant health and vitality in some of its limbs, and still maintain the appearances of wellbeing. At the same time, peo-ple associated with the organisation can be easily misled into believing that all is well in the entire system simply because all appears to be well in the subsystem of which they are a part.

Often, then, a mandated change from outside - things like Royal Commissions, Boards of Review, committees of inquiry, wholesale restructuring - come as a relative surprise to some peo-ple in organisations. In the same way, external agents - and they are often politicians or lobby groups - frequently call for such in-quiries and reforms because they do not know the extent of the health in all the inward parts of the organisation under scrutiny.

To summarise, then, loosely coupled systems like schools can be healthy in several of their parts while at the same time har-bouring quite serious organisational dysfunctions in others. They have very powerful strengths. Such systems can be better led and organised if their complexity is respected, if the need for accoun-tability is honoured, if indicators are chosen which satisfy the ap-propriate publics and if the manager proceeds with caution and honesty to reconcile the competing demands of good teaching and of demonstrating that the organisation is worthy of public and client confidence. But the leader also needs to know that it is virtually impossible to control completely the system or the school by conventional administrative structures, and it might destroy the quality of education if he or she tried to do so.

Conclusion

In this chapter, we have discussed the new corporate management structures which, where accurately deployed, have appropriately supplanted many of the now outmoded bureaucratic practices. The new structures encourage autonomy, entrepreneurship, creativity and enterprise within broadly defined frameworks, and they spin off free-standing, smaller-sized units as atoms making up the whole. We have shown that the functional design, contemporaneous parallel structures and loose coupling are all consistent with the new ideas about structures.

We have indicated that school managers now operate in an increasingly more complicated environment. We do not need to be daunted by that fact; indeed we can use these developments to good effect and there are new techniques to assist us. But they will impose on administrators the need to acquire new skills and to build up coherent strategies and structures to handle the different areas of school organisation. Probably we will have to reject at long last the idea that there is one and only one structure which any organisation has; it will in fact operate in several modes depending on what business it is confronting at the time.

Key persons like principals, bursars, and some teachers will be called upon to work in several of these domains and will be expected to adapt their behaviours accordingly to fit the business in hand. School managers, in short, must be multi-modal. It is salutary to remind ourselves that the school as we know it, especially the secondary school, and large-scale bureaucracy were both products of the industrial age. They did not exist like this in the pre-industrial period, and it seems highly unlikely that they will be appropriate in their present form for the post-industrial age. That being the case, those involved in the management of schools do not have the choice of standing still. Yet, 'if we can learn to make uncertainty our friend,' says Naisbitt (1982: 252) 'we can achieve much more than in stable times.'

So our discussion has come full circle. The essential purposes of school are instruction and learning; the excellent schools are simply excellent in these two areas. And the principal is first and foremost an instructional leader in a multi-modal school, in which there exists a great amount of autonomy for each unit or person and where the glue bonding the whole together is a strong corporate culture. The principal is, in the final analysis, the custodian of a culture. It is appropriate, then, that transformational leadership should be the concept addressed in the next chapter.

5

Leadership

Outstanding leadership has invariably emerged as a key characteristic of outstanding schools. There can no longer be doubt that
those seeking quality in education must ensure its presence and
that the development of potential leaders must be given high priority.

Setting aside legend and anecdote, there was by the early
1980s a surprisingly narrow base of knowledge to guide practice.
Theories of leadership, often resulting from painstaking empirical
research, rarely excited the practitioner and even more rarely
shaped practice. Indeed, several of those theories were difficult to
explain in language which could be understood by practitioners or
even agreed upon by scholars. However, there is now a far richer
body of knowledge winning the confidence of scholars and practitioners alike. This has been achieved with more expansive, multidisciplinary study of organisations and leaders rather than what
had become an increasingly narrow focus on a small number of
measurable variables in research conducted within the framework
of a single field of inquiry. Leaders, aspiring leaders and others
with an interest in leadership can now proceed with much greater
confidence than was the case a decade before.

The purpose of this chapter is to describe and illustrate the
major features of what is now known about leadership in a way
which should provide a guide to action in the school setting.
Emphasis is given to the broader, emerging view although attention is given to some products of the earlier 'theory movement'
which, while of limited utility, are nevertheless part of the larger
picture. Prominent in this larger picture is vision in leadership:
outstanding leaders have a vision for their schools - a mental picture of a preferred future - which is shared with all in the school

community and which shapes the programme for learning and teaching as well as policies, priorities, plans and procedures pervading the day-to-day life of the school. The major part of the chapter is devoted to ten generalisations about leadership which have emerged from recent studies. Illustrations in the school context are offered in each instance. The final section of the chapter gives special attention to description and illustration of vision in leadership and the ways in which vision may be articulated. Chapter 6 contains a description of a systematic approach which will help ensure that vision is institutionalised through the policies and plans of the school. The manner in which vision may shape the educational programme through instructional leadership is addressed in Chapter 7.

Consistent with a pattern of school governance emerging in several countries and which is the preference of the authors, most illustrations of the actions of leaders assume a high level of school autonomy or 'self-management' where, among public schools or a system of private schools, there is significant and consistent decentralisation to the school level of authority to make decisions related to the allocation of resources, with resources defined broadly to include knowledge, technology, power, *materiel*, people, time and money. This decentralisation tends to be administrative rather than political, with decisions at the school level being made within a framework of local, state or national policies and guidelines, while the school remains accountable, within the framework functions outlined in the previous chapter, to a central authority for the manner in which resources are allocated.

Leader and leadership defined

A useful starting point is to clarify the concepts of 'leadership' and 'leader'. The large number of meanings which may be discerned in print and in everyday use is often a source of concern. It seems that each scholar and practitioner has a different personal opinion. The view taken here is that there is no one 'correct' meaning and that differences in definition reflect different contexts as well as different perspectives.

Dubin (1968: 385) saw leadership as 'the exercise of authority and the making of decisions' while Fiedler (1967: 8) considered the leader to be 'the individual in the group given the task of directing and coordinating task-relevant group activities'. According to these definitions, principals, headteachers and other senior staff who have formal authority by virtue of their appointments are leaders and may exercise leadership. Dubin and Fiedler offer a view which is constrained by the source of power (authority), scope (task-relevant) and function (decision-making, directing, coordinating). Stogdill (1950: 4) had a broader context in mind when he defined leadership as 'the process of influencing the activities of an organised group toward goal setting and goal accomplishment'. While this view includes the contexts envisaged by Dubin and Fiedler, it acknowledges that people without formal authority may exercise leadership. The source of influence or power may be their expertise, or their capacity to bring rewards or benefits, or their capacity to apply sanctions, or their personal qualities which make them liked or respected as people. Such leadership may emerge in many contexts in a school and may involve people other than the principal and senior staff.

Stogdill's view also included the setting of the goal itself as well as the influence of activities associated with the accomplishment of the goal. This aspect of leadership is important in effecting change. Lipham (1964: 122) focused exclusively on change when he defined leadership as 'the initiation of a new structure or procedure for accomplishing an organisation's goals and objectives'. In this view, a principal will not be a leader at all if activity is limited to the maintenance of existing means and ends. Management rather than leadership may be a more appropriate description of such an activity.

More recent attempts to explain the concept of leadership penetrate more deeply than 'the organisation' and the activities associated with goal setting and goal accomplishment. Attention now is also given to meanings and values. Pondy (1978: 94), for example, considers that the effectiveness of a leader lies in 'ability to make activity meaningful . . . not to change behaviour but to give others a sense of understanding of what they are doing'. The exercise of leadership by the principal thus involves making clear the meaning of activity in the school by posing and securing answers to questions such as the following. What are the purposes of our school? How should we as teachers work with students to reflect our purposes? What should be the relationship between our school and its local community?

To Greenfield (1986: 142) 'leadership is a willful act where one person attempts to construct the social world for others'. He suggests that 'leaders will try to commit others to the values that they themselves believe are good. Organisations are built on the unification of people around values' (*ibid*: 166). Greenfield challenges us to think of leaders in terms very different from those in the traditional view. For example, debate on a school's discipline policy may be seen as a contest of values reflecting different beliefs about 'what ought to be'. Those representing each set of values are leaders in that debate. The outcome of the contest is reflected in the words of the policy. The principal may be a leader in debate and, once policy is determined, becomes a leader in another sense. The policy is presented to all parents and students as an expression of the values of the school and an attempt is made to build commitment to that policy: an attempt to bring about 'unification of people around values' and to 'construct the social world for others'.

An example of each definition of leader and leadership can thus be found in the school setting. Whereas earlier definitions focused on the exercise of formal authority related to the setting and accomplishment of goals, more recent perspectives invite us to consider at a deeper, more personal level what actually transpires when decisions are made and people try to make sense of their work. Concise definitions and descriptions are difficult, if not inappropriate. As Duke (1986: 10) observed, 'Leadership seems to be a gestalt phenomenon; greater than the sum of its parts.'

Leadership traits and theories: part of the picture

Studies until the late 1970s and early 1980s yielded useful but limited information about leaders and leadership. Attempts to identify the traits of leaders led to a relatively small list of attributes to guide the selection process. A quarter-century of careful research focused on two dimensions of leadership behaviour, generally concerned with tasks and people, with some measure of success in determining which particular behaviours or styles are the more effective in different situations. Some findings of these earlier studies are summarised here, with brief illustrations of their utility in the school setting. Attention is then turned to the larger picture which emerged in the 1980s.

Traits of leaders

Studies in the first half of the century compared the physical and psychological characteristics of leaders and non-leaders. An analysis of many of these studies by Stogdill (1948) found little consistency in their findings. The search for traits in leadership continued, however, with different approaches to measurement and an effort to distinguish among leaders on the basis of their effectiveness. Analyses of these later studies by Stogdill (1981) revealed a number of traits which consistently characterise more effective leaders. These include:

- sense of responsibility
- concern for task completion
- energy
- persistence
- risk-taking
- originality
- self-confidence
- capacity to handle stress
- capacity to influence
- capacity to coordinate the efforts of others in the achievement of purpose.

While these characteristics may be used with a relatively high degree of confidence in the selection and development of leaders, they are but a small part of the picture and provide little to guide the day-to-day activities of leaders in the school setting. More detail was added as attempts were made in the 1950s and 1960s to develop theories of leadership.

Theories of leadership

Some major findings of the 'theory movement' in leadership are briefly summarised here. Details may be found in books which deal in comprehensive fashion with this movement as far as its contribution to knowledge in educational administration is concerned (see, for example, Hoy and Miskel, 1987).

Research has consistently revealed the importance of two 'dimensions' in describing the behaviour of leaders. These behaviours reflect a concern for accomplishing the tasks of the organisation and a concern for relationships among people in the organisation. It is generally accepted that both kinds of behaviour are required for successful leadership. Attempts to develop theories have involved the careful study of situations in which leadership is exercised, acknowledging that there is no one best way to lead in all situations but that in any particular situation, one approach to leadership may be more effective than another. The challenge has been to identify particular attributes of leadership and circumstances which are important in establishing these situational contingencies. Two well-regarded contingency theories (Hersey and Blanchard 1982, Fiedler 1977) are summarised briefly, with illustrations of their utility in the school setting.

Hersey and Blanchard (1982) proposed in their situational theory that leadership behaviour should be varied according to the maturity of subordinates or followers. The situation in this theory is thus defined by maturity, with two dimensions proposed: professional maturity and psychological maturity. There are also two dimensions of leadership behaviour: task behaviour, in which the leader emphasises or specifies the task; and relationship behaviour, in which the leader invests time in developing good interpersonal relationships with and among the group. The theory proposes four general types of leadership behaviour, each of which is appropriate to a particular level of maturity. With increasing maturity, the leader should move through styles designated 'telling' (high task, low relationship); 'selling' (high task, high relationship); 'participating' (low task, high relationship); and 'delegating' (low task, low relationship).

Application of the Hersey and Blanchard theory calls for a highly personalised approach to leadership behaviour. In the school setting, for example, there may be high variability among staff in terms of maturity so that different behaviours will be required for different people. Particular members of staff may have different levels of maturity for different tasks. Furthermore, maturity levels will change from year to year as staff acquire professional and psychological maturity.

Surprisingly, the Hersey and Blanchard theory has not been subjected to rigorous validation. However, its propositions are intuitively well received and have become the focus of widely used management training programmes. The capacity carefully to diagnose maturity levels of staff and then to select matching leadership behaviour according to these propositions would appear to be a worthwhile addition to the repertoire of the school leader.

To understand the contingency theory of leadership formulated by Fiedler (see Fiedler, Chemers and Mahar, 1977, for more detailed explanation and illustration), we need to distinguish between leadership style and leadership behaviour. To Fiedler, leadership style is an innate, relatively enduring attribute of our personality which provides our motivation and determines our general orientation when exercising leadership. Leadership behaviour, on the other hand, refers to particular acts which we can perform or not perform if we have the knowledge and skills, and if we judge them appropriate at the time (this is the sense in which leadership behaviour is used in the Hersey and Blanchard theory).

Fiedler found that task-motivated leaders (those whose primary, driving motivation is to ensure that the task at hand is addressed) tend to be best suited to situations which are either highly favourable or highly unfavourable according to the extent to which tasks are structured, where there are good leader-member relations and when the leader has position power. Relationship-motivated leaders (those whose primary, driving motivation is to ensure that there are good relations with and among members of the work group) are best suited to situations which are moderately favourable on these dimensions. The Fiedler theory has implications for matching leaders to situations and for encouraging leaders to modify their situation where possible to ensure consistency with style. These applications rest on such fine distinctions, and represent such a small aspect of all that must be considered, that the theory seems unlikely to have major impact, despite its validation through research in a variety of settings.

Hodgkinson (1983: 200) summed up the theory movement in leadership as embodied in what he judged to be the finest of its products:

> I am prepared to acknowledge that the general productive effort of this type of research, particularly as it is embodied in Professor Fiedler's work, yields us the best theory we have to date in the domain of psychological discourse. I would suspect, however, a paradox. The closer such theory approaches the truth, the more incomprehensible it will become.

A decade of study: the larger picture

Retaining for a moment the metaphor of a picture, it seems that attention for some twenty-five years or so was turned to just one part of the scene (leadership behaviour, narrowly defined on two dimensions) which was then studied through a series of lenses with increasing power in terms of their capacity to discern detail, resulting in the precision of theories such as that offered by Fiedler. There seemed to be little impact on practice as the result of such efforts. Then followed a decade of study in which observers, in effect, stepped back and examined the whole picture, or at least a much broader canvas of activity, in an effort to describe and explain what makes organisations and their leaders successful. The outcomes do not yet constitute a new theory in the strictly scientific sense, but the generalisations which have emerged seem to hold much greater promise for shaping practice. They are intuitively well received by experienced practitioners, and have a richness and vibrancy which inspire action to a larger extent than the findings of earlier attempts to develop theories of leadership.

Emerging generalisations

Emerging from these studies are several generalisations which can shape leadership in schools where excellence is valued. Ten are offered here, with acknowledgement of their source in the literature described above. A summary with brief illustration is contained in Table 5.1. Guidelines and further illustrations are provided in the next section and in the two chapters which follow.

1. *Emphasis should be given to transforming rather than transactional leadership*
This important distinction was made by James McGregor Burns (1978) in his study of leadership and followership. According to Burns, leadership is transactional in most instances, that is, there is a simple exchange of one thing for another: jobs for votes in the case of a political leader and the electorate; a congenial working atmosphere and security in return for keeping central office, parents and students happy in the case of a principal and teaching staff. The transforming leader, while still responding to needs among followers, looks for potential motives in followers, seeks to satisfy higher needs, and engages the full person of the follower. The result of transforming leadership is a relationship of mutual stimulation and elevation that converts followers into leaders and leaders into moral agents (Burns 1978: 4).

The transforming leader may motivate citizens to make new commitments to help those in need (Mother Teresa) or to achieve a breakthrough in civil rights (Martin Luther King Jr.) or to achieve independence (Mahatma Gandhi). The principal who is a transforming leader may secure substantial commitments of time and energy from teachers in a drive to change attitudes of students and parents to school in a community where previously there were low levels of achievement and little value was placed on education. Illustrations of this thrust in transforming leadership are contained in Table 5.1.

2. *Outstanding leaders have a vision for their organisations*

Providing a vision was one of four strategies or themes in the study by Bennis and Nanus (1985) of ninety transforming leaders in a variety of settings. A vision is:

> a mental image of a possible and desirable future state of the organisation . . . as vague as a dream or as precise as a goal or mission statement . . . a view of a realistic, credible, attractive future for the organisation, a condition that is better in some important ways than what now exists (Bennis and Nanus 1985: 89).

The vision of Martin Luther King Jr. was captured in his stirring 'I have a dream' speech on the steps of the Lincoln Memorial in Washington. The vision of John F. Kennedy concerning space exploration was precise: a man on the moon before the end of the decade.

The importance of vision is a recurring theme in studies of excellence and leadership in education. The vision of a transforming principal may be a dream expressed in written form as 'our school will be a learning centre in the community, where every child will enjoy coming to school and will acquire the basic skills, and where parents and other members of the community can engage in educational programmes for their personal improvement and enjoyment.' This vision is illustrated in Table 5.1. The vision may, alternatively, be a more precise statement of mission: 'our students are presently performing far below those in schools in comparable social settings on tests of basic skills; we aim to come in the top ten among these schools on system-wide tests of achievement.'

3. *Vision must be communicated in a way which secures commitment among members of the organisation*

Bennis and Nanus (1985: 28) highlight the compelling nature of what is involved:

Table 5.1 Generalisations and Illustrations
Reflecting Recent Advances in Knowledge about Leadership

Generalisation	Illustration
1. Emphasis should be given to transformational rather than transactional leadership	Principal takes action to change community attitudes towards school
2. Outstanding leaders have a vision for their organisation	Principal envisages school as a learning centre for whole community
3. Vision must be communicated in a way which secures commitment among members of the organisation	Principal seeks commitment of teachers in devoting time and energy to change community attitudes towards school
4. Communication of vision requires communication of meaning	'Community' is metaphor for school; Principal rewards related teacher activities
5. Issues of value - 'what ought to be' - are central to leadership	Principal has strong commitment to equity in terms of access to schooling
6. The leader has an important role in developing culture of organisation	Principal involves members of community in all ceremonies at the school
7. Studies of outstanding schools provide strong support for school-based management and collaborative decision-making	School policy is determined by group representing parents, teachers, students and community at large
8. There are many kinds of leadership forces - technical, human, educational, symbolic and cultural - and these should be widely dispersed throughout the school	Planning for the various programmes in school carried out by teams of teachers, each having its own leader
9. Attention should be given to institutionalising vision if leadership of the transforming kind is to be successful	The vision of the school as a learning centre for the community is reflected in goals, policies, plans, budgets and activities
10. Both 'masculine' and 'feminine' stereotype qualities are important in leadership, regardless of the gender of the leader	Principal is sensitive and caring about personal needs ('feminine' stereotype); principal fosters competitive, team approach in raising school's academic standing ('masculine' stereotype)

Their visions or intentions are compelling and pull people toward them. Intensity coupled with commitment is magnetic . . . [Leaders] do not have to coerce people to pay attention; they are so intent on what they are doing that, like a child completely absorbed in creating a sand castle, they draw others in. Vision grabs.

Starratt (1986) includes the same requirement in his theory of leadership, emphasising that the shared vision must pervade day-to-day activities. One facet of this theory is that 'the leader articulates that vision in such compelling ways that it becomes the shared vision of the leader's colleagues, and it illuminates their ordinary activities with dramatic significance.' In a school, for example, a vision of high levels of self-esteem for every child in a community marked by severe disadvantage requires the shared commitment of all teachers. This commitment must shape every interaction of teacher and student; every word and every action must reflect that vision. Vaill (1986) coined the term 'purposing' to describe what is required of leaders in helping to achieve commitment. Purposing is 'that continuous stream of actions by an organisation's formal leadership which have the effect of inducing clarity, consensus and commitment regarding the organisation's basic purposes' (Vaill 1986: 91). One can imagine the very careful attention to 'purposing' in a school where the achievement of self-esteem is part of the vision, since that achievement is dependent on 'clarity, consensus and commitment' among the staff as they carry out their 'ordinary activities'.

4. *Communication of vision requires communication of meaning*
According to Bennis and Nanus (1985: 33) 'the management of meaning, [the] mastery of communication, is inseparable from effective leadership'. In reviewing the significant changes which have occurred over a decade of study in leadership, Sergiovanni (1987: 116) asserted that:

At the heart of these changes is the view that the meaning of leadership behaviour and events to teachers and others is more important than the behaviour and events themselves. Leadership reality for all groups is the reality they create for themselves, and thus leadership cannot exist separate from what people find significant and meaningful.

Particular attention has been given in recent years to the use of metaphors and symbols in the communication of meaning. Spoken and written words have always been regarded as important in the sharing of purposes and intentions, but the choice of metaphors takes on special significance, not only in expressing a vision but also in shaping the climate of the school and the meaning of ordinary activities. Some of the metaphors employed in describing a school are familiar: factory, hospital, family, community, war zone, or even a prison. The student is portrayed, respectively, as a worker, patient, family member, young citizen, soldier or prisoner. Teachers may be seen as factory supervisors, doctors, parents, community leaders, sergeants or warders. There will be debate and conflict about the choice of metaphors since they reflect values and views about the nature of people, society, schooling and education. Gaining consensus and commitment to the particular metaphors which will shape the ordinary activities of the school is thus an important concern for the principal and other leaders in the school.

Symbols are also important for the communication of meaning by leaders. A recent study of the management of symbols by school principals led Kelley and Bredeson (1987: 31) to describe symbolic leadership in terms of integrated messages 'communicated through the patterned use of words, actions and rewards that have an impact on the beliefs, values, attitudes and behaviours of others with whom the principal interacts'. The principal who seeks commitment among teachers to a vision which includes raising the levels of self-esteem will give careful thought to words, actions and rewards. For example, verbal interaction with students will be characterised by praise and encouragement. The principal will choose to attend and, where appropriate, participate in a wide variety of activities involving students with low levels of self-esteem. The presence of the principal will communicate to teachers, students and parents that these activities are valued. Rewards will come in the form of praise and encouragement of teachers who use similar words and engage in similar activities.

5. Issues of value - 'what ought to be' - are central to leadership
Greenfield (1986: 166) asserted that 'organisations are built on the unification of people around values. The business of being a leader is therefore the business of being an entrepreneur of values.' For transactional leadership, where there is a simple exchange between leader and followers ('votes for jobs'), these

values will be what Burns (1978: 426) called modal values or values of means such as honesty, responsibility, fairness and the honouring of commitments. For transforming leadership, where the pursuit of higher goals calls for full engagement and commitment, he suggests that the leader must be more concerned with end values such as liberty, justice and equality (Burns 1978: 426).

Much of the principal's work will involve transactional leadership. The aforementioned values of honesty, responsibility, fairness and the honouring of commitments are a basic requirement if the support of teachers is to be gained. If excellence is the goal, then transforming leadership and associated end values are needed. Excellence, however conceived, is itself an end value and, along with other end values, will be the subject of debate. Sergiovanni *et al.* (1987: 7) recognised this when, writing in the American context, they stated that 'at the heart of educational policy debates are four widely held but conflicting values: equity, excellence, efficiency and liberty'. Similar debates occur in other countries. Managing conflict over basic values will be as much part of the principal's role as it will be of leaders at local, state and national levels. For example, the value of excellence, conceived in terms of high levels of achievement in a relatively narrow range of academic studies, may conflict with the value of equity, conceived in terms of access to a range of educational programmes for all students, regardless of social and economic circumstance. Alternatively, substantial investment in resources with the intention of achieving excellence and equity might conflict with the value of efficiency. These conflicts, however resolved, will be followed by leadership acts designed to achieve what Greenfield (1986: 166) described as the 'unification of people around [these] values'.

6. *The leader has an important role in developing the culture of the organisation*

The nature of organisational culture and guidelines for building the culture of a school are offered in another chapter. As with the management of meaning, 'cultural leadership' has emerged as a major theme in studies over the last decade. Indeed, generalisations offered thus far are all embodied in the special attention which is accorded this aspect of leadership. While acknowledging that technical and managerial conceptions have their place, Sergiovanni (1987: 127) believes that:

Cultural leadership - by accepting the realities of the human spirit, by emphasising the importance of meaning and significance, and by acknowledging the concept of professional freedom linked to values and norms that make up a moral order - comes closer to the point of leadership.

The opportunities for cultural leadership in the school may be briefly illustrated. While definitions of culture are as varied as the definitions of leaders, there is general agreement that shared values and beliefs lie at the heart of the concept. There is also agreement that the extent to which values and beliefs are shared cannot be easily measured or directly observed. We can only rely on what Deal (1987: 6) called 'tangible cultural forms' or Sathe (1985: 17) described as 'manifestations of culture' in making inferences about culture in an organisation.

Deal listed six tangible cultural forms, each of which can be developed by the principal: shared values as reflected in shorthand slogans ('we care for every child in this school'), heroes in the life of the school or in society at large who embody the values which are held to be important ('former teacher Beth Hanson visited the home of every child she taught in twenty years of service'), rituals in the form of repetitive activities in which shared values are experienced ('new students are made welcome each year at a party where they are served by teachers'), ceremonies where values and heroes are highlighted and celebrated ('every child has the opportunity at least once each year to be recognised in some way at the Monday morning assembly'), stories illustrating, for example, where values and heroes triumphed in adversity ('the principal recounted to beginning teachers how Beth Hanson visited the parent of one of her students, the father, who was in prison at the time'), and cultural networks of people ('gossips, spies, storytellers') who in a variety of ways serve to protect the ways things are done.

7. Studies of outstanding schools provide strong support for school-based management and collaborative decision-making within a framework of state and local policies
While acknowledging that much research remains to be done, Purkey and Smith (1985: 355) believe that existing research on school effectiveness 'is sufficiently consistent to guide school improvement efforts based on its conclusions'. They offer a model for creating an effective school, with implications for school

leadership among its thirteen elements. One strategy for the development of school culture is the adoption of collaborative planning and collegial relationships. Another in the same vein is school-site management wherein:

> The staff of each school is given a considerable amount of responsibility and authority in determining the exact means by which they address the problem of increasing academic performance. This includes giving staffs more authority over curricular and instructional decisions and allocation of building resources (Purkey and Smith, 1985: 358).

These recommendations are consistent with those of scholars such as Theodore Sizer and John Goodlad following their respective studies of schooling in the United States. Sizer (1984: 214) believes that one 'imperative for better schools' is to give teachers and students room to take full advantage of the variety among them, a situation which 'implies that there must be substantial authority in each school. For most public and diocesan Catholic school systems, this means the decentralisation of power from headquarters to individual schools.' Goodlad (1984: 275) proposed 'genuine decentralisation of authority and responsibility to the local school within a framework designed to assure school-to-school equity and a measure of accountability'. He noted that 'the guiding principle being put forward here is that the school must become largely self-directing' (Goodlad 1984: 276).

School-based management calls for approaches to school leadership which encourage and support high levels of collaboration among teachers and, where appropriate, parents and students.

8. There are many kinds of leadership forces - technical, human, educational, symbolic and cultural - and these should be widely dispersed throughout the school

Symbolic and cultural aspects of leadership have been a feature of recent studies as reflected in most of the generalisations offered thus far. However, other aspects which have been part of more traditional perspectives must also be sustained. Sergiovanni (1984: 6) provided a useful classification of what he called 'leadership forces', each of which 'can be thought of as the means available to administrators, supervisors and teachers to bring about or preserve changes needed to improve schooling'. Technical leadership forces include the capacity to plan, organise, coordinate and schedule. Human leadership forces include building and maintaining morale, encouraging growth and creativity and involving people in decision-making. Educational leadership forces include the capacity to work with staff to determine student needs and develop curriculum and to provide supervision.

The technical, human and educational aspects of leadership in the Sergiovanni classification encompass the task and relationship dimensions of leadership behaviour used in earlier attempts to develop theories of leadership. Sergiovanni suggested that these three forces alone may ensure an effective school but, if excellence is desired, symbolic and cultural forces should also be evident.

It will be rare for a single leader such as the principal to exercise all of the leadership forces. Consistent with evidence of benefit from collaborative approaches, Sergiovanni (1987: 122) suggests that highly successful leaders recognise the importance of 'leadership density' which refers to 'the extent to which leadership roles are shared and the extent to which leadership is broadly exercised'. There will thus be many leaders in an excellent school.

9. *Attention should be given to institutionalising vision if leadership of the transforming kind is to be successful*
This generalisation takes up implications of those listed previously that point to the importance of what Burns called 'transforming leadership', with the principal having a vision for the school, and being able to articulate that vision in such a way that others become committed to it and day-to-day activities are imbued with its meanings and values. It is necessary, of course, that the vision be sustained or 'institutionalised', with its meanings and values embedded in the culture of the school. Starratt (1986) combined all of these perspectives in a simple, eloquent model for leadership as the 'communal institutionalising of a vision':

• The leader's power is rooted in a vision that is itself rooted in something basic to human life
• That vision illuminates the ordinary with dramatic significance
• The leader articulates that vision in such compelling ways that it becomes the shared vision of the leader's colleagues, and it illuminates their ordinary activities with dramatic significance
• The leader implants the vision in the structures and processes of the organisation, so that people experience the vision in the various patterned activities of the organisation

• The leader and colleagues make day-to-day decisions in the light of that vision, so that the vision becomes the heart of the culture of the organisation
• All the members of the organisation celebrate the vision in ritual, ceremonies and art forms.

This model may be shaped further by other generalisations related to collaborative decision-making as well as to density of leadership and the variety of leadership forces (technical, human, educational, symbolic, cultural). The principal may work with others to establish the vision for a school. The principal should work with others to implant the vision in the structures and processes of the school, something that calls for the technical and human skills of policy-making and planning. The making of day-to-day decisions in the areas of curriculum and instruction in a manner which reflects the vision will call for density of the educational leadership force; that is, a number of teachers will be leaders as the purposes, policies and priorities of the school are reflected in the various areas of the curriculum and in approaches to teaching and learning.

10. *Both 'masculine' and 'feminine' stereotype qualities are important in leadership, regardless of the gender of the leader*
The shortcomings of research and theory on the basis of their limited focus on males has been documented (Shakeshaft and Nowell, 1984). A cultural bias toward leadership by males is also evident, with Burns (1978: 50) noting that 'femininity has been stereotyped as dependent, submissive and conforming, and hence women have been seen as lacking in leadership qualities'. Burns believed that 'male bias is reflected in the false conception of leadership as mere command or control'. He sees promise of a shift in bias as other conceptions of leadership take hold, especially those which deal with the relationship between leader and followers. An examination of this relationship was central to his own study of leadership which led to the important distinction between transactional and transformational leadership. Burns concluded that as 'leadership comes properly to be seen as a process of leaders engaging and mobilising the human needs and aspirations of followers, women will be more readily recognised as leaders and men will change their own leadership styles'.

Some valuable insights on this issue were provided by Lightfoot (1983) in her investigation of 'the good high school'.

115

She described her studies as 'portraits' because 'I thought it would allow us a measure of freedom from the traditions and constraints of disciplined research methods, and because I thought our work would be defined by aesthetic, as well as empirical and analytic, dimensions' (Lightfoot 1983: 13). This approach enabled her to capture aspects of leadership which may have eluded the researcher who employed a more constrained methodology. She found that the six principals in her investigation, all of whom were male, were stereotypically male in some respects (images included 'the raw masculinity of the coach', 'the paternalism of the father-principal', 'the imperial figure'). Yet, she observed, 'in all cases, the masculine images have been somewhat transformed and the arrangements of power have been adjusted. In the most compelling cases, the leaders have sought to feminise their style and have been aware of the necessity of motherly interactions with colleagues and staff'. Lightfoot (1983: 333) concluded that the 'people and context demand a reshaping of anachronistic patterns':

> The redefinition includes softer images that are based on nurturance given and received by the leader; based on relationships and affiliations as central dimensions of the exercise of power; and based on a subtle integration of personal qualities traditionally attached to male and female images.

While the need for further research is evident, a generalisation which acknowledges the importance of both masculine and feminine qualities in leadership can be offered with confidence. It seems especially relevant to leadership in a shift toward more autonomy for schools, with school-based management characterised by collaborative approaches.

Vision in school leadership: guidelines and illustrations

The final section of the chapter provides guidelines and illustrations of three generalisations related to vision in school leadership:

- Outstanding leaders have a vision for their organisations (See Generalisation No. 2 on p. 107)
- Vision must be communicated in a way which secures commitment among members of the organisation (Generalisation No. 3)

• Communication of vision requires communication of meaning (Generalisation No. 4).

In most instances, these guidelines and illustrations are for the school as a whole, with the principal as leader. The same guidelines and similar illustrations may be developed for units within the school and their leaders.

The nature of vision

Bennis and Nanus (1985: 89) considered vision in broad terms to mean:

A mental image of a possible and desirable future state of the organisation . . . as vague as a dream or as precise as a goal or mission statement . . . a view of a realistic, credible, attractive future for the organisation, a condition that is better in some important ways than what now exists.

Some writers such as Block (1987) would prefer to distinguish between a vision, a mission and an objective, but the broader view is adopted here. It is acknowledged, however, that the term 'vision' as it now appears in the literature on leadership has the same or similar meaning as has been usually ascribed to words like 'goal'. Scheive and Schoenheit (1987), for example, wrote about vision and leadership after interviewing twelve educators, including five principals, who were widely regarded as leaders. These interviews began with a question which asked about the leader's goals as an educator, after which the subject was asked 'Is your vision, then, to . . . ?' (Scheive and Schoenheit 1987: 96). In this chapter we are not ascribing to the term 'vision' any special characteristic which has recently been discovered, although we accept its usefulness in describing a 'mental picture' which is shaped by one or more goals.

The study by Scheive and Schoenheit is a useful starting point for providing illustrations of visions for schools. Those interviewed shared two kinds of vision, one related to their own organisation and the other to the world beyond their own organisation; the former embodied a vision of organisational excellence, the latter centred on the issue of equity and was concerned with 'righting a wrong'. It would seem that the specific vision for the school is shaped in part by a more general vision which reflects some basic values and beliefs held by the leader. This is consistent with the model for leadership proposed by Starratt (1986) which suggested that 'the leader's power is rooted in a vision that is itself rooted in something basic to human life'. At the broadest level, these basic values and beliefs seem to fall into constellations which are often in conflict. These 'competing visions' in society as a whole were described by Sowell (1987).

Roueche and Baker (1986) obtained 'profiles of excellence' of 154 schools selected in the 1983 National School Recognition Program in the United States and found that principals tended to have visions not only of a preferred outcome but also of the process of change through which that outcome would be attained. Processes of change include preferred approaches to teaching and learning as well as preferred approaches to the management of change. As with vision related to outcomes, preferences in terms of process reflect different values and beliefs held by the leader. Both kinds of vision - process and outcome - seem to include what Sergiovanni and Starratt (1983: 227) described as the leader's 'educational platform', a set of assumptions and beliefs which 'deal with the way children and youth grow, with the purposes of schooling, with the nature of learning, with pedagogy and teaching, with educational programmes, and with school climate'.

Guidelines - 1

Drawing together this research and writing, we offer the following as a guide to the nature of vision for a school:

• The vision of a school leader includes a mental image of a possible and desirable future state of the school
• The vision will embody the leader's own view of what constitutes excellence in schooling
• The vision of a school leader also includes a mental image of a possible and desirable future state for the broader educational scene and for society in general
• The vision of a school leader also includes a mental image of a possible and desirable process of change through which the preferred future state will be achieved
• Each aspect of the vision for a school reflects different assumptions, values and beliefs about such matters as the nature of humankind; the purpose of schooling; the roles of government, family and church in schooling; approaches to teaching and

learning; and approaches to the management of change
• There will be competing visions of schooling reflecting the many, often conflicting differences in assumptions, values and beliefs.

Illustration - 1

The following is an example of one leader's vision for a school, illustrating each of the elements listed above:

Ruth Griffiths has been appointed principal of a high school in a lower socio-economic area of the city. The school buildings are becoming dilapidated because of their age as well as from increasing vandalism. Parents and other members of the community rarely visit the school. Ruth would like to see a quite different scene in five years. She has committed herself to stay for five years and would like to assemble about her a staff which will develop a similar commitment. She wants to create a school in which children can take pride and which parents and others will visit regularly and support. She acknowledges that student achievement may never be as high as that in more favoured areas but she is convinced that most of the children can do well and can enjoy their schooling. She has the same view for education in general, believing that the quality of life for all will be enhanced if this can be achieved. Ruth Griffiths believes that it is possible for all parents to be involved in the school in a variety of ways, including direct involvement in their children's learning and in the planning and implementation of change. She would especially like to engage the many businesses and industries in the community in a major effort to improve the school. She believes in a partnership of government, community, home and school since all have an interest in what the school accomplishes for its students, each of whom should be able to make a contribution to the community at large at the same time as being satisfied and challenged as an individual. Ruth expects that curriculum and instruction should reflect the needs and interests of all children but that high expectations can be pursued with consistency and enthusiasm. She acknowledges, however, that her views are different from those of many of her teachers who believe that little more can be expected of the school than is being achieved at present.

The term 'vision', as we have illustrated it above, is not describing a new phenomenon in leadership. It is simply attaching a label to the sort of dream or constellation of goals or scenarios that form in the mind of everyone from time to time. What we now know is that these form readily in the minds of leaders who succeed in transforming their organisations. Before progress can be made, however, the leader must succeed in communicating that vision in ways that secure commitment among others.

Communicating the vision

The ways in which the principal may work with others to 'institutionalise' the vision in the structures, policies, priorities, plans, budgets, approaches to teaching and learning, and everyday activities in the school are addressed in Chapters 6 and 7. Here are some guidelines, with brief illustration, of what is not only a necessary first step but also a continuing requirement, namely communicating the vision in ways which are likely to gain the commitment of others.

Symbolic leadership

A simple presentation, both rational and eloquent, to a meeting of staff, or a carefully constructed discussion paper for distribution to staff prior to such a meeting, are useful contributions but constitute only a narrow range of leadership behaviour. Among the generalisations which have emerged from recent studies of leaders was the importance of symbolic leadership and the communication of meaning, especially through the use of metaphor, and it is to acts of symbolic leadership that the principal should turn in an effort to communicate a vision for the school. The definition of symbolic leadership offered by Kelley and Bredeson (1987) is a useful starting point for developing some guidelines. They described symbolic leadership in terms of integrated messages which 'are communicated through the patterned use of words, actions and rewards that have an impact on the beliefs, values, attitudes and behaviours of others with whom the principal interacts' (Kelley and Bredeson 1987: 31).

Guidelines - 2

This view of symbolic leadership, and the recognition that it is the meanings others attribute to actions rather than the acts themselves which are significant, produces guidelines like the following:

• Words, both oral and written, are important for effective communication of vision, giving particular attention to metaphors which describe what is preferred, especially in relation to people, behaviours and relationships
• Vision can be communicated through actions which, quite separate from any words which might accompany them, can communicate meaning in very powerful ways - the way the school leader dresses, how the school leader arranges an office and greets visitors, events which the school leader chooses to attend, people with whom the school leader is seen to associate, ceremonies which the school leader decides to conduct, and how the school leader allocates time during the school day
• Vision can be communicated through rewards. What words and behaviours of others the school leader chooses to reward and in what manner will readily convey a picture of what is preferred. These rewards may be bestowed on students, members of staff, parents and other members of the school community and may come in the form of simple words of thanks or praise as well as through the granting of some privilege or favour
• It is important for the school leader to demonstrate consistency among these elements of symbolic leadership and be consistent over time with different people in different circumstances. It is also important for others in the school to see consistency between these acts of symbolic leadership and what they discern as the personality and underlying motives and values of the leader.

Illustration - 2

The view of a preferred future by Ruth Griffiths, a recently appointed principal of an inner-city high school, was offered as an illustration of a vision for a school. What follows here are illustrations of how elements of that vision might be communicated through words, actions and rewards.

• *Element of vision*: 'Ruth Griffiths sees a school in which all children can take pride.'

Words: Ruth Griffiths openly articulates to staff and students her commitment to improving the condition of the school buildings.

Actions: Ruth Griffiths rescinds a previous decision to paint and repair the wing of the school where her office is located and arranges for the work to be done instead on two common rooms used by the students.

Rewards: Ruth Griffiths encourages students to make their own improvements in their common rooms and classes. She secures funds and donations from local business to upgrade the facilities used by students.

• *Element of vision*: 'Ruth Griffiths would especially like to engage the many businesses and industries in a major effort to improve the school.'

Words: Ruth Griffiths arranged invitations to speak at meetings of the Chamber of Commerce for herself, a parent, a teacher and a student. The benefits of close links between school and community were stressed. Metaphors such as 'community' and 'partnership' were used here as well as in meetings of staff and in communications with parents.

Actions: Ruth Griffiths attends seminars organised to promote local business and asks to be invited to management seminars for leaders in the community. She invites a highly-regarded business executive to speak at a staff seminar on trends in the use of technology.

Rewards: Ruth Griffiths ensures that the seminar involvement of staff and business is noted in newspaper accounts. She makes favourable comment on each occasion staff develop these and similar linkages.

These examples illustrate just two elements in the vision for the school offered by Ruth Griffiths. Since there are several elements in that vision, it is evident that there is a rich array in the repertoire of symbolic acts available to the principal. This aspect of leadership will demand time and energy, requiring a sharing of leadership in what Sergiovanni described as 'leadership density' in the distribution of leadership forces. Over time, however, this commitment by the principal will become the shared commitment of staff and others in the community, setting the stage for 'institutionalising' the vision in the structures and processes of the school. How this might be done is the subject of Chapter 6.

Summary

Our purpose in this chapter has been to demonstrate how recent advances in knowledge about leadership can contribute to the achievement of excellence. Earlier views about the nature of leadership itself were rather constrained and superficial, tending to emphasise the exercise of formal authority in achieving the goals of the school. This view gave way to recognition that leadership involves influence and that many who are not formally designated as such may serve as leaders. More recently, we have gained a deeper appreciation of leadership by examining the relationship between leaders and other members of staff, noting the importance of meanings which are derived from leadership acts.

So theories of leadership have provided only a small part of the total picture. We know, for example, that it is important for leaders to give attention to two dimensions: accomplishment of the tasks at hand, and establishing good relationships with and among members of staff. So-called 'contingency theories' offer refinements which are helpful but are somewhat narrow in their potential for application and impact. For example, the situational theory of Hersey and Blanchard reminds us of the importance of varying leadership behaviour according to the maturity of staff for the task at hand; the more mature in a personal and professional sense, the less directive and more participative the leader should be. Fiedler's contingency theory tells us that the relatively unchanging, somewhat innate aspects of our leadership style make us better suited to some situations than to others.

However, it is the larger picture which has resulted from leadership studies of the last decade which will prove most helpful to the leader who wishes to make a contribution to excellence in the school. It seems that emphasis should be given to transforming rather than transactional leadership, with the intent being to change attitudes and bring about commitment to 'a better state' which is embodied in a vision of excellence for the school. We know that outstanding school leaders have such a vision and that they succeed in communicating it in a way that secures the commitment of others in the school and its community. The most important aspect of communication is the meaning it conveys. So it is important for the school leader to decide on the meanings which are intended and then to choose acts which will ensure the intended outcome. Leadership is concerned with gaining commitment to a set of values, statements of 'what ought to be', which then become the heart of the culture of the school. Gaining this commitment can be achieved in a number of ways, especially with collaborative approaches to decision-making and with placing at the school level high responsibility and authority for making decisions related to the allocation of resources in the school. We know that there is a variety of what Sergiovanni called 'leadership forces' - technical, human, educational, symbolic and cultural - and all should be present and widely dispersed in the school ('leadership density') if excellence is to be attained. Having a vision and securing commitment to that vision is just the starting point. That vision must then be 'institutionalised' so that it shapes the everyday activities in the school. All of these approaches call for masculine and feminine qualities of leadership, regardless of the gender of the leader.

This chapter also contained some guidelines and illustrations for forming and communicating a vision. The vision should be concerned with a possible and desirable future state for the school, should embody a view of excellence and a view of a preferred future for education and society in general, should incorporate a picture of the process of change through which the vision for the school will be achieved, and will reflect different assumptions, beliefs and attitudes which are basic to life and education. There will be competing visions of what is preferred, reflecting a variety of assumptions, beliefs and values. In communicating the vision, the school leader should use a wide range of symbolic leadership acts, broadly classified as words, actions and rewards, with consistency in their use being important.

The stage is now set for considering ways in which the shared vision for the school can shape everyday activities in learning and teaching.

6

A Model for Managing
an Excellent School

The vision for a school, however determined, must be brought to reality. The view of excellence which is envisaged should be reflected in statements about the philosophy and goals of the school. The educational needs of children and instructional programmes for the school will be determined in the light of these statements which will also give substance to important management processes wherein policies are formulated, priorities are set, plans are made, resources are allocated and teaching and learning proceeds, with regular, systematic appraisal of the programme. With the view of leadership offered in Chapter 5, the vision will be articulated in a manner which secures the commitment of all in the school community, with opportunities for leadership widely dispersed in the school. This commitment will be enhanced, as will the quality of decisions, with appropriate involvement of others in the decision-making process.

This chapter contains guidelines and illustrations for helping to bring vision to reality. We recommend a model for school management which provides a framework for accomplishing the following aspects of leadership considered in Chapter 5:

• *Purposing*
'. . . that continuous stream of actions by an organisation's formal leadership which have the effect of inducing clarity, consensus, and commitment regarding the organisation's basic purposes' (Vaill, 1986: 91)

• *Values*
'Organisations are built on the unification of people around values' (Greenfield, 1986: 166)

• *School-site management and collaborative decision-making*
'The staff of each school is given a considerable amount of responsibility and authority in determining the exact means by which they address the problem of increasing academic performance. This includes giving staffs more authority over curricular and instructional decisions and allocation of building resources' (Purkey and Smith, 1985: 358)

• *Leadership density*
'. . . the extent to which leadership roles are shared and the extent to which leadership is broadly exercised' (Sergiovanni, 1987: 122)

• *Institutionalising the vision*
'The leader implants the vision in the structures and processes of the organisation, so that people experience the vision in the various patterned activities of the organisation' (Starratt, 1986).

Since bringing vision to reality may frequently involve changing the existing way of doing things, a model for school management must also contain strategies for the successful management of change. It is necessary, then, to review briefly what is now known about such strategies before describing and illustrating the model we recommend.

Management of change

The ten generalisations about successful leadership set out in Chapter 5 were offered with a high degree of confidence since they describe what has consistently been found in studies of leadership in a variety of organisations, including schools. One might ask: 'Are there generalisations about successful change which can be offered with the same degree of confidence?' We believe there are, and the purpose of this section of the chapter is to summarise the findings from one of the most recent and credible pieces of research about the management of change.

What follows is a summary of the findings of the *Project on Improving Urban High Schools* (Miles, 1987) which has been in progress for some time in the United States. We have chosen to share these findings for the following reasons:

• the project involved field-based research in schools which have been highly successful in implementing change

• the changes which had been successfully implemented fell into categories generally described as school improvement or school effectiveness or teacher effectiveness, and are thus relevant to the issue of excellence as it is addressed in this book
• the findings are consistent with guidelines for the management of change which have been generally regarded as widely transferable
• the leader of the project, Matthew B. Miles, Center for Policy Research in New York, is one of the outstanding researchers and writers about organisational change, especially in education
• as noted by Miles (1987: 17), though the studies were carried out in urban high schools, there is no apparent reason why the findings should not be relevant to any kind of school in any setting (although we, with the reader, will put this observation to critical test).

The findings summarised below were derived from survey data from a national sample of 170 schools which had achieved varying degrees of success in implementation and from detailed case studies of 5 schools having a high degree of success with change of the kind described above.

Factors leading to successful implementation

Miles and his colleagues identified sixteen factors which seemed to account for successful implementation. Most are within the control of the principal and most call for particular patterns of working with and through staff. These factors are as follows, with the first four in the list being preconditions:

• Leadership   (precondition)
• School autonomy   (precondition)
• Staff cohesiveness   (precondition)
• Good programme / fit   (precondition)
• Power-sharing
• Rewards for staff
• Vision
• Control over staffing
• Control over resources
• Staff willingness / initiative
• Evolutionary programme development
• External networks

- Coping
- 'Good implementation'
- Institutionalisation
- Organisational change

The first four factors were described as 'preconditions' because they can only be partly influenced by people at the school level. Successful implementation calls for principals (assuming they have the necessary leadership skills) generally having the capacity to do the kinds of things outlined in Chapter 5. We believe that most of these skills can be developed by a principal after appointment. The extent of school autonomy is often determined by policies formulated at the system level. Another precondition, staff cohesiveness, can be shaped to some extent by the principal and members of staff but is also influenced by the manner in which staff are appointed. The fourth precondition, a good programme/fit, refers to the extent to which the programme to be implemented is suited to schools in general and the particular community or culture. Miles and his colleagues found that major decisions related to programmes were generally made by people at the system level or by the principal.

A number of causal relationships were observed or hypothesised as summarised in Table 6.1 and illustrated in Figure 6.1. The following findings are noteworthy:

- Power sharing tended to occur after the major decisions about programmes were made but was critical to securing staff willingness/initiative which, in turn, was crucial to stabilising the change after implementation (institutionalisation)
- School autonomy extended to at least some control over staffing and other resources
- Programme development was evolutionary - 'a strong bias toward steady adaptation' (Miles, 1987: 13) - rather than implementation which was planned in detail at the outset
- The shared vision included a vision of the process of change as well as of a preferred and possible future for the school
- Empowerment of staff was important, with 'a critical mass of actively engaged people, usually up to a dozen or so' (*ibid*: 14), with expansion over time; bottom-up, departmentally based, planning groups and school councils were cited as examples of such empowered groups

• Internal and external assistance tailored to the special needs of the school was sought and sustained when success was achieved; assistance tended to be uniform in nature and limited to the 'front end' of the change process in less successful attempts at implementation

• Coping with problems was important if implementation was to be successful; successful schools used 'deep coping' strategies such as restaffing, securing greater control over resources, empowering, team building, and redesigning roles or the organisation itself; unsuccessful schools tended to use 'shallow coping' strategies such as avoiding, denying, procrastinating or people-shuffling.

These findings are consistent with generalisations on leadership set out in Chapter 5, especially in regard to a shared vision, power-sharing ('leadership density'), and institutionalising the vision. They also identify other factors which can be influenced by leaders if change is to be successful, namely, staff cohesiveness, ensuring a good programme which 'fits' the school setting, rewards for staff, coping, and the formation and utilisation of external networks. We believe the model for school management described and illustrated in the pages which follow incorporates the generalisations on leadership and strategies for the successful management of change which are suggested by the findings of the Miles study.

Table 6.1 Relationships between Factors in Successful
Implementation of Change (based on Miles, 1987)†

Factor	Is influenced by	Has influence on
Leadership	Precondition	Staff cohesiveness Good programme/fit Power sharing Rewards for staff Vision, Coping External networks Institutionalisation
School autonomy	Precondition	Good programme/fit Control over resources
Staff cohesiveness	Precondition (Leadership)	Vision
Good programme/fit	Precondition Leadership School autonomy Evolutionary programme development	Power sharing Rewards for staff
Power sharing	Leadership Good programme/fit	Staff willingness/ initiative (Institutionalisation)
Rewards for staff	Leadership Good programme/fit	Staff willingness/ initiative
Vision	Leadership Staff cohesiveness Control over staffing	Evolutionary programme development Staff willingness/ initiative
Control over staffing	School autonomy	Vision Staff willingness/ initiative
Control over resources	School autonomy	Evolutionary programme development

Factor	Is influenced by	Has influence on
Staff willingness/ initiative	Power sharing Rewards for staff Vision Control over staffing External networks	Evolutionary programme development 'Good implementation'
External networks	Leadership	Evolutionary programme development Staff willingness/ initiative Coping
Coping	Leadership External networks	Evolutionary programme development 'Good implementation' (Institutionalisation)
Evolutionary programme development	Vision Control over resources External networks Staff willingness/ initiative Coping	Good programme/fit Organisational change 'Good implementation'
'Good implementation'	Evolutionary programme development Staff willingness/ initiative Coping	Institutionalisation
Institutional- isation	Leadership (Power sharing) (Coping) 'Good implementation' Organisational change	
Organisational change	Evolutionary programme development	Institutionalisation

† All relationships were observed causal relationships, except those in brackets which were hypothesised.

Figure 6.1 Illustration of Relationships in Successful
Implementation of Change (Miles 1987: 6)

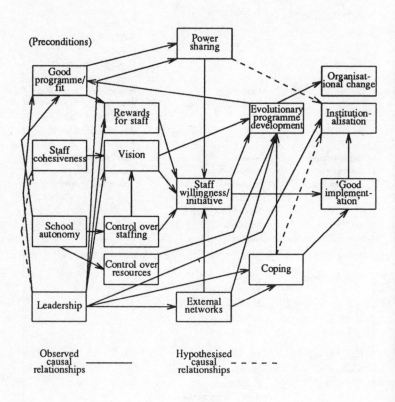

The recommended model

We recommend the *Collaborative School Management Cycle* of
Caldwell and Spinks (1988) as a model for school management
which incorporates the generalisations and strategies related to
leadership and change. An outline of the model is provided here
along with a brief account of the research and development effort
which led to its identification. The model is described as the Collaborative School Management Cycle and is illustrated in Figure
6.2. The cycle has six phases:

• Goal-setting and needs identification
• Policy-making, with policies consisting of statements of purpose
and broad guidelines
• Planning of programmes
• Preparation and approval of programme budgets
• Implementing
• Evaluating.

Three special characteristics of the model are:

• the clear and unambiguous specification of those phrases which
are the concern of the group responsible for policy-making ('policy group') and of other phases which are the concern of the
groups responsible for implementing policy ('programme teams'),
• a definition of policy which goes beyond a statement of general
aims or purposes but is not so detailed as to specify action - it
provides a brief statement of purpose and a set of broad guidelines, and
• the organising of planning activities around programmes which
correspond to the preferred patterns of work in the school.

The distinction between 'policy group' and 'programme teams'
provides the framework for an approach to school management
which is consistent with the generalisations about leadership and
the strategies for the successful management of change. The people who constitute the policy group will vary from setting to setting. In Britain, under the provisions of the 1986 Education Act
and the intentions of the national government as far as budgets in
publicly funded schools are concerned, the policy group is the
governing body. In government schools in Victoria, Australia, the
policy group is a school council. In other places, the policy group

*Figure 6.2 The Collaborative School Management Cycle
(Caldwell and Spinks, 1988)*

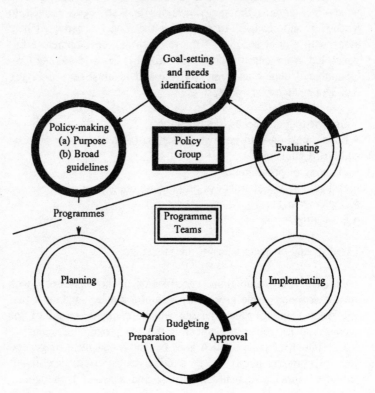

may be the principal alone, principal and senior staff, or principal and senior staff with advice from teachers and other members of the school community. There may, in some instances, be different policy groups in the school, each addressing different sets of issues.

The activities of the school associated with learning and teaching and the support of learning and teaching are divided into programmes. The policies and priorities set by the policy group shape the planning of these programmes by members of programme teams who will be teachers in most instances, with a

leader who may be designated as a head of department or programme coordinator, depending on local terminology and practice.
It is this feature of the model which provides for power-sharing,
with a 'critical mass' of actively engaged people (a finding of
Miles and his colleagues on successful change) and 'leadership
density' (generalisation about leadership). Programme teams are
responsible for preparing a plan for the implementation of policies
related to their programmes and for identifying the resources
required to support that plan. A programme plan and the proposed
pattern for resource allocation together constitute a programme
budget. The model thus affords a framework wherein a school can
exercise control over the allocation of resources (a factor identified in the study reported by Miles), subject to the limits of school
autonomy.

While programme budgets are prepared by programme
teams, they must be approved by the policy group; they must
reflect the policies and priorities established earlier by that group.
This aspect of the model is consistent with the finding in the
study reported by Miles that power-sharing in schools which successfully managed change tended to follow the making of 'major'
decisions. Following implementation by programme teams, the
evaluating phase is again a shared responsibility, with programme
teams gathering information for programme evaluation and the
policy group gathering further information as appropriate to make
judgments on the effectiveness of policies and programmes.

In general, the policy group has responsibility for those
phases which are emphasised in black in Figure 6.2 - largely those
above the diagonal line - while programme teams work within a
framework of policy to take responsibility for the remaining
phases - largely those below the diagonal line. While a clear distinction is made between the responsibilities of the policy group
and programme teams, there will in reality be a high degree of
overlap as far as personnel are concerned and a continuing high
level of formal and informal communication.

Identification of the model

The model was an outcome of the Effective Resource Allocation
in Schools Project (ERASP), a joint endeavour in 1983 of the
Education Department of Tasmania and the Centre for Education
at the University of Tasmania, funded as a Project of National
Significance by the Commonwealth Schools Commission. Its

purpose was to prepare a professional development programme for principals and other school administrators to help ensure the efficient and effective allocation of resources at the school level. While resources were conceived somewhat narrowly in the early stages of ERASP, the model which provides the centre-piece of the professional development programme takes a broader view, with the resources of the school being knowledge, power, people, time, space, buildings, material and money.

The approach adopted in ERASP was to conduct studies of highly effective government (public or state) and non-government (private or independent) schools in two states, Tasmania and South Australia, where there was at the time a relatively high degree of decentralisation to the school level of responsibility for resource allocation. Schools selected for case study were considered to be highly effective in a general sense as well as in the manner in which they allocated resources. Schools were nominated for study by panels of people who were generally regarded as highly knowledgeable about schools in the two states. Guiding their selections were lists of characteristics of highly effective schools which had been gleaned from the literature on school effectiveness. The schools selected for study were those nominated most frequently in categories which reflected differences in size, type, location and socio-economic environment.

It was found that highly effective schools in the project had adopted approaches to resource allocation which involved a clearly identifiable and systematic approach to matching resources to educational goals and student needs, with opportunities for staff and often community involvement in the process. The process at Rosebery District High School under the leadership of the principal, Jim Spinks, was selected for special attention because it contained all of the characteristics of highly effective resource allocation which had been identified in the literature. This school had earlier received the most nominations as a highly effective school of any school in its category in the Tasmanian component of the project.

Utilisation of the model

The model was the focus of an important initiative in school management in one large school system and seems to have wide application. Caldwell and Spinks conducted seminars from 1984 to 1986 in Victoria, Australia, for representatives of more than 1,100 schools as part of a government initiative in that state to introduce programme budgeting in schools at a time when there was also the intent to devolve substantial management powers to schools. A total of 71 per cent of all schools in the system responding to a survey in early 1987 had made a decision to adopt the approach, with the majority making good progress, even though adoption was not required until 1989 (see Ministry of Education, Victoria, 1987). Continuing support is now provided by senior officers in the regions of the state as the system moves toward adoption of the approach in all schools. The model seems relevant to initiatives which encourage school-site management in Canada, United States and Britain, where it is the intent of the national government to give control over their budgets to headteachers and governing bodies of all secondary and most primary schools. Caldwell (1987) provided a comparative study of these developments, giving particular attention to Britain.

Guidelines and illustrations

In this section of the chapter we use for illustrative purposes a vision for excellence that was offered in Chapter 5 to illustrate vision in leadership. Included in the vision of the principal was the statement: 'Ruth (the principal) expects that curriculum and instruction should reflect the needs and interests of all children but that high expectations can be set and pursued with consistency and enthusiasm.' We shall provide illustrations for a primary school on this occasion.

Following some of the approaches illustrated in Chapter 5, the principal may use a variety of strategies which result in general acceptance among staff and others that this vision should shape the programme of the school. This acceptance may take time, especially if some staff do not initially believe that it is possible to set high expectations for all students. However, these attitudes will change, especially as a result of sustained leadership of a symbolic nature including the use of rewards, choice of language and careful attention to the design of activities such as school ceremonies. Accomplishing this change of attitude is the essence of transforming leadership and a hallmark of excellence.

In time, then, this vision may be embodied in a statement of philosophy of the school. A school's philosophy is a statement of assumptions, values and beliefs about the nature and purpose of schooling, of learning and teaching processes, and processes which support learning and teaching. Included in a school's philosophy might be the following which reflects the aforementioned statement of vision.

We believe that it is desirable and possible to develop an educational programme at the school which will meet the needs and interests of every child in our community. Moreover, we believe that every child can achieve success in every learning experience in those parts of the school programme which have been selected as appropriate to the needs and interests of the child. We hold it important that every member of staff provide such learning opportunities for each child and that all parents and others in the school community be encouraged to give their strong support to the achievement of these expectations.

The goals, policies, plans, priorities, budgets and everyday activities in the school should all be consistent with the school's philosophy. That philosophy is the most fundamental benchmark for identifying needs and for programme evaluation.

Goal-setting

A goal is a statement of broad direction, general purpose or intent; it is general and timeless and is not concerned with a particular outcome at a particular point in time. Goals are usually formulated to reflect desired learning experiences and outcomes for the student. Some goals may also be concerned with the support of learning and the process of management.

The following are sample goals which reflect those parts of a statement of vision and school philosophy concerned with the setting of high expectations for all students:

• To ensure that each student enjoys learning and other experiences offered by the school
• To ensure that each student can attain a high level of reading ability, taking account of age and any special personal circumstances.

It is desirable that all in the school community be committed to goals as well as to the vision and philosophy of the school. Similar strategies for building commitment should therefore be followed, with formal adoption of goals being the outcome of a decision-making process designed to achieve consensus.

Another aspect of the first phase of the Collaborative School Management Cycle is identification of needs. Though we will qualify this definition, a need is considered to exist if 'what is' falls short of 'what should be'. Consider, for example one of the goals illustrated above: 'To ensure that each student can attain a high level of reading ability, taking account of age and any special personal circumstances.' For a particular primary school, the mean score on a standardised reading test given in Grade 3 was at the thirtieth percentile among mean scores for all primary schools in the state, that is, in only thirty per cent of primary schools was the mean score lower. This is a statement of 'what is' as far as levels of reading skill are concerned. Does a need for change exist? The answer depends on a judgement as to 'what ought to be' for such a school. Suppose a further comparison revealed that the mean score for the school in question exceeded the mean score for ninety per cent of all schools located in similar communities as far as student social and family background characteristics were concerned. The policy group might decide that investment of additional resources is unlikely to bring the school to the very top when such comparisons are made and that discrepancies between 'what is' and 'what ought to be' as far as other goals are concerned are such that other needs are greater or of higher priority. The group is likely to make a different judgement, however, if the second comparison reveals that mean reading scores exceed those of only fifty per cent of similar kinds of schools.

In general, the policy group must ask a number of questions before a need for change can be specified. A goal is just the starting point. The group must decide in practical terms 'what should be'. It must gather information about 'what is'. A judgement must then be made as to whether a gap is large enough for action to be taken. Will some harm be done if the gap is not closed? Can the gap be closed given a reasonable investment of resources? How important is this need compared with others?

Policy-making

Caldwell and Spinks (1988) describe a school policy as a statement of purpose and one or more guidelines as to how that purpose is to be achieved which, taken together, provide a framework for the operation of the school or programme. A school will have a number of policies, depending on its size and programme. Most policies will provide a framework for decisions related to the curriculum in areas such as mathematics, science and language. Other policies will affect all areas of the curriculum; for example, homework, assessment and reporting. Other categories of policy will concern the management of students (for example, discipline, field trips) and management processes in general (for example, a policy on decision-making or community involvement).

A primary school may have a policy on the development of reading skills which reflects that element of the statement of vision concerned with the setting of high expectations for all students and a goal or aim such as 'to ensure that each student can attain a high level of reading ability, taking account of age and any special personal circumstances'. A sample policy on reading is contained in Figure 6.3.

Caldwell and Spinks recommend a model for the formulation of policy according to whether the issue at hand is contentious or non-contentious. A non-contentious issue is one for which there is general satisfaction with current practice in the school. A contentious issue is one for which there is disagreement on current practice among staff or others in the school community, or disagreement about the approach which should be taken if the issue is not currently addressed in the school. For non-contentious issues, Caldwell and Spinks recommend the simple documentation of existing practice in the agreed format for a policy statement. They suggest that a statement of policy should not exceed one page; any longer and it will be rarely read or changed. They also stress the importance of keeping, the statement free of jargon so that it can be read and understood by all members of the school community.

For policy-making on contentious issues, Caldwell and Spinks recommend the appointment of a working party to prepare options for consideration by the policy group. The working party should be representative of those with expertise and a stake in the issue and it should obtain information from a variety of sources in preparing policy options. The desired outcome is consensus on a policy which is both desirable and feasible. The recommended approach provides a mechanism for empowering staff and others in preparing policy which provides a framework for action in bringing vision to reality.

Figure 6.3 Sample Policy on Reading in a Primary School

LEARNING TO READ

Purpose

Reading is one of the most important skills to be learned by children attending our school. We believe that the home and school are partners in helping children learn to read and that all teachers have the opportunity and responsibility to make a contribution in this partnership. Accordingly, the purposes of this aspect of our school programme are:

1. To ensure that each child learns to read at the highest level possible, given his or her age and any special personal circumstances.
2. To involve parents wherever possible in reading activities involving their children, both at home and at school.
3. To ensure that each teacher takes every opportunity to foster the development of skills in reading.

Guidelines

1. At least one hour per day will be set aside in every classroom for the development of reading skills. A variety of learning and teaching approaches will be employed during this time. These include large and small group teaching as well as individual reading and tutoring.
2. Parents and others in the school community will be invited to assist in the reading programme in each classroom. The parents of every child will be encouraged to assist their children in reading at home. Teachers will provide advice on how this might be done when parents visit the school and in specially written guides for parents.
3. Every teacher will encourage and assist children in reading at times other than that set aside in the daily timetable. That reading is an enjoyable and worthwhile activity will be stressed on all occasions.
4. Achievement levels in reading will be determined regularly through tests given to all children. Special programmes of assistance will be provided for those who fall below the benchmarks established for their age / grade group.

Planning

Different levels of planning are possible in the recommended model for school management. These include corporate planning, strategic planning, programme planning, curriculum planning and instructional planning.

The most comprehensive approach is contained in the notion of corporate planning, defined by Caldwell and Spinks (1988) as:

> a continuous process in administration which links goal-setting, policy-making, short-term and long-term planning, budgeting and evaluation in a manner which spans all levels of the organisation, secures appropriate involvement of people according to their responsibility for implementing plans as well as of people with an interest or stake in the outcomes of those plans, and provides a framework for the annual planning, budgeting and evaluation cycle.

A school may establish a corporate plan for, say, three years which will provide the framework for annual planning. Consider, for example, a school which has adopted the goal 'to ensure that each student can attain a high level of reading ability, taking account of age and any special personal circumstances'. Where evaluation has revealed that outcomes in the current reading programme fall well short of expectations, the school may plan to address the need over three years. Part of the corporate plan will refer to current levels of achievement in reading, desired outcomes at the end of three years, strategies for change to achieve the desired outcomes and the priority which is to be assigned to this initiative.

While distinctions between corporate planning and strategic planning are often unclear, we suggest that strategic planning is that aspect of corporate planning which involves the assessment of needs, the identification of desired outcomes, the determination of strategies to achieve desired outcomes and the assignment of priorities to various programmes and initiatives.

Schools throughout the western world are now faced with the need for ongoing curriculum change, especially at the secondary level. In Britain, for example, all publicly funded schools must now respond to the expectations embodied in a national curriculum. Government schools in most states of Australia now have a centrally determined curriculum framework. Adoption over three to five years is a normal expectation, an aspect of state or national 'strategic plans' which allows for an evolutionary approach to programme development at the school level. Such an approach was a characteristic of these schools which have successfully managed the process of change in studies conducted in the United States by Miles and his colleagues. The preparation of school-level corporate plans is thus consistent with what is known about successful management of change and with government expectations in a number of countries.

Distinctions can now be made between programme planning, curriculum planning and instructional planning. Programme planning is determining in general terms how a programme is to be implemented, specifying such things as the manner in which students will be grouped vertically (among class or year levels) and horizontally (within a class or year level); the number and nature of teachers and support staff associated with the programme; the supplies, equipment and services required; and initiatives (additions or deletions) which are noteworthy. Curriculum planning provides a relatively detailed specification of intended learning experiences, with details, for example, of what will be learned, how it will be learned and when it will be learned. Instructional planning is considered here to be the planning undertaken by individual teachers when implementing a curriculum plan in their own classrooms.

In the Collaborative School Management Cycle recommended by Caldwell and Spinks, a programme is an area of learning and teaching, or an area which supports learning and teaching, corresponding to the preferred patterns of work in a school. For example, since mathematics is taught in a secondary school, it is appropriate to refer to 'the Mathematics Programme'. Since a number of people will be involved in administration - a collection of activities which support learning and teaching - it is also appropriate to refer to 'the Administration Programme'. The programmes found in a school will or should reflect the philosophy and goals in that school which will, in turn, reflect the vision for the school. Rarely will two schools have the same set of programmes, even where schools must reflect state or national as well as local expectations.

In the Collaborative School Management Cycle, teachers and others involved in the implementation of a programme form a 'programme team' to prepare a programme plan which is consistent with the policies and priorities of the school as determined by the policy group. Each team will have a leader who usually, but not necessarily, has a position of formal responsibility in the staffing arrangements of the school. With many programmes in a school, there will be many programme teams and many programme leaders, thus providing further opportunity for empowerment and 'leadership density'.

Budgeting

A school budget may be viewed as a financial translation of an educational plan for the school. Budgeting is thus one aspect of planning but is shown as a separate phase of the management cycle in Figure 6.2. A programme budget is simply a financial translation of a programme plan. In the approach recommended by Caldwell and Spinks, programme teams will prepare a programme budget as part of the programme planning process.

Figure 6.4 contains an illustration of a programme plan and budget for an Individualised Learning Assistance Programme in a primary school which has adopted the vision and one of the goals which are the subject of illustration in this section of the chapter: 'Ruth (the principal) expects that curriculum and instruction should reflect the needs and interests of all children but that high expectations can be set and pursued with consistency and enthusiasm' (element of vision) and 'to ensure that each student can attain a high level of reading ability, taking account of age and any special personal circumstances' (goal). It is likely that these expectations will be addressed in several programmes, one of which might make provision for offering highly individualised assistance to children who may encounter major difficulty in a particular area of learning such as reading. There may, for example, be one or more teachers who have special responsibility for a programme designated as the Individualised Learning Assistance Programme.

In preparing a programme plan and budget, members of the programme team in the Individualised Learning Assistance Programme must take account of policies and priorities adopted by the policy group, the formulation of which would have seen their involvement. The plan and budget illustrated in Figure 6.4 contains:

• A statement of purpose and broad guidelines for the programme, being a summary of school policy on Individualised Learning

Assistance
• A plan for implementing the programme in the forthcoming
year, with elements in the plan arranged in order of priority and
the plan being consistent with the aforementioned policy and
priorities for the school
• A listing of resources required: a specification of staff, supplies,
equipment and services to implement the plan, with 4.1-4.5 being
the resources and estimated costs for 3.1 to 3.5, respectively, in
the plan for implementation
• A plan for evaluating the programme, with the general approach
following guidelines for programme evaluation.

An important feature of Figure 6.4 is that no programme plan and
budget should exceed two pages. The aim is to minimise paper-
work. Another feature is the costing for staff, even though the
illustration might be for a school which does not directly 'pay' for
staff. In this instance, the time allocation (40 units or periods) has
been converted to a monetary equivalent on the basis that the
average cost of instruction in offering a unit or period per week
over the year is $700. Many schools may wish simply to list the
number of units or periods per week.
    Plans and budgets will be prepared for all programmes in
the school. These will be consolidated in a collection of two-page
proposals. A process of 'reconciliation' must then occur, with estimates of expenditure adjusted in the light of estimates of revenue.
This reconciliation is best carried out by a small body of people
appointed by the policy group. The consolidation of plans and
budgets, with estimates of revenue and expenditure reconciled, is
then forwarded to the policy group with a recommendation for
adoption. The policy group is involved again at this point to
ensure that plans and budgets are consistent with policies and
priorities established earlier in the Collaborative School Management Cycle. With refinements, the programme plan and budget
can be adopted before the commencement of the school year.
Essentially then, the educational plan will reflect the vision, philosophy, goals, needs, priorities and policies of the school.

Implementing the plan

With the adoption of the educational plan by the policy group,
programme teams have the authorisation to proceed with implementation in the year which follows. The major aspect of

Figure 6.4 Programme Plan and Budget for Individualised Learning Assistance Programme

---

1. Purpose

We intend to help all children attain the highest level of achievement of which they are capable. While learning activities in each classroom will be designed to meet the needs and interests of every child, we recognise that some will require extended periods of individual assistance in areas of basic learning such as reading, writing, spelling and mathematics. We have established an Individualised Learning Assistance Programme to meet these needs.

2. Broad Guidelines

2.1   Achievement levels in areas of basic learning will be determined regularly through tests given to all children.

2.2   While every teacher will provide assistance to all children on an individual basis, the Individualised Learning Assistance Programme will be provided for those who fall below benchmarks established for their age / grade group.

2.3   Benchmarks will be established each year by the policy group after receiving recommendations from members of programme teams in areas of basic learning.

2.4   Teachers in the Individualised Learning Assistance Programme will work with students whose need for assistance has been identified. This assistance will be given either in the regular classroom or, in exceptional circumstances, in learning areas away from the classroom.

3. Plan for implementation

3.1   A review of achievement tests last year suggests the need for the equivalent of two full-time teachers to work in the programme.

3.2   Supervision of the programme will be provided by a member of senior staff.

3.3   A part-time teacher aide will be provided to assist in the preparation of learning materials.

3.4   Additional supplies and equipment will be required in the two rooms which will be devoted to the programme. These include reading and mathematics materials and the purchase of a large-print typewriter.

3.5   All teachers in areas of basic learning seek the assistance of a consultant in determining benchmarks for tests of achievement.

4. Resources required

	Element	Teaching staff	Support staff	Supplies	Equipment	Services
4.1	Teachers: 50 units @ $700 / unit	35000				
4.2	Supervision 2 units @ $900 / unit	1800				
4.3	Teacher aide 5 hrs / week 40 weeks @ $10 / hour		2000			
4.4	Supplies, reading and mathematics materials; typewriter			500	750	
4.5	Consultative assistance: 3 hr seminar with travel costs @ $50 / hour					200
		36800	2000	500	750	200
	Programme total	= $40250				

5. Plan for evaluation (minor)

Teachers will review results of achievement tests in the areas of reading, spel-
·ling and mathematics in the light of benchmarks recommended last year and
adopted by the policy group. This review and a general appraisal shall form the
basis of recommendations for this programme next year.

implementation is, of course, learning and teaching which is the life blood for the school. As far as resources are concerned, there is no need for further reference to the policy group unless a need for major change emerges. Revenue and expenditure are monitored, with programme teams and the policy group receiving regular financial statements.

Evaluating

Evaluation is the gathering of information for the purpose of making a judgement. In the Collaborative School Management Cycle, evaluation is not a discrete activity carried out in isolation from other phases of management. The judgements which are made are important factors in decisions on the formulation of goals, the identification of needs, the setting of policies and priorities, the preparation of plans and budgets, and in the ongoing implementation of school programmes.

Caldwell and Spinks distinguish between minor evaluations carried out annually and major evaluations carried out less frequently on, say, a three- or five-year cycle. They suggest that all programmes be placed on such a cycle. The emphasis is on a manageable and usable approach to programme evaluation, in contrast to the frequently exhausting approach to school review and evaluation which is often encountered when an attempt has been made to evaluate all programmes in a single year. It is recommended that the report of a minor evaluation be a maximum of one page and that a report of a major evaluation be a maximum of two pages. Minor evaluations may be conducted informally and subjectively by members of the programme team who report on simple indicators of success, areas of concern and recommendations for change. A major evaluation in the same programme would be carried out more comprehensively and objectively by a team which is broadly representative of the school community, including members of the policy group.

More detailed consideration of approaches to evaluation is contained in Chapter 7 in the context of instructional leadership, supervision and the support of learning and teaching.

The model in operation

This approach has now been successfully adopted in hundreds of schools, notably in Victoria, Australia. The schedule of activities in schools which have now fully adopted the model is generally along the following lines. In Term 1, the policy group reviews reports of programme evaluations from the previous year to identify areas for action. Policies are then amended as appropriate, new needs identified and priorities established for the school year which follows, that is, which commences twelve months hence.

In Term 2, programme teams prepare programme plans and budgets for the following year. They work within the framework of policies and priorities set by the policy group, together with estimates of all of the resources to be available in the following year. Toward the end of Term 2, programme plans and budgets in proposal form are consolidated and reconciled against estimates of resources. The programme plan and budget is adopted in Term 3. Refinements will be made at the start of the next school year once final enrolments and revenue are known. Programme evaluation will be completed in Term 3 for consideration by the policy group in Term 1 to follow, thus ensuring the continuation of the cycle.

Schools need to set aside three to five years to adopt a model for management such as that outlined above. This time span is consistent with guidelines for the management of change in schools, including those which emerge from studies such as those by Miles and his colleagues reported earlier in the chapter.

Summary

The purpose of this chapter was to outline a model for school management which would help bring a vision of excellence to reality. Such a model should be consistent with what is known about outstanding leadership (as summarised in Chapter 5), especially those aspects concerned with ensuring clarity, consensus and commitment to the purposes of the school (Vaill's concept of 'purposing'); the unification of people around values (an important role for leaders described by Greenfield); responsibility and authority at the school level (the characteristic of school-site management and collaborative decision-making contained in Purkey and Smith's model for creating an effective school); the sharing of leadership roles (Sergiovanni's concept of 'leadership density'); and implanting the vision for a school in policies, plans, budgets and processes so that day-to-day activities are shaped by the vision (Starratt's view that the leader must 'institutionalise' the vision).

Any model for management must be consistent with what is known about successful approaches to the management of change. The findings of recent studies by Miles and his colleagues in the USA were chosen to identify additional requirements for such a model. In addition to leadership of the kind considered in Chapter 5, these requirements included a large measure of school autonomy, including some control over staffing and resources; staff cohesiveness; a school programme which was a good 'fit' with the school setting and needs in the community; power sharing among staff; rewards for staff; staff willingness and initiative and evolutionary programme development.

The Collaborative School Management Cycle described by Caldwell and Spinks was offered as a model for school management which is consistent with these requirements. This model integrates the processes of goal setting and needs identification, policy-making, planning, budgeting, implementing and evaluating in a continuous cycle. The vision for a school as it may be expressed in a statement of school philosophy becomes the driving force in school management, thus shaping day-to-day activities in the school. Power-sharing is evident in policy groups but, especially, in programme teams of people who have the responsibility for implementing policy. Leadership is widely dispersed. The approach provides a framework for evolutionary programme development. Some guidelines and illustration were offered for operation of the model which has now been successfully implemented in hundreds of schools and seems broadly transferable and adaptable.

This model for management provides a framework for day-to-day activities in the school, especially those described as the 'life-blood' of the school: learning and teaching. Chapter 7 shifts the focus of management to promising approaches to the support of learning and teaching.

7

Focus on Learning
and Teaching

The achievement of excellence in a school is dependent in the final analysis on the quality of the educational experience of each of its students. Every approach to management under consideration in this book is directed toward enhancing that experience. The starting point in this chapter is the assumption that excellent schools require excellent teachers. The aim is to describe and illustrate some ways in which this requirement can be met.

The first part of the chapter provides a brief review of trends in the management of education in western countries. The intent is to show that the school and the classroom have become the focus of educational reform, with energies increasingly devoted to improving the quality of learning and teaching. Then follows a summary of a useful model for instructional leadership and some guidelines for the design and delivery of programmes to provide the necessary capability at the school level. Account is then taken of the view that schooling and education in general are likely to be substantially different at the end of the century. The chapter concludes with an illustration of how these practices and possibilities might be seen in action at the start of the twenty-first century.

This chapter is set within the general framework of leadership and management offered in Chapters 5 and 6. The intention in Chapter 5 was to describe and illustrate some emerging generalisations about leadership, giving particular attention to the importance of vision and the capacity of school leaders, especially the principal, to work with others to develop that vision and to gain commitment to it. That vision must shape the philosophy, goals, policies, priorities, programmes, plans and budgets of the school if it is to be brought to reality. A promising model for school management has been described and illustrated. As Starratt (1986) noted, vision must be implanted in structures and processes 'so that people experience the vision in the various patterned activities of the organisation'. At the most fundamental level, these activities in a school are associated with learning and teaching and they are the focus of attention in this chapter.

New patterns of management in education

There is evidence of a major shift in the way education is managed in western countries. It may, indeed, be a shift of historic proportions following more than a century of sustained growth and success in relatively centralised public or government systems of education. It has important implications for instructional leadership at the school level.

It seems that governments are responding to changes in values which shape public policy in education. These values include quality, equity and efficiency. The outcome is that, increasingly, energies at national, state or local levels of government are devoted primarily to setting broad goals and expectations, specifying outcomes and establishing frameworks for accountability. Major responsibility for achieving these outcomes, including authority to make decisions on programmes and resources, is shifted to schools. Within this framework, central and local authorities must become highly responsive in providing support to schools.

These patterns of management are essentially shifts in the centralisation-decentralisation balance in educational governance. Shifts (in some instances, a return) to the centre include the setting of state or national curriculum frameworks and testing requirements. Devolution to the school level of responsibility for planning and budgeting is an example of a shift away from the centre. These shifts have occurred simultaneously in some instances. The Thatcher government in Britain, for example, called for a national curriculum and testing programme and, at the same time, for governing bodies and principals of all secondary and most primary schools to have control over their own budgets. The government in Victoria, Australia, granted power to school councils to set educational policies for the school, within guidelines provided by the Minister, and with the intention of increasing the school's responsibilities in budgeting. At the same time, the government has provided a curriculum framework and a general policy that all schools give priority to the redress of disadvantage.

Change in the USA in the early 1980s was centralising in the first instance, with the first wave of educational reform being the welter of state commissions and regulations which, at least in the public mind, followed the report of the National Commission on Excellence in Education (1983). Toward the end of the decade, however, there was growing acceptance of the fact that the intentions in the first wave could only be achieved if changes occur in the classroom. In the second wave of reform, the focus was the school and the support of the school. The powerful National Governors' Association (1986) called for school-site management. The largest teacher organisation in the United States, the National Education Association (NEA), joined with the National Association of Secondary School Principals (NASSP) in a commitment 'to the principle that substantial decision-making at the school site is the essential pre-requisite for quality education' (NASSP - NEA, 1986: 13). Following his national study of schooling, John Goodlad (1984: 275-6) proposed 'genuine decentralisation of authority and responsibility to the local school within a framework designed to assure school-to-school equity and a measure of accountability', noting that 'the guiding principle being put forward here is that the school must become largely self-directing'.

Account has been taken in some of these developments, especially in the USA, of research on effectiveness in education. Studies in school effectiveness and school improvement by Purkey and Smith (1985) and Miles (1987) were cited in support of the model for school management which was described in Chapter 6. Studies in teacher effectiveness have led to a variety of practices which are intended to enhance the quality of learning in these new patterns of management. Some of these practices are examined in the pages which follow.

A model for instructional leadership

These developments suggest that learning and teaching must be the focus of leadership acts in a school. Given also the importance of leadership density - 'the extent to which leadership roles are shared and the extent to which leadership is broadly exercised' (Sergiovanni, 1987: 122) - it is clear that a school where excellence is the goal will seek a model for instructional leadership which will have this focus and which can shape the role of a number of people in addition to the principal. Duke (1987) proposed 'a vision of instructional leadership' which seems to satisfy these requirements.

Duke drew from research on school and teacher effectiveness to suggest that instructional leadership should involve two broad interrelated areas of activity: the fostering of excellence in teaching; and the capacity to deal successfully with certain 'key situations'. Each is briefly described and illustrated, with more detailed attention given to strategies for developing the capability for this kind of leadership in a school.

Excellence in teaching

For Duke (1987: 66-70), the fostering of excellence in teaching calls in the first instance for a vision of excellence. His vision provides a picture of capable teachers who are involved in six types of activity:

- *Clinical assistance:*
a capacity to diagnose student needs and provide learning experiences to meet the needs of each individual

- *Planning:*
the selection of appropriate objectives, learning experience and assessment procedures

- *Instruction:*
successful communication and achievement of expectation for all students

- *Classroom management:*
maintaining an orderly environment for learning

- *Monitoring of progress:*
a continuous process of assessment and reporting for all students, providing information for the ongoing process of clinical assistance, planning and instruction

- *Caring for students:*
actions on the part of the teacher which reflect values such as respect, acceptance, support, and recognition.

A first requirement for instructional leadership is that the leader should have a vision for excellence in teaching such as that offered by Duke. It was established in Chapter 5 that effectiveness depends among other things on shared commitment to a vision. A second requirement, then, is that instructional leaders work with other teachers to develop a shared commitment to a common vision of excellence in teaching. Guidelines for gaining commitment to a vision are contained in Chapter 5. Going further, however, a third requirement is that instructional leaders and their teaching colleagues have the knowledge and skill to bring that vision to reality. This requirement has significance because for most it will mean a level of knowledge and skill that goes well beyond what is typically involved in pre-service programmes. The need for ongoing professional development is evident.

An increasing number of school systems are offering programmes for professional development based on findings from recent research on teacher effectiveness. It is not our intention here to provide a detailed specification of knowledge and skill in areas such as those listed above. The reader is referred to the work of people such as Adler (1984), Biggs and Telfer (1987), Brady (1985), Good and Brophy (1984), Hunter (1985), Joyce and Weil (1980), Purkey and Novak (1984). We return later in the chapter to the design of professional development programmes when we consider strategies for the development of capability in this aspect of instructional leadership.

Key situations in instructional leadership

Deriving his list from findings in research on effective schools, Duke (1987: 81-4) identified seven 'key situations' with which the instructional leader must deal:

• *Teacher supervision and development:*
working with teachers in a variety of ways in the gathering of information to guide efforts to enhance the quality of learning; working with teachers in the design and delivery of school-based programmes for professional development of individuals and groups

• *Teacher evaluation:*
evaluation of teachers to the extent required in the policies of the school system

• *Instructional management and support:*
the formulation and implementation of policies (on matters such as discipline) to support the learning process, the aim being to create a climate for excellence

• *Resource management:*
ensuring that resources are acquired and allocated in a manner consistent with goals, needs, policies, priorities and plans

• *Quality control:*
a continuous process of programme evaluation to provide information on the extent to which goals, needs, priorities and standards have been addressed and achieved, including the monitoring of pupil progress and the evaluation of teachers but much broader in scope

• *Coordination:*
planning across programmes, both horizontally and vertically, to ensure the most efficient and effective use of resources (staff, time, space, money, services, curriculum)

• *Trouble-shooting:*
the anticipation and solution of problems which may impair the quality of learning and teaching.

As with particular skills and knowledge required in bringing vision of excellence in teaching to reality, it is not our intent to provide a detailed specification. Duke addresses each in separate chapters of his book as do other writers such as Sergiovanni and Starratt (1983). We deal, instead, with two aspects of Duke's model which are different in significant ways from traditional approaches to instructional leadership. These are concerned with the contemporary view of supervision and with the special emphasis which is given to evaluation. We have some hesitation in dealing with these in isolation because, as Duke notes, the 'key situations' described above are complex and interrelated:

Handling each of these situations well requires far more than a particular skill or set of competencies. The situations constitute complex configurations of intentions, activities, people and interrelationships.

They call for a variety of technical skills and professional judgements, adapted to the particular needs of the moment. Since these needs are everchanging, no single prescription for dealing with a given situation will suffice. And, while each situation is somewhat discrete, all may occur simultaneously, blurring lines between, say, teacher evaluation and trouble-shooting (Duke, 1987: 81-2).

Contemporary view of supervision

The traditional view of supervision has a connotation of direction and control. The Oxford English Dictionary defines 'to supervise' as '. . . to oversee, have the oversight of, superintend the execution or performance of (a thing), the movements or work of (a person).' The emphasis tended to be on the exercise of authority by the supervisor in a supervisor-supervisee relationship. After reviewing various 'images' of supervision, Sergiovanni and Starratt (1983: 12) suggest that, in the contemporary 'human resources' view, the 'crucial aspect that differentiates supervisory behaviour from other forms of organisational behaviour is action to achieve goals through other people. Attention is shifted to others whose committed involvement is required for an effective outcome.'

In a school where concern for excellence is a driving force, supervision is the process of working with and through others to achieve to the greatest extent possible a quality education for all students. 'Working with and through others' is a characteristic of a host of practices which are now evident in this drive for excellence. It is central, for example, to so-called 'clinical' approaches. Writing about clinical supervision, Smyth (1984: 2-3) contrasts 'the in-class nature of assistance provided to teachers to help them make sense of the complex processes of teaching and learning . . . in the clinic of the classroom' with the ineffectual 'one-shot visits to classrooms by well-meaning outsiders (principals and inspectors)'. This assistance comes in the form of a cycle of four stages in which the teacher works with a trusted colleague who may have a formal designation in a supervisory role. These stages are:

• *Pre-observation conference:*
the teacher and colleague aim to reach a common understanding of the objectives, approaches to learning and teaching, and intended outcomes in a lesson or part of a lesson

• *Observation:*
the colleague gathers information through observation while the teacher conducts the lesson as planned

• *Analysis:*
the teacher and colleague reflect on and draw inferences from what transpired and was observed

• *Post-observation conference:*
the teacher and colleague meet to share their analysis and draw implications; intentions on the part of the teacher are the basis for discussion and judgements are avoided. (Based on Smyth, 1984)

An array of techniques has been developed for clinical supervision (see, for example, Acheson and Gall, 1980). These give particular attention to observation and the conferences. An association has also been made between the cycle of clinical supervision and the model for effective teaching developed by Hunter (1985). Hunter's model of clinical teaching embodies a number of 'principles of learning' related to motivation, reinforcement, sequence, practice, discipline and transfer. While acknowledging criticism of the approach, Duke (1987: 62) observed that 'Madeline Hunter's vision of teaching has gained widespread acceptance around the United States as a sound basis for teacher development'. An example based on that vision is offered later in the chapter.

Clinical supervision is just one example of 'working with and through others' in contemporary approaches to instructional leadership and supervision. The model for school management described in Chapter 6 is another, emphasising a cycle of goal-setting, policy-making, planning, budgeting, implementing and evaluating.

The importance of evaluation

We address the wider issue of evaluation of schools and teaching in a later chapter. At this point, however, we note the importance attached to evaluation when the focus of management is learning and teaching and the goal is the highest possible quality of learning for every student in the school.

Studies of effectiveness, however conceived, invariably yield the finding that effective schools have adopted a systematic approach to evaluation and assessment. Programmes of reform have generally made provision for more extensive and open evaluation than traditional reliance on classroom tests, with reporting to the student and parent, and an external examination on one or two occasions at the secondary level. For example, there is now widespread use of standardised tests in basic skills in the USA, with public reporting of results on a school-by-school basis in many instances. Opponents of such practice are concerned that it gives undue attention to a small number of cognitive skills and that unhealthy competition between schools is encouraged. A closer examination of how these results are used, however, suggests that, as intended, they become the basis for planning to bring about improvement. Published accounts of the tests place as much emphasis on schools where improvement has occurred and factors which led to that improvement as they place on schools where levels of achievement were the highest. For example, the results of reading tests in 613 elementary schools in the City of New York were published in the New York Post on 22 January, 1987. This is a highly visible public reporting since the newspaper has the highest circulation of any in that city. The account included short feature items on the school with the highest ranking, and on the school which had shown the most improvement (from 529th to 217th).

A more comprehensive approach is evident in the school system gaining international attention as a model for school-based decision-making. In the Edmonton Public School District in Alberta, Canada, system-wide standardised tests are conducted in language, social studies, mathematics and science in Grades 3, 6 and 9 (in addition to province-wide external examinations at the end of Grade 12). A standard is determined for each test, this being a target level of performance for every student in the system. Schools receive the results of the tests for each student, with additional information about the number of students who reached the standard compared to previous years and to other schools. It is intended that schools use these results as the basis of planning for improvement. Central and regional services are available to assist schools in this effort. Other information to guide the improvement effort comes from district-wide opinion surveys conducted every year among all principals, teachers, parents, students, ancillary staff, and staff at central and regional levels. These surveys seek opinions on the quality of education, climate and service at the school and system level.

Other initiatives in evaluation and reporting, especially in Britain (England and Wales) and Australia, seek an even broader approach. These encourage the compilation of 'records of achievement' for every student: documents or portfolios which exhibit a range of accomplishments by each individual of a kind and in a manner which cannot be recorded in the traditional brief school report or list of results. This broader approach is well supported by teachers even though it entails more work. Currently, however, the government has proposed a system of nationwide standardised tests and is seeking an approach which is acceptable to the teaching profession.

If the new patterns of management in education outlined at the start of the chapter are taken as a guide, it is evident that more comprehensive and open approaches to evaluation and reporting are expected. While a number of concerns have been expressed, it is important to note that such approaches have support in models of school effectiveness and instructional leadership, and that schools in systems which have moved in this direction do indeed use results in the manner intended as far as improvement is concerned. Critical considerations from an educational point of view are that the testing programme should be as broad as possible, reflecting the breadth desired in a vision of excellence; that emphasis should be placed on improvement as much as on overall levels of achievement; and that staff at the school level should have the capability, resources, and support to bring about improvement for all students.

Developing capability at the school level

Attention is turned now to ways in which people can develop the capability to work in the way we have described in Chapters 5 to 7. To some extent, this is development of a capacity for 'self-management' at the school level. Three general areas are addressed; first, areas of knowledge and skill for instructional leadership of the kind we have described; second, the nature of support for schools when the focus in management is placed on learning and teaching; and third, strategies for professional development.

Areas of knowledge and skill

It is clear that very careful attention must be given to pre- and in-service education and to ongoing professional development if processes of the kind outlined in this chapter are to be effective. As far as instructional leadership is concerned, areas of knowledge and skill to be addressed in such programmes will be comprehensive and far broader than those in most post-graduate programmes which offer specialisation in educational administration or management. Five key areas are identified here on the basis of principles and practices we have described in Chapters 5 to 7. They assume a relatively high level of authority and responsibility at the school level. A detailed listing of general teaching and management skills is not included.

• *Approaches to learning and teaching:*
knowledge about a wide range of approaches to learning and teaching, including those embodied in a 'vision of excellence' in teaching such as that described earlier in the chapter. A capacity to apply that knowledge in different ways will be required, depending on authority and responsibility. Telecommunications and computers will be an increasingly important component of learning in schools and in the home, requiring teachers and leaders, as well as those providing support, to be expert in their use

• *Curriculum design and delivery:*
a capacity to work within national, state or system-wide frameworks and priorities to design and deliver programmes of learning to meet the needs of every student. Included here is an understanding of trends in society, especially as they concern the economy and the nature of work

• *Evaluation:*
a capacity to make an ongoing and systematic approach to programme evaluation a feature of the management process. Evaluation must become part of the school culture. A comprehensive programme of assessment and reporting is included

• *Leadership and supervision:*
a capacity to address in practical terms the ten generalisations on leadership set out in Chapter 5, especially that on gaining

commitment to a shared vision of excellence. Included here is knowledge and skill in instructional leadership which places emphasis on the contemporary view of supervision, for example, on the so-called 'clinical' approaches described earlier in this chapter

• *Policy-making and planning:*
a capacity to design and implement an ongoing, cyclical approach to goal-setting, policy-making, planning, budgeting, implementing and evaluation of the kind described in Chapter 6. Included here is knowledge and skill in the management of change.

Two special areas of knowledge and skill are identified for those at central and regional levels. These are included in the key areas listed above but are specified further here. The first, strategic planning, calls for a capacity to identify needs, formulate policies and establish priorities for the system as a whole, taking account of the general environment for education in the nation as well as of particular trends and issues at the state or local levels. A framework for accountability having three interfaces must also be established: between the system and the national or state government, permitting the gathering of information and the making of judgements on the extent to which national or state priorities are being addressed in the system; between the system and its community on the extent to which local goals and priorities are being addressed; and between the system and the school on the extent to which national or state or local goals and priorities are being achieved at the school level.

A second area of knowledge and skill for those employed at central or regional levels is concerned with the provision of support for schools. At one level this will call for staff to help schools develop a capacity for management of the kind we have described, essentially a capacity to become 'self-managing'. At another level, however, specialist support to schools must be provided through curriculum and student services. Areas of knowledge and skill may be defined in part by the 'requirements for a responsive central support service' as identified in Edmonton, Canada, following a trial of school-based planning for the use of such services. These include a vision of central support which, among other things, provides for the support of good assessment practice; needs assessment, with school-by-school planning and provision for schools to 'pay'; service agreements with schools, with provision for evaluation of services; flexible staffing patterns in the support of schools; and monitoring the quantity and quality of services, making a contribution to the setting of standards for such services as well as for outcomes in schools (based on Smilanich, 1988). Further details of central and regional support for schools in Edmonton are given below.

Support for schools

Capability at the school level is dependent to an important extent on the quality of support from staff at the central and regional levels of a school system. Some requirements for a responsive approach were noted in the context of needs as far as knowledge and skills are concerned. Taking the issue further, however, a key question is 'What structures and processes at these levels are helpful in providing support to schools?'

What has occurred in Edmonton, Alberta, is of particular interest, with the evolution over ten years of a far-reaching and comprehensive form of school-based decision-making, with an emphasis on school-based budgets and approaches to evaluation described earlier in the chapter. Of special interest in Edmonton was the decision in 1986 to pilot the extension of the initiative to include curriculum and student services. These central services are normally available to schools upon request and are not usually considered in a school's annual educational plan and budget. Fourteen schools reflecting diversity in the district were selected for the pilot from eighty-four volunteers. Those selected had their lump-sum budget allocations supplemented by amounts which reflected the historical use of these services according to type of school and level of student need. Standard costs for various types of service were then determined, on a per hour or per incident basis, with costs charged to the school as service was provided. Participating schools were free to acquire these services from any source: from the central office, from other schools or from outside the system. The aim of this pilot project was to ensure the effective and efficient deployment of curriculum and student services, to improve capacity at the school level to plan for services, and to improve the way services were accessed and delivered. It is noteworthy that the level of utilisation of central services declined in the first year of the pilot, with schools opting in many instances to acquire other resources to solve their problems; for example, additional teachers were deployed, or schools turned to other schools in their search for expertise.

The initiative in Edmonton illustrates the high level of support required if schools are to meet the learning needs of all students. A different kind of initiative was under way in 1987 in Victoria, Australia, where the most recent of several attempts to restructure the system of government schools saw a further movement of staff from centre to regions and an even stronger emphasis on the role of regional staff in supporting the work of schools. A significant development in each region was the establishment of large school support centres. Their major functions, in addition to general support, place emphasis on evaluation and assisting schools in becoming accountable to local communities as well as to the Minister. Accountability to the Minister reflects the need for schools to operate within a curriculum framework for the system and to address the priorities of government.

Strategies for professional development

One aspect of support for schools is provision for professional development in key areas such as those listed earlier. It is evident that new strategies are required in many systems since very large numbers of teachers must acquire the necessary knowledge and skills in a relatively short period of time if schools are to develop the capability described in this chapter. One- or two-day seminars and postgraduate programmes for volunteers will not have major impact. Two alternative approaches are described here.

The need for a far-reaching and comprehensive programme in Pittsburgh, Pennsylvania was recognised in the early 1980s after a system-wide assessment. Nearly two years was spent in planning the approach in what appears to be a model partnership of the local school authority, the teacher union and the private sector through business and industry. The outcome was a 'mini-sabbatical' of eight weeks for every high school teacher in the system (see Hovey, 1986). A feature of this programme at the Schenley High School Teachers Centre was the development of skill in clinical approaches to teaching based on the model of Hunter described earlier in the chapter. A similar programme has been established at Brookline Elementary School for all teachers in the system at the primary level. Another feature of management in this district is its approach to 'decision-oriented educational research', with capability at the school level for a comprehensive approach to programme evaluation (see Cooley and Bickel, 1986).

The trend in Pittsburgh seems to be toward self-directing schools which are managed within a framework of district policies and priorities, with high levels of expertise at the school level in the areas of curriculum and instruction, a format consistent with what we described in Chapter 4.

Another example of a comprehensive programme of professional development is in Edmonton, Alberta, where the public school district has established a teacher effectiveness programme. Commencing in 1981 as a small centrally-funded project, by 1986-87 most schools were represented in the one-half-day per week professional development programme, with funding from school-based budgets. It is estimated that about half of all teachers in the district had been involved as expertise was shared within schools.

The scope of approaches such as those in Pittsburgh and Edmonton, and the associated high level of responsiveness in meeting needs at the school level, suggest implications for those outside the school system with an interest in and capacity to provide management training. These include universities and other institutions at the tertiary level as well as individuals and organisations in the private sector. Given the size of the task, it is likely that many at the tertiary level in particular will have to devise approaches to the delivery of management training which will:

• be more responsive to the needs of neighbouring schools and school systems
• integrate programmes in management, curriculum and learning
• provide options through off-campus and year-round study.

Recommendations for a more responsive tertiary sector were made in the USA by the *National Commission for Excellence in Educational Administration* (1987).

Approaches to learning and teaching in the future

It is likely that schooling and education in general will be different in significant ways by the end of the century. Account should be taken of these changes in planning an approach to management which has a focus on learning and teaching.

Fantini (1986: 104-117) identified what he considered to be 'state-of-the-art concepts' which have implications for excellence and reform in education. These and others will shape education and schooling over the next decade. Included in Fantini's list were the following, with each expressed as a possible and desirable outcome in the future:

• There will be acceptance of the principle that all people can learn under the right conditions. An implication is that 'if a program does not achieve the intended goals, then it is redesigned until it does. There are no learner failures, only program failures' (Fantini, 1986: 105)

• Choice and the provision of alternatives and options within and among schools are necessary if there is acceptance of the principle that all people can learn under the right conditions

• Acceptance of the existence of multiple intelligence or talents will mean approaches from school organisation which are vastly different from those in many schools which are shaped by a relatively narrow view of intelligence. Fantini (1986: 107) cites Gardner's seven areas of intelligence: linguistic, musical, logical-mathematical, spatial, bodily-kinesthetic, interpersonal ability and intrapersonal ability. Traditionally, there has been a narrow focus on the linguistic and logical-mathematical

• Acceptance of individual difference and diversity will render obsolete those approaches to structure and organisation which limit access by many students to learning experiences in which they have an interest and capacity to achieve

• School organisation will accommodate the accelerating technological revolution. Fantini (1986: 110) contrasts the speed of the computer with that in the school in noting that 'computers are capable of achieving solutions to problems in microseconds . . . At best, activity in the classroom moves at the speed of sound . . . While it might be argued that more computers are being used in school, and therefore schools are catching up, it must be recognised that most of the computers are being put into a traditional school structure, which limits their use and effectiveness'

• Advances in telecommunication and computers will mean that 'school and nonschool learning become part of an overall curriculum that is both formal and non-formal, in which learning takes place at any time and in multiple ways' (Fantini, 1986: 111)

• 'We are now entering an age of education in which learning will be the most valued and important of all lifelong processes' (Fantini, 1986: 113).

Developments along these lines may well bring to reality the achievement of excellence as conceived in this chapter: a quality education to meet the needs and interests of all students. The implications are staggering in some instances. For example, it is likely that technological advance will allow students to acquire in their own homes much of the knowledge and skill currently addressed in schools. Such technology is likely to provide higher and more effective levels of individualisation than is possible in the classroom setting with the best of teachers. What patterns of management will support such a focus in learning? One possibility is illustrated in the final section of the chapter.

A vision for the twenty-first century

A useful way to synthesise the various practices and possibilities is to offer a vision of schooling for the start of the twenty-first century, with a focus on management to support quality of learning for all students. We have chosen to recast the vision of Ruth Griffiths, principal of a high school in a lower socio-economic urban setting, as it was outlined in Chapter 5. It was noted that 'Ruth would like to see a quite different scene in five years. She acknowledges that student achievement may never be as high as that in more favoured areas but she is convinced that most children can do well and can enjoy their schooling. Ruth Griffiths believes that it is possible for all parents to be involved in the school in a variety of ways, including the support of and direct involvement in their children's learning. Ruth expects that curriculum and instruction should reflect the needs and interests of all children but that high expectations can be set and pursued with consistency and enthusiasm.' The situation now envisaged is that Ruth has seen good progress in bringing that vision to reality and is now working with many individuals and groups to anticipate events in the final years of the century and the beginning of the next. What follows is just one possibility to illustrate how responsive the school and school system must become and that approaches to instructional leadership such as those we have described can be applied. The vision is largely written in the present tense, with the present being, say, the year 2001.

Ruth Griffiths anticipates a dramatically different setting for the school at the start of the twenty-first century. Major factors which will shape this setting include an acceleration of the revolution in telecommunications and computers as well as general acceptance that programs can indeed be developed to meet the needs and interests of every student ('There are no learner failures, only program failures'). The number of programs available to each student in a particular area of learning has grown geometrically to number in the hundreds compared with a handful at the start of the 1990s. All can be accessed within seconds, with every student from the earliest age having what are now routine skills at the keyboard. The variety, responsiveness, colour and excitement of interactive television, for example, have ensured a level of individualisation that was never possible or even dreamt of with a single teacher and a class of fifteen to fifty students.

Developments along these lines have meant that learning for some 'intelligences' (following Gardner's classification offered by Fantini), notably the linguistic and logical-mathematical, can be addressed as well in the home as in the school. Indeed, the majority of students at all levels now acquire in the home much of the learning formerly acquired in a school building. This has had a number of implications for the management of schools. One is the abolition of laws related to compulsory attendance at a school. Initially reluctant to do so, governments had little alternative when the possibilities of non-school learning became a reality.

The pattern of management which started to emerge in the 1980s continued, with governments setting general goals and a broad curriculum framework for all students along with a comprehensive testing and reporting system. By the end of the 1990s, these tests were being taken in the home as well as in the school building, making the process of assessment and reporting at once more complex in the sense of mode and access but simpler for the student, who was no longer a prisoner of the lock-step system of learning by year and grade. Another implication is that schools are now able to address many of the other 'intelligences' which in years past were at the periphery. These include the musical, bodily-kinesthetic, interpersonal and intrapersonal. Programmes in the arts (art, music, drama, physical education) as well as personal and spiritual development are flourishing to the extent that they form most of the programme in many schools. Examples started to appear in the USA in the 1980s with the so-called 'magnet school'. These developments have allayed fears that the revolution in telecommunications and computers would bring an unduly narrow focus to learning and teaching. Indeed, it has led to the flourishing of important areas which were formerly given lip service.

Another feature of management which emerged in the 1980s was concerned with planning and resource allocation. School-site management became a reality in the early 1990s, with each school receiving a lump-sum to be allocated according to needs and priorities at the school level. There was no alternative, given the new view of equity that required all students to have a programme to satisfy their individual learning needs. However, schools had little time to adjust to these new opportunities and challenges in management. With non-school as well as school learning and with students selecting programmes from multiple sources, including more than one site when the programme was school-based, what was once described as a 'voucher system' quickly became a reality. Allocating money to schools on a per pupil basis became meaningless with high levels of non-school and multiple source/site learning. Instead, the money went, initially, directly to the student (or parent), with different levels of allocation according to the educational needs of the student. Schools then levied charges according to the service provided, a process made easy for schools, as for all other human services, given that by the end of the century money was handled entirely by electronic means.

Schools soon accommodated to the concept of lifelong learning as parents - indeed, citizens of all ages - became involved. In some instances, governments made grants to citizens for purposes of continuing education in areas of skill which made a contribution to the economic wellbeing of the nation. In most instances, however, citizens participated in the system of lifelong learning using their own resources.

All of these developments had far-reaching implications for school management, instructional leadership and the role of the teacher. In most respects however, these were but an extension of principles and practices which emerged in the 1980s. A vision of excellence in teaching demanded more than ever before the highest level of skill in clinical assistance, planning, instruction, monitoring of progress and caring for students. Critically important was a capacity to diagnose the learning needs of each individual and then make a selection of appropriate learning programmes, especially those delivered through telecommunications and computers. The so-called 'clinical' approaches to teaching and supervision became the norm. Evaluation was now a strong element in the culture of education, being a prerequisite for a capacity to individualise the learning process, with attention to a much broader range of intelligence and talents, the preparation by teachers and students of 'records of achievement', with a diversity of test results and examples of accomplishments in many fields of learning.

The traditional design of buildings became obsolete in the 1990s. Schools generally became smaller and more flexible. Although teachers were assigned to a school site, their work frequently took them to other schools and into the community, often working in home groups with children from different families. With non-school learning, teachers were, however, able to use the latest systems of telecommunications to maintain contact with students in their homes for many aspects of the learning programme. School support centres were established to assist schools in their pursuit of excellence, giving particular attention to helping teachers assess the needs of students and then select appropriate learning programmes. Staff in school support centres as well as in schools now require a capability to work with all agencies in the community.

Collaborative approaches to goal-setting, policy-making, budgeting and evaluating were used in the critically important task of ensuring that resources were acquired and allocated in the most efficient and effective way. This capability was more important than ever before when governments allocated money to students rather than to schools. Such approaches also called for a high level of responsiveness as the environment for schools tended to change more rapidly than ever before. A capacity for strategic planning at the school level was a prerequisite.

Most school systems recognised the need for a comprehensive and ongoing programme of professional development for teachers, with many following the example of Pittsburgh in the mid-1980s in providing 'mini-sabbaticals' for all. Ongoing development is now necessary for professional survival, with most teachers able to participate in their own homes through the latest systems of telecommunication and computers. Schools which did not acquire the capability to respond were restaffed or closed when their services were not sought.

Conclusion

We cannot be certain, of course, that such a vision will come to reality. We are confident, however, that its major features will emerge, especially as far as technology is concerned. It is reassuring, however, that models for instructional leadership and the management of schools which are emerging in the late 1980s seem resilient enough to cope with whatever transpires.

In describing how state-of-the-art concepts will shape educational reform, Fantini (1986: 117) concluded that 'schools need structural transformation. The process involves not only a recommitment to excellence but an expansion of the view of education'. Gaining a shared commitment to a new vision for education, with its focus on the highest quality of learning for every student, is the challenge for instructional leaders in the years ahead.

8

How to Enhance School Culture

Each school is different, just as each child is different! Recent writings on organisational theory and administrative behaviour have emphasised that every organisation is unique; discussions about phenomenology, organisational individuality and uniqueness go well beyond the stereotypical positivistic approach which suggests that all organisations can be fitted into typologies and that all of a type are fundamentally the same. The subtle and subjective quality of personal and interpersonal values, attitudes and actions, together with other contextual elements, contribute to the unique *gestalt* of a particular organisation, including a school.

Since Greenfield's courageous and far-reaching 1974 International Intervisitation Programme (IIP) paper in Bristol, the theory of educational administration has been more seriously concerned to incorporate those elements which are conceptually based, non-quantifiable and value-laden, alongside those elements which are quantifiable and/or are empirically verifiable. Many researchers and writers in the field have adopted this so-called non-positivistic approach, while many others have softened the hitherto hardline approach to educational research and analysis to accommodate this more flexible viewpoint (Willower, 1980; Hills, 1977, 1980; Griffiths, 1975, 1979).

In consequence organisations are now less frequently conceived of as reified entities (that is, as things), having substance and power of their own and being distinct and apart from the human beings who inhabit them. Instead, the organisation is seen as a conceptual entity which people collectively create and maintain largely in their minds. Organisations are essentially collectivities of people, who define policies, generate structures, manipulate resources and engage in activities to achieve their desired ends in

172

keeping with their own individual and collective values and needs. In the human service organisation called a school, one of these desired ends is helping people to learn.

An increasing number of the writers in organisation theory and in educational management/administration in particular have adopted the term 'culture' to define that social and phenomenological uniqueness of a particular organisational community - be it a factory or a hospital, a bakery or a school - and which comprises numerous intangible and symbolic elements (such as values, philosophies and ideologies) as well as those which are more tangible, and are given behavioural and visual expression. We have finally acknowledged publicly that uniqueness is a virtue, that values are important and that they should be fostered and taken into account in any analysis of an organisation's purpose or performance.

Articles which address the uniqueness of organisations or organisational culture now abound. Indeed, the whole of the September 1983 issue of *Administrative Science Quarterly* (ASQ) was devoted to the concept of culture. Increasing numbers of texts either include the word 'culture' in the title or have major sections, or the whole of the content, related to culture (Sergiovanni and Corbally, 1984; Giroux, 1981; Freire, 1972; Meyer, 1978; Wolcott, 1977; Peters and Waterman, 1982; Deal and Kennedy, 1982; Myer and Rowan, 1977; Starratt, 1986; Greenfield, 1975, 1979; Morgan, 1980 and many more).

Culture - the tangible, intangible and symbolic elements of organisational life - includes characteristics such as:

- the underlying philosophy and/or ideology espoused by the leaders and members
- the ways in which that philosophy is translated into an operational mission or purpose
- the respective value-sets of leaders and others (both within the organisation and those directly or indirectly affected by its operations) and the resonance between these
- the quality (as well as the nature) of personal and interpersonal actions and interactions
- the metaphors which consciously or unconsciously serve as frameworks for thinking and action
- the sagas, myths, stories, folk heroes and celebrations which serve to generate or bolster incentive and motivation
- the many other tangible and intangible manifestations which have hitherto been given scant importance but have both potential

173

and power in the organisation (Millikan 1985, 1987).

Any educator - indeed any sensitive person - knows that all schools are in fact intrinsically quite different from each other, and that their simplistic group-classification as schools *per se* fails to take into account their uniqueness and individuality. Schools comprise people, the activities of schools are people oriented and people centred, the mission of schools is people development and each person brings an idiosyncratic values-focus, experience and contribution to the particular school. So schools are different in every aspect of their operation because each is a non-replicable admixture of diverse, interacting elements.

Every school, then, small as well as large, new as well as old has a particular culture, determined by the individual values and experiences which each person brings to it, the ways in which its people act and interact and the footprints they leave behind them.

However, there are some identifiable symbolic elements which can and do significantly influence the nature and quality of that culture. Putting sensitive emphasis upon and making adjustments to some of these organisational characteristics can result in a constructive and coordinated school culture which will visit benefits on students, teachers and parents. On the other hand adjustments can also be made to achieve student control and staff manipulation; in other words, culture can be misused in the interests of power and influence; but good or bad, it is a culture nonetheless. Figure 8.1 suggests that there are two basic categories of characteristics which are components of school culture: those in the inner space are conceptual and intangible in character and comprise values, philosophy and ideology, whilst those in the outer space are capable of more tangible expression and can be further subclassified into verbalised expressions, visual expressions and enacted or behavioural expressions. The broken circle between the intangible and the tangible acknowledges that there are no specific boundaries and that these elements are in dynamic interaction. Further, the broken outer boundary of the framework similarly reflects the interchange between the school and its wider community.

A unique culture will be apparent in any ongoing organisation. It may not, however, be in keeping with the stated aims or written objectives of the organisation. For a strong and coordinated culture, there needs to be a close correspondence between the intangible, foundational elements and the tangible, outward expressions and symbols, between the espoused values, philosophy and ideology on the one hand, and the actual manifestations and practices on the other. Significant unrelatedness is possible and indeed not uncommon; and in any case most elements are subject to constant subtle modifications as the continually changing contextual variables impinge upon the school's dynamic interactions.

Several aspects of schooling can be seen to fall into more than one subgrouping. For example, curriculum and language (sometimes called 'organisational vocabulary') are both predominantly conceptualised/verbalised expressions but they also qualify for the enacted/behavioural category. Similarly, whilst educators may not be aware that they favour a particular metaphor or metaphors to interpret what the school stands for or does, nevertheless this kind of language constitutes both a verbalised and a behavioural expression. Hence, the subgroupings shown in Figure 8.1 are not intended to be clear cut, but they do provide a useful tool for diagnosing the elements which seem to make up the school's culture. In large part, aims and objectives, language, curriculum, sagas, metaphors and myths are in fact conceptual, but their expression will be tangible - that is, behavioural, verbal, material or visual.

The elements listed within the groupings of Figure 8.1 are present in all schools in one form, or another. What is important is the degree to which their respective significance is apparent to and is acted upon by the members of the school community; the nature of the relationship between these elements; the effect each has upon the development and maintenance of the school's culture; and the impact that culture has on individual students. For if we isolate the elements, then we can come to terms with them and do something about them.

Culture

It is now possible to be more systematic about the concept of culture. It has until now largely attracted the attention of two groups of researchers and writers, namely anthropologists and sociologists on the one hand, and literati and artists on the other. Both groups have attempted to generate definitions for their own purposes, but the fact that the word 'culture' remains a generic term used for two quite different conceptualisations perpetuates its ambiguity. The term now embodies notions both of ethnicity and tribal

*Figure 8.1 Conceptual Framework for Assessing
and Developing School Culture*

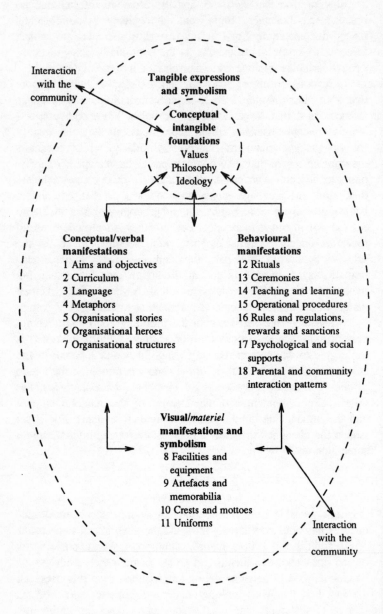

behaviours, and also of artistic expression in its many and varied forms.

From the anthropological/sociological standpoint, culture is that system of shared meanings, cognitions, symbols and experiences which are expressed in the behaviours and practices of the members of an affiliated group (a 'tribe') and which give them both social definition and a sense of association. Culture is that collectivity of images which serves both physiological and psychological needs and which governs interpersonal interaction and social support. It is expressed through rituals, ceremonies, imagery and symbols, all of which can serve to reinforce and maintain each other. Culture is the distinct way of life which gives meaning and order to the particular group or community. Culture is not static but is in a continual state of flux - indeed of development. It is subject to perpetual testing, evaluation, modification and refinement by the tribal members - both as individuals and as a collectivity. Culture consists of beliefs, language and knowledge, within which and through which the members establish and maintain their sense of community. Taken in its wider ethnographic sense, culture is that complex whole which includes arts, morals, laws, customs, beliefs, knowledge and all the other capabilities and habits acquired by people as members of a society.

Culture is in part inherited, and is often a system of conceptions transmitted in symbolic forms and which enables human beings to develop, communicate and perpetuate their knowledge and attitudes towards life, both now and for the future. Culture therefore comprises energy systems, objective artefacts, modes of thought and the transactional patterns of the members of a community. Culture is socially oriented and socially maintained. Every continuing group of people develops and maintains a unique culture; as the membership changes, so the culture will reflect both the particular contributions of the new members and the loss of the idiosyncratic qualities of the old. Culture is present both by intent and by default. It constitutes both an interpretation of behaviour as well as a focus for behaviour. Bates (1982: 6) describes the resources from which social and individual identities are constructed as 'cultural baggage'. So culture is complex and always situationally unique. It will be so for each school.

From the aesthetic/artistic/literati standpoint, the word 'culture' is used to refer to those actions and outcomes, expressions or products which are defined within the all-embracing classification of 'the fine arts', and which are deemed to have intrinsic value in and of themselves, aside from any actual or personal commercial value. The fine arts, or 'high culture', generally includes painting, music, ballet, opera, engraving, embroidery, poetry, literature, architecture, sculpture and all other areas of refined artistic and creative expression. Matthew Arnold (1869) defined culture as the pursuit of perfection by means of getting to know, in matters which interest us most, the very best which human beings have thought or said. In the artistic and intellectual sense, culture refers to the intentional and sustained effort to achieve an ideal, to create a 'reality' which reflects the highest ideals which a human being can envisage. Cultural perfection, then, is the synthesis of the ethical and the rational, the state which transports us, at least conceptually, beyond the limitations of human frailty to a superior level of creativity, artistry or intellect. Culture, then, embodies the determination to achieve the ideally good both in morality and in taste, through continual practice and study of the best of all civilizations, and also to develop a discerning appreciation of artistic expressions. Arnold believed that the pursuit of culture provided the means whereby the individual could pass beyond the normal limitations of the self, that it was a force to preserve and promote humane values and to raise people above base desires. The pursuit of culture (by this definition) is associated with a search for both excellence and refinement and in both artistic and moral endeavours. Not surprisingly, then, other nineteenth-century literary figures saw the promotion of culture as a major responsibility of schools, as the means whereby young people gain meaning and guidance for their actions. Culture should provide a pattern for life, based upon a clear understanding of individual potentialities and limitations and measured against the highest ideals of human endeavour. To be 'cultured' meant having achieved a quality of life-style, in both thought and activity, which far surpassed mere animal existence. In fact, schools have preserved this approach to culture in many of their policies and practices, both intentionally and unintentionally and over several centuries.

A central factor of culture, whether in terms of the anthropological or the aesthetic approach, is the sharing of special experiences and values - ethnic, aesthetic, artistic, moral and emotional. Schools can purposefully develop and maintain an awareness of the importance and value of culture in both its anthropological and its artistic meanings. Anthropologically, each school constitutes a unique entity with respect to:

- the specific admixture of ethnicity, values, experience, skills, aspirations, energies and potential of all personnel
- the socio-economic and geographic location and lay-out of the school within its environment
- the unique history of achievements and traditions, past heroes and sagas, associated with the particular school
- the special rituals and ceremonies, symbols and metaphors which constitute its operational procedures and structure.

Artistically, academically and aesthetically, each school will similarly be phenomenologically unique in terms of:

- the breadth, content, and emphases of its curricular offerings, and its extra-curricular activities
- the apparent and latent, expressive and artistic skills and knowledge of all personnel
- the nature and extent of its cultural support and its sponsored interactions within the immediate and its extended communities
- the outward and visible expression of the school's culture through the activities of the school within and with its community (Millikan 1987).

Schooling is concerned with the development of individual potential, and in the widest possible range of knowledge and skills. It cannot be restricted to rational and pragmatic studies and to activities directed primarily towards vocational preparation; it does include those artistic and aesthetic studies which develop sensitivity to beauty and refinement. It seems impossible to constrain schooling to a narrowness of approach or to intense specialisms, for it seems always to be spilling over into comprehensiveness, into breadth as well as depth, into creativity and self-expression, within a wide range of modes and media. So schools, almost in spite of themselves, seem to have a responsibility to clarify and coordinate these various cultural elements because as organisations they espouse, either directly or indirectly, a composite of values, philosophy and ideology which purports to educate intellectually, socially and skilfully the children who place their faith and their futures in the school's care and nurture. Schools, both purposefully and incidentally, are powerfully cultural places.

School culture: conceptual intangible foundations

As we have already indicated, the framework in Figure 8.1 contains two sets of characteristics which are present in all schools. Ideally, the first set (values, philosophy and ideology) should influence what is done in the school, the shape of its buildings, its sponsored behaviour patterns, its ceremonies and its symbols, and should provide a rationale and justification for all its functions. Values, philosophy and ideology are closely related terms, but the last two have greater specificity than the first.

Values

Values are guidelines for behaviour. They are criteria against which we evaluate (and reflect upon) our actions, either proposed or taken, and on the attitudes and behaviours of others. Values are weights: the priorities we place on things. Values are learned, internalised through experience, education and observation, and are subject to continual reappraisal. With the exception of spontaneous and instinctive reactions, our attitudes and our actions are reflections of our values, though the spontaneous and instinctive are considered by some to be imprinted and therefore automatic-response values. However, like culture, values are not genetically inherited but are learned and inculcated from birth.

Hodgkinson (1978 and 1983) provides a useful framework within which to analyse and interpret values. He defines values as 'concepts of the desirable with motivating force', and as motivating determinants of behaviour (Hodgkinson 1983: 36). They are thus preferred states of affairs, what we believe 'ought' to be. We value things or states not so much because they have worth in and of themselves but because we choose to assign a worth to them. In so doing, we superimpose on to an objective thing a subjective element to indicate its level of significance for us. To be collectively valuable, others must similarly assign degrees of value to this same thing or state; shared or social values are an aggregation of individual values or preferred states.

The assigning of values is in response to personal belief structures, accepted social standards or other criteria, but in every case the degree of value assigned is a very personal decision. Hodgkinson (1978) reminds us that values are different from facts; that facts can be true or false, but that values will be good or bad, right or wrong; that values cannot be scientifically proven or logically verified. In assigning values we make judgements about the worth of things from our peculiar perspective. Hodgkinson (1978 and 1983) suggests that we operate a hierarchy of values; some have absolute or non-negotiable quality, whereas others are subject to social negotiation, or merely to personal preference.

Hodgkinson offers two values paradigms - one (which he published in 1978) deals with individual values and the other (published in 1983) sets them within an organisational context. The earlier model (1978: 111) (see Figure 8.2) has three levels - transrational, rational, and subrational.

At the *transrational* level, values are conceived of as follows:

• they are metaphysical and conative, having a quality of absoluteness, enlightenment and volition
• they are based on will, aesthetic sense, principle, ethical code and moral insight
• adoption of transrational values implies an act of faith, belief and commitment
• these values are entirely personal and individual, unique to the value holder, and cannot be verified by scientific techniques or logical argument.

At the *rational* level, values are viewed as follows:

• they enlist the faculties of reason and cognition
• they are grounded within a social context of norms, mores, customs, expectations and standards
• they depend upon collective justification
• they are disciplinary and organisationally oriented
• their philosophic base is in humanism, pragmatism and utilitarianism
• they are buttressed by the *status quo*, ethos, customs, beliefs, laws and *mores* of a particular culture
• reason and compromise are venerated, as are prudence and expediency.

At the *subrational* level:

• values are seen as being grounded in feeling and personal preference. Typically, what feels good is valued

- they are almost entirely behaviouristic in character
- they are rooted in emotion, are basic, direct, affective, and individual
- they are basically asocial and amoral.

In practice, we tend to move between these various levels constantly, as our emphasis shifts from beliefs/idealism (level 1) to the cognitive/social (level 2) to the affective/preferential (level 3).

Whether they are happy to accept the responsibility or not, those concerned with the management of schools - which are clearly 'people places' - need to be very sensitive to personal values, for everyone associated with the school has them, and they directly influence what kind of a place that school is. At the least, then, the first Hodgkinson model provides the school manager with a framework for diagnosing how powerful any person's value-set will be in any given situation. Generally speaking, the higher the level, the more formidable the influence. More awesome still, schools themselves are powerful manufacturers of values and value-sets, especially in children.

Hodgkinson's more recent model (1983: 24) (see Figure 8.3) is similar to the earlier attempts to reconcile personal (ideographic) values with the organisational (nomothetic) elements of organisation made initially by Getzels and Guba (1957) and later expanded by Getzels and Thelen (1960). The model (consisting of five levels) addresses the relationship between the leader, the organisation and its official mission or purpose. Level V1 reflects the values-stance of the individual within the organisation; V2 represents groups of all sorts and sizes within the organisation; V3 is the organisational or nomothetic level; V4 depicts the social subculture within which the organisation operates; and V5 is the overarching societal ethos which, while not impinging upon the particular organisation, can be influential through the subculture (V4) level. In discussing the role of the leader, Hodgkinson raises the possibility of a sixth (V6) level which (like level 1 in the 1978 model) represents the transrational/transcendental. Both models acknowledge that there is overlapping between the respective levels.

The second model therefore indicates what complications might occur when personal and group values are mediated through an organisation such as a school. In the end, adopting a 'school philosophy' is a far from simple exercise, especially if it is to become the basis of the school's operation; mere adoption of a

Figure 8.2 Analytical Model of the Value Concept

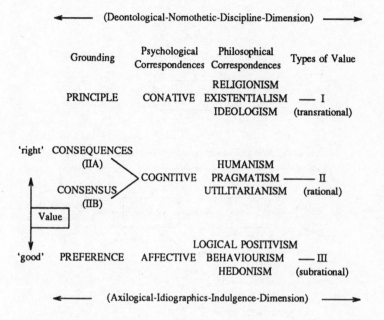

◄─────── (Deontological-Nomothetic-Discipline-Dimension) ───────►

Grounding	Psychological Correspondences	Philosophical Correspondences	Types of Value
PRINCIPLE	CONATIVE	RELIGIONISM EXISTENTIALISM IDEOLOGISM	── I (transrational)
'right' CONSEQUENCES (IIA) CONSENSUS (IIB)	COGNITIVE	HUMANISM PRAGMATISM UTILITARIANISM	── II (rational)
'good' PREFERENCE	AFFECTIVE	LOGICAL POSITIVISM BEHAVIOURISM HEDONISM	── III (subrational)

Value

◄─────── (Axilogical-Idiographics-Indulgence-Dimension) ───────►

*(Permission to reproduce this figure kindly granted
by the author C. Hodgkinson and publisher
Basil Blackwell, Oxford)*

*Figure 8.3 The Total Field of Action: Values placed
within the Organisational Context*

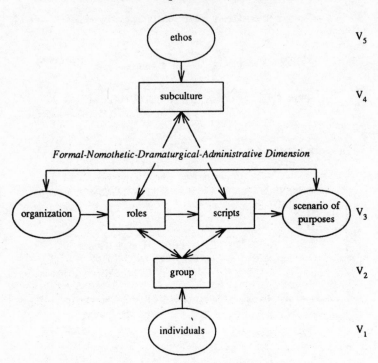

*(Permission to reproduce this figure kindly granted by
the author C. Hodgkinson and publisher
Basil Blackwell, Oxford)*

philosophy will usually not achieve that outcome. Principals and their school communities, singly and collectively, need to be clear about their own and their shared values if they are to ensure that the school's practices genuinely reflect what the school says it stands for. Complicated though the process might be, the discrepancy between what schools say and what they do is one of the major causes of parent and student criticism. It is an area the school manager cannot avoid.

Philosophy

For our purposes here, a philosophy (from the Greek 'love of wisdom') is a coherent statement about one's values, usually the higher order values of level 1; a statement that engages lower order values usually is not accorded the status of a philosophy.

Some schools operate according to the philosophy of a particular writer (like Steiner, Montessori, Rousseau), but most have a less targeted and usually less presumptuous statement of the ideals which mobilise them. Some base their functioning on academic rigour, for example, to be developed through the study of the classics, logic, calculus and so on. Others have adopted a laissez-faire philosophy with an emphasis on personal and social development. Others emphasise the expressive arts in their philosophy. At the most simplistic level of definition, a school philosophy provides a theoretical or conceptual focus for the school's activities, and reflects a set of formally espoused values.

Ideology

Ideology (literally, the study of an idea) has a more specific connotation than philosophy, sometimes addressing causes and effects in thought systems, and deliberately forcing thought and action along particular lines. It tends to adopt a predetermined position or belief structure and is generally more focused and more limited than a philosophy; indeed we frequently develop an ideology from a more general philosophy. Thus, values underlie the statement of beliefs which we call a philosophy, and an ideology usually focuses upon an idea or ideas contained within a philosophy.

In summary, then, we tend as individuals, as organisations, and as social groups to derive a philosophy from our values, and ideologies from our philosophy. We then try to operationalise them; that is, we turn them into particular practices - into tangible outcomes - and it is by these means that we bring a measure of coherence and identity to what we have called culture. The process is of course reversible; those outward manifestations of culture send very clear signals about what we value, what ideals we espouse and by what ideas we are infatuated. Every school is full of such signals.

An agenda for action: tangible expressions and symbolism

The tangible manifestations of school culture are generally verbal, visual and behavioural. If school managers are seriously concerned about transforming leadership, about organisational and personal excellence, about admirable learning and teaching outcomes, then they cannot avoid becoming involved in developing, maintaining and reshaping the things and symbols which express what the school stands for. The transformational leader must become sophisticated about cultural symbolism and about how to handle it.

Conceptual/verbal manifestations

The first group of symbolic and expressive manifestations of culture are those which have been committed to writing or are conveyed in words among the members of the school community. We give here a check list for the school principal to consider.

1. *Aims and Objectives*
An obvious place to start is with the statements of aims and objectives of the school. Aims tend to be the more abstract while objectives are usually more pragmatic, operations-oriented statements of intent. Aims tend to be broad and often express intentions that go well beyond the school's resources or capacities. Their usefulness lies in their ability to inspire endeavour and to focus effort. Objectives translate the aims into achievable activities; indeed they provide direction for all school activity. Aims and objectives statements should not be immutable, and ought to be subjected to periodic reconsideration. But most important of all, the school managers need to be satisfied that the official aims and objectives embody their values and that it is a statement to which they are willing to commit themselves without reservation.

2. *Curriculum*

The curriculum, and the emphases and balances within it, is the prime vehicle for conveying the school's educational purposes. Subtle inclusions and exclusions can colour its impact, and its strength can be subverted by unplanned factors like administrative expediency or the teaching range within the staff. Most schools try to provide an appropriately wide and balanced range of subject offerings and learning experiences but a decision to weight some subject areas or activities as more or less important than others can skew that balance; similarly, the absence of teaching expertise or physical facilities may also unintentionally distort the desired balance.

The curriculum is much wider than the formal, timetabled, subject offerings, and is usually taken to include all activities, both formal and informal, which are experienced by the child during the school day. Indeed, what students are most likely to remember with clarity about their schooldays will rarely be the day on which they first understood Pythagorean theorems or memorised a passage from Shakespeare, but rather the extra-curricular events in which they were involved, or which were ceremonial in character; and these things become the sagas or stories which are the carriers of culture. Imaginative teaching can ensure that the formal studies are also interesting and memorable, that the academic programme does in fact play its part in culture building.

Many schools have sports, clubs, and societies which also constitute a part of the curriculum even though they are often labelled as extra-curricular. There is also the 'hidden curriculum' - those other non-timetabled features which can be intentional or unintentional, which are sometimes knowingly concealed, which are infrequently given public acknowledgement but which are powerful in conveying culture. So the managers of excellent schools will be very aware of the range and impact of all curriculum experiences on students, and will attempt to harness their power in the interests of improving the quality of every child's education.

3. *Language*

The language which people inside an organisation repeatedly use, and the ways in which it is used also reflect, either directly or indirectly, intentionally or unintentionally, a values base. In fact, there is an 'in-language', an organisational vocabulary, which develops inside a human group. It is the easiest means of dividing who belongs to the organisation from those who do not. Language is our chief means of interaction with others, but not all communication is verbal; there is also, for example, body language, eye contact, gesticulation and so on. We need to consider the tenor of our communications very carefully indeed, for our use of language admits some to the culture and excludes others. Of course, language is of prime importance in the learning experiences of students: it can enlighten or confuse; it opens and closes opportunities; it can be descriptive or prescriptive; it can promote intellectual development or stifle it. 'Teacher talk' is all-pervasive in schools. Teachers and especially the principal must therefore be most sensitive about the language they use and what impacts it may have.

4. *Metaphors*
Metaphors are analogies and our language is full of them. It is the way we make sense of our world, by comparing one thing with another, by classifying and by linking qualities. Our values are most powerfully revealed by means of the comparisons we make.

Metaphors are rarely consciously chosen, nor is the significance of their inherent symbolism always clearly understood. Importantly, teachers use metaphors to describe teaching, learning, individual students and the school. If students are not to be confused or cowed by the school's approach to learning, there ought to be some commonality among the metaphors used in the school, as well as some agreement about the metaphors which are condoned or favoured and those which are not to be used.

The recurrent imagery which one uses gives a clear indication of the templates which one is carrying in one's head, the patterned way in which one thinks about a subject. There are some frequently used analogies about schools and their implications which ought to be appreciated by principals. When, for example, people talk about a school using military terms to describe it, they have a model in their minds about how the school operates and its style. Schools are also likened to a prison, a factory, a monastery, a family and a free market. Let us consider what these terms mean. Here are the the most common metaphors associated with schools:

- *Military* - regimented; authoritarian; hierarchical; inflexible; directly specific ; tending to stifle creativity and innovativeness; an expectation of uniformity; directive; often insensitive; ignoring the specific and the individual; bureaucratic
- *Prison* - highly coercive; untrusting; non-risk-taking; punitive; authoritarian; operates from a presumption of guilt; stringently observant of rules and regulations; inflexible; bureaucratic; lacking in compassion and consideration; basic and spartan; over-controlled
- *Factory* - mechanistic and routine; an expectation of uniformity; predetermined standards for behaviours and outcomes; production-line mentality to teaching and learning; a systems approach to organisation; cost-benefit orientation; efficiency rather than effectiveness; expectations of sameness; little concern for the special case; rigid expectations; quantitative rather than qualitative approach and focus
- *Monastic* - austere; spartan; self-denying; expectations of strong self-control; strong systemic control; clear assumptions of right and wrong; inflexible interpretation of rules and regulations; strong moral overtones; an unquestioned expectation of understanding and conformity; penances exacted for laxity or non-conformity; unemotional and unbending on matters of principle; rigid commitment to an ideal
- *Happy Family* - human-ness and humaneness; consideration in all things; supportive and forgiving; strong emphasis on individuality and creativity; flexible; condoning of aberrant behaviour; concern for the needy, helpless and insecure; strong emphasis on interpersonal relations; encouragement for self-direction and self-motivation; frequently weak in the giving of directions, in meeting deadlines, and in performance efficiency
- *Laissez-faire* - a 'do-your-own-thing' mentality; 'anything-goes', an absence of rules and regulations; encouraging of creativity, innovativeness and self-awareness; non-bureaucratic; non-specific; non-directive; encouraging of self-expression; unhurried and unflappable; a lack of concern for efficiency and effectiveness; personal experience and expression are of paramount importance.

Teachers and principals do not have to accept these metaphors; in fact, the most positive response they can make is to select deliberately a metaphor which affirms the way they image the school and then repeatedly to use it, reinforcing each other's assertions by overtly introducing the same analogy into their conversations.

Keep it simple: One simple picture, constantly repeated, which affirms that 'This is what our school is like.'

5. *Organisational Stories*

Every organisation collects its share of apocryphal stories, just as every tribe and every nation does. In fact, these stories gather remarkable power as they are embellished in the telling and begin to acquire archetypal meanings. Consider how difficult it often is, for example, to refute a case based upon anecdotal evidence; the anecdote often carries more evocative power than argumentation or statistics. It is for this reason that every culture in the world and every major religion abound with stories, for, regardless of background or learning in the hearer, those things which are most difficult to put into words - like values, for example - can be imaged in a story. So allegories, parables, myths and fables, epics and the like are weapons in the armoury of the transformational leader just as they are the stuff of religion and culture.

Myths may be fictitious but in many respects they are more 'true' than real-life stories. Stories of this kind are inventions which encapsulate the aspirations of individuals or groups and which make sense of their reality, as they perceive it; indeed they systematise those perceptions and serve as surrogates for them when the hearer has no first-hand personal experience to go on. These myths are alive and active in every school; some of them are powerfully positive influences in learning. Myths of course often embody an ideology, indeed, give it substance; and they can reinforce a philosophy. There are also legends abroad, elaborated and selective distortions of some prior and actual events or exploits or persons.

In summary, then, story-telling is one of the universal methods for conveying values and meanings, often religious, quasi-religious or value-laden meanings. Note how widespread is the device of illustrating a generalisation with an anecdote. Indeed, some stories gather such power through constant telling that they acquire epic or mythic overtones; in just such a way the Arthurian cycle grew. In its own way, every school cultivates its own cycle of legends to encapsulate what is transcendent about its own culture. And every transformational leader encourages the evocative story about his or her organisation and the people in it, reinforcing the culture by repeated tellings of it. Indeed when these stories are garbed in ceremony of some kind, they become very powerful, unifying symbols. Every leader should learn how to use them.

6. *Organisational Heroes*

Sagas are stories about heroes and heroic exploits; and in educational settings they are stories ostensibly about the school and its people. Burton Clark (1975) used the term 'organisational saga' to explain how three liberal arts colleges had preserved their identity over time in spite of upheavals and changes in leadership. Sagas vary dramatically in their intensity and durability. Those having greatest strength and permanency tend to be built slowly within a structured and ongoing context, and are maintained, strengthened and embellished through regular retelling and in combination with other ritualistic and ceremonial behaviour, each reinforcing the other.

The heroes (and anti-heroes) around whom a saga is built personify the values, philosophy and ideology which the community wishes to sustain. So the heroic figures are depicted as dragon-slayers, or as knights-errant. Heroes become role-models for the tribal members, epitomising leadership, bravery in the face of great odds, chivalry, thoughtfulness, charity, service. Sagas and the hero stories are based on actual events, but become creatively distorted through frequent retelling. The hero figure invites emulation and helps to sustain group unity. Every school has its heroes and its potential heroes; they can be found among principals and staff, both present and past; among students and especially old scholars who have gone on to higher successes; and among parents and others associated with the school. Every school honour board contains hero material. And every school principal would do well to cultivate some if he or she is serious about the excellence of the school.

There are always others who will undertake the task of cultivating folk heroes. Every school has its cultural high priests, some of them quite unexpected. Within the school staff, among parents and also in the student body, certain people acquire the status of both the conservators and the creators of local culture; they counsel others; they pass on information (often in the form of gossip, or as messages from, or messengers for, the grapevine); they operate a network of contacts and spread stories. They are the go-betweens, the creators of folklore. They mediate culture and meaning, they help to build the emotional bonds which hold the tribe together and, in so doing, they emphasise the closeness of community and the uniqueness of belonging. So the transforming leader, concerned about school excellence, learns not only how to identify the organisation's high priests but also to value what they do. They usually select themselves because they need a peculiar set of characteristics before they can assume the role within the culture, but the wise leader will know intuitively how to capitalise upon that priestly role once a role incumbent has emerged.

7. *Organisational Structures*

A curriculum philosophy will be supported by organisational structures and by operational procedures which are in keeping with that philosophy. Organisational structures find their tangible expression through the behaviours and actions of the members of the particular organisation; and those structures are therefore usually accurate indicators of the world map inside the heads of the leaders, revealing the way decision-making is conceived, the favoured communications patterns, the preferred power-authority relationships and so on. In consequence, the school managers need to ask, concerning every new and existing procedure, whether it is conveying the right impressions and whether it is consistent with the school's prime aims.

Visual/materiel *manifestations and symbolism*

8. *Facilities and Equipment*

Facilities typically comprise buildings and grounds; their distinctive configurations, as well as their quality, architecture and furnishings make an immediate and usually lasting impression. The messages a school signals to a person who visits it for the first time are important, especially the approaches, the reception area, and the office and classroom furnishings.

The term 'equipment' generally relates to hardware or materials which the school possesses. Even so, facilities and equipment have a symbiotic relationship with each other. For the school's resources - its possessions, as it were - both human and material, reflect the priorities, values and philosophy underlying the school's curricula. In some instances, and to some degree, schools can indicate their educational priorities through factors such as, for example, academic emphasis and numerical strength (department by department) and the special expertise of its teaching staff. It may also be clearly apparent what qualities are valued in the staff members and whether qualities like personality, adaptability, creativity and team work are commonly shared characteristics. Every school also attempts to develop its resources and facilities in keeping with a particular curricular focus. Some schools advertise their academic priorities by means of indicators like teacher strength, the facilities for specialised activities and the predominance or otherwise of language laboratories, specialised science or computer facilities, fine arts and performing arts studios, physical education gymnasia and out doors arenas, stables, boat-sheds, chapel, and so on. However, it must be acknowledged that flexibility and feasibility in many of these areas, particularly those affecting plant and facilities, are often extremely difficult for government schools to wrest from constrained education ministry budgets. Wealthy non-government schools in Australia and North America have much greater negotiability in being able to shape the physical characteristics of their facilities and resources. Many other schools in England, Australia, Canada and the USA can do little to modify even their academic curriculum because of staffing and facilities constraints. The intention must always be there to modify and change the physical learning environment in the developmental interests of the students.

It is important to note that particular specialisations and facilities frequently develop under the influence of an individual teacher or principal; the physical features sometimes become a trademark of a period of the school's history, and are thereafter a part of the school's cultural baggage. The community comes to associate certain offerings and activities with the school, especially where specialised facilities and equipment have been developed to sustain that activity. Facilities, once established, are fairly permanent and making changes in configuration or quality can be both time-consuming and costly. It can thus become a matter of symbolical importance as to where a school is able to construct its halls, pools, playing-fields, laboratories, studios, camp-sites, and teaching spaces such as science wings, computing centres and home economics centres. As Christopher Wren could claim about London, if you want to see memorials to the educational ideas which have motivated the school now and in the past, just look around you at the school's buildings and its equipment. Indeed, it is not only what the school has but how those resources are configured; it is the pattern rather than the individual pieces which reveals the picture. A transforming leader will almost certainly wish to make some changes to the physical envelope of the school and its furnishings if he or she is concerned about cultural impacts, and providing there is the physical and economic opportunity to so do.

9. *Artefacts and Memorabilia*

For many schools these are features of past eras, yet a school's culture is also evident in the form of artefacts and memorabilia in the school, including conventions like sports blazer pockets (where uniforms are still worn), school song-books (where formal assemblies are a regular feature), awards and achievement certificates. Most schools produce a magazine or newspaper, for example. In others, photographs of student and staff groupings are on display. Some schools develop old boy or girl, ex-student, or alumni associations to maintain strong affiliations with the school. Honour boards, trophies cabinets, galleries for artwork, flags and pennants, and display boards are visible in many of the older and more traditional schools and, where present, contribute as pieces in the mosaic of the particular school: what its values are, and what things it regards as admirable. The transforming leader will consider all of these in attempting to create a unique learning environment, and will be constantly vigilant about the consistency of the message these visual signs are sending out to those both inside and outside of the school community.

10. *Crests and Mottoes*

Similarly, crests, mottoes, uniforms and other visual symbolism constitute the 'livery' of the school. These are usually displayed in a more formal way in the pageantry of ceremonial occasions - those behavioural observances of a school's culture - but for many schools these are now a thing of the past. However, where they are still present, they constitute a valuable means of culture development and of community affiliation.

Crests are a visual summary of the values, philosophy and ideology of the school. They can vary widely depending upon whether the school has sacred or secular origins. Some use Christian symbolism such as the cross, a Bishop's mitre, a shepherd's crook, an open Bible, or other ecclesiastical imagery. Some in a kind of carry-over from medieval origins use military symbols like knights on horse-back, swords and pikes, castle-keeps, cannon, ships, rampant lions (as associated with Royalty) and the like. Most crests are based upon an heraldic coat-of-arms, although more recently established schools have used a logo rather than a crest as the school identifier, a fact that signals modernity rather than tradition or conservatism.

Mottoes are similarly varied, and range in sentiment from the challenging to the reflective and contemplative. They have traditionally included injunctions like 'For God and Home', 'Dare to be Wise', 'By our Works are we Known', 'Enlightenment and Service', and whilst many heraldic mottoes are still to be found (some of them in ecclesiastical Latin), the emphasis has clearly shifted from physical to intellectual battle. Mottoes often occur in association with crests, and aim to encapsulate the school's philosophy and values through an aphorism.

11. *Uniforms*

Many schools, especially those based on the English tradition, for either philosophical or throughly utilitarian reasons, opt for a school uniform, both to provide a sense of identity for students and to establish a standard code of dress. They constitute a visual expression of a student's affiliation with a particular school. Uniforms, on the other hand, can often convey unintended impressions; if the school feels militaristic in its mode of operation, the existence of a uniform heightens the analogy of the army. In some Catholic schools, the uniform was sometimes identified with a cassock or habit thereby confirming an impression that the students are like monastic novices. Perhaps fortunately, such examples are now very rare.

In summary, then, those charged with the management of schools must be aware that the saying 'What you see is what you get' does not always hold true for a person conscious of organisational culture. Physical facilities repeatedly acquire a colouring that reflects deeper meanings. In fact, educational facilities are more prone than most to become iconic, physical symbols of deeply held, quasi-religious values, largely because education and schooling are associated with the impressionable years of one's growing-up, and because parents invest in the future of their children. With such emotive expectations the wise manager, far from submitting as a victim of these characteristics, can intervene powerfully to ensure that the icons preach a consistently ennobling, consistently integral gospel about learning.

Behavioural manifestations

The enacted expressions of culture can be so intrinsic to the operation of the school that we tend to view them as routine or purely functional and overlook their collective impact. On the other hand, sometimes the enactments are deliberately contrived, such as to acknowledge the achievements of a school hero or to celebrate an important event.

12. *Rituals*

Much of what is done in schools is ritualistic; indeed many of the procedures and routines of school organisation are ritualised for efficiency and ease of administration. These are functional, utilitarian practices, but they imply that there is a 'best' way of doing things, in harmony with the philosophy, ideology and values of the school. The procedures may have been devised for purely pragmatic reasons, but there is a fine-grained relationship between espoused values and philosophy and what is regarded as normal organisational processes. When organisational behaviour, formal or informal, fits well, then it tells us a great deal about the environment with which it harmonises.

There are of course other rituals which are easily recognised as such - like various forms of housemeetings and pastoral care programmes, small group meetings of students for the primary purpose of providing individual support, or to enhance group affiliation within the larger school organisation. Rituals can also become instruments of control. Rituals and ceremonies can build *esprit de corps* and pride of association, but they can similarly manipulate and distort, confuse ends with means, and serve less public agenda. Where rituals are coupled with high ideals and a philosophy of educational excellence and social justice, they are powerful tools for education.

13. *Ceremonies*

Ceremonies are celebrations of the life of an organisation, and may be staged to pay tribute to particular members, to acknowledge special events, to commemorate past achievements, to build support for current programmes or to launch a new activity. While rituals are regular and routine, ceremonies can be infrequent, special, are often elaborate in their form of presentation, can be formalistic, and are usually staged at the times of greatest impact. Ceremonies are a public display of culture. They are never in the strict sense accidental or perfunctory.

There are many occasions when a school's activities can be celebrated and promoted through ceremony. If ceremonies are seen by students and staff to be disruptive to the normal routines and out of keeping with the formal curriculum or timetable, then too little attention has been given to their authenticity. Every organisation needs formal enactments of its culture, and some pageantry reinforces the impact.

14. *Teaching and Learning*

The primary purpose of the school is the teaching and learning activity of the staff and students. As we discovered from the effective schools research, a major task for school principals, teachers and support staff is creating a safe environment maximally conducive to learning. Its features include the following:

- the relevance and appropriateness of the curricular content to which the students are exposed
- the relevance and appropriateness of the teaching techniques and methodologies employed
- the appropriateness of time-frames within which the activity takes place
- the availability of support materials and resources
- the appropriateness of evaluative and assessment mechanisms and techniques
- the quality of the modelling role of teachers and significant others
- the appropriateness of reporting procedures for both students and parents
- the appropriateness of rewards for both students and teachers.

By whatever philosophy or methodology, and within whatever context teachers engage in their professional interaction with students, it is useful to conceptualise this broad range of activities as 'teaching'. Similarly, the range and variety of activities by which students learn are usefully conceived of as 'learning'. It is important that assessment and evaluation procedures also enhance teaching and learning and are recognised as contributors to the school's culture and ethos.

15. *Operational Procedures*

These are a working-out in practice of the conceptual structures underpinned by the organisation's aims and objectives. They include factors like communication patterns, decision-making procedures, techniques for dealing with conflict and accommodating changes, accountability and evaluation techniques, the audit of the efficiency and effectiveness of operations, staff development and so on. The association between espoused aims and actual processes should be close. Whereas many schools include in their statements of aims and objectives reference to individualised instruction and the maximising of individual potential, their real practices embody, for example, large-group instruction, insufficient individualised attention, and bureaucratic procedures which frequently overlook the subtle needs of individuals. Excellent schools tend to be more ambitious, creative and flexible about meeting the individual educational needs of their students.

16. *Rules and Regulations, Rewards and Sanctions*
To ensure consistency in the behaviours of members inside an organisation, rules and regulations are generally drawn up to define boundaries for activity and to guarantee predictable performance and outcomes. Ideally rules and regulations should be conceived of as guidelines rather than as prescriptions for behaviour. In autocratic or bureaucratic environments they are often interpreted as absolutes, with little room for variation appropriate to the particular circumstance or context. A rigid observance of rules and regulations may be character building, but such rigidity can remove the element of trust in relationships, maturity, and the kind of growth which can only come through accepting responsibilities. Of course, rules and regulations are forced on schools by litigation, by industrial awards, and by disputes; the legal answer usually is to spell out responsibilities in explicit language. So it is worth noting that confrontation may well leave an unwanted legacy in the school's ethos.

The corollary to rules and regulations is rewards and sanctions. The latter are outcomes of the observance or non-observance of the former.

17. *Psychological and Social Supports*
Schools often claim in their official statement of aims that they are caring places; but, if this is a serious affirmation, the school will need to give sufficient attention to matters of psychological, social, emotional, moral or spiritual support for both students and teachers. In many Australian schools such support structures typically take the form of a school counsellor, school chaplain, pastoral care groups, house groups or home groups, and the like. English state schools do not have school chaplains, and they are becoming increasingly rare in the public schools as well. However, all organisations provide personal support of one form or another for their members; it can be institutionalised or discretionary, formal or incidental. The former include mechanisms to

establish and honour industrial agreements, and to cover members against physical or psychological harm of one form or another. The later category can include active and visible caring procedures within the day-to-day activity of the organisation.

18. *Parental and community interaction patterns*
The final element incorporated into this check list for a constructive school culture pertains to the quality of interactions between the school and its parents and community. The traditional contacts through assessments and reports of student's academic progress, and the (sometimes confrontationist) term or annual parent-teacher nights have now been expanded to include curriculum information evenings, psychological guidance and advice, open days and fairs, concerts and displays of student's achievements, and a more genuine, open-door policy whereby parents have access to teachers and to the school's administration.

The parent body of any school constitutes a rich fund of skills and expertise, knowledge and experience, which goes well beyond the capacities of its teaching staff, and excellent schools are now creating opportunities to enrich the educational experiences of their students by tapping this resource. Where the resource is unused, the school may be sending signals to its public that it sees learning as closeted, esoteric, and bound by teacher possessiveness. Beware that the signals your school broadcasts, perhaps unwittingly, are constructive and positive.

Coda

A school's culture is the *gestalt* of all of the foregoing. As indicated earlier, culture is present in one form or another in all ongoing communities. It is capable of modification and transformation through the intentional manipulation of emphases and weightings of the various elements, which produce the observable differences among schools, even though they operate with the same fundamental resource base.

A coordinated culture develops from a dynamic combination of strong, imaginative and transforming leadership within a forward looking school community, in which consistent values, philosophy and ideology permeate all decision-making.

It should be noted that a strong culture may be contrary to the officially articulated philosophy and values of the school and, in such a circumstance, a kind of counter-culture will develop which will be at variance with the official philosophy and values. If a counter-culture continues and gathers sufficient support, it can result in significant cultural confusion for the members of the school and may ultimately become the predominant culture - a situation which indicates the absence of strong formal leadership and the presence of strong informal leadership. The role of leader in cultural development is potentially very powerful and fundamentally very important.

Recent writings on the development of organisational culture and on excellence of operation point to the crucial role of the leader as a visionary, as having strong and clearly articulated values and a clear perception of the mission of the organisation. Such leadership attributes may also be shared by the other members of the organisation. In this chapter, we have tried to show that the development of a coordinated and constructive school culture can be a matter of deliberate intent.

9

Performance Indicators
and Accountability

Would you recognise a good school when you saw one? What would you look for as evidence of that quality? There are several answers one could expect. Some people, indeed many parents, will say that the 'feel' of the school is one of the best indicators; school style, school tone, school morale are qualities which one picks up in incidental ways and do not need to be quantified, they would say. Others argue that the learning outcomes or academic results signal whether it is a good school: 'by their fruits shall ye know them.' So these people will look for success rates in academic performance, reading scores, language skills, the numbers who compete successfully somewhere beyond the school and so on. Thirdly, some people will argue that there are several key characteristics or indicators which will demonstrate a school's quality, like behaviour patterns, the cleanliness of the school grounds, a lack of noise, insistence on school uniforms. But in every case, the person making the appraisal of quality assembles, either formally or informally, some evidence or data as indicators of 'goodness'. As Harlen warned in 1973, 'If you are teaching skills that cannot be evaluated, you are in the awkward position of being unable to demonstrate that you are teaching anything at all' (Harlen, 1973: 230).

Objectives

As we indicated in the first chapter, the terms 'effectiveness' and 'efficiency' are related, 'Effectiveness' means that one has set a goal and achieved it. In consequence, it is impossible for an organisation or a person to be effective unless there has first been a specification of goals.

When these two terms are used by economic rationalists, it is assumed that the objectives are capable of clear definition and, usually, also of quantification. It should then be possible to collect numerical or financial data which will indicate overtly whether the objectives have been achieved. And that is one of the problems with education, for some of the most highly regarded objectives of learning are personal, self-transforming and intangible. How does one quantify a child's tears, or the wonder of great music, or a shift in one's value system, or an attitudinal change, or a religious experience? Frequently these learning experiences come from a process which by its very nature must look inefficient, sometimes haphazard, often experimental. Those who are concerned to measure learning outcomes or to assess both the effectiveness and efficiency of schooling must somehow accommodate these intensely personal and transcendental aspects of education. Educators have always had difficulty in defining both the objectives of education and some of the most desired outcomes, and they always will.

Even so, it is important to recognise this essential characteristic about effectiveness; it assumes a prior definition of objectives and some means of measuring to see whether those objectives have been achieved. Indeed the effective schools movement has been based upon that premise, namely that schools have objectives and they ought to be tested. Because educators have been unable to define and measure some of the desired outcomes of schooling, the measurers seized upon the indicators which were available and were being used already. Since all teachers seemed to be involved with teaching reading, writing and arithmetic, the effective schools movement has used the standardised test scores for reading and number skills as the prime indicator of effectiveness. In doing so, the movement has in effect defined the prime purpose of schooling as the raising of literacy and numeracy skills. Those schools which grind away at these purposes to the exclusion of other, more intangible aims are likely to come out on top in terms of 'effectiveness'. Yet an effective school on this measure may well be one where you would not like to send your child; it could have a stifling and repressively narrow focus which both belies and belittles what we really look for in a liberal, liberating education.

A third term, 'excellence', has now completed a trilogy. Excellence implies that some are better than others, that there are peaks of achievement which only the superlatively skilled or endowed can reach, and that it is not only possible but also desirable to draw up rank orders to demonstrate this characteristic. What is more, excellence is defined on a scale that someone selects; it may not be a scale which you are happy to accede to or agree with.

This point was well demonstrated in a commentary on the book *Fifteen Thousand Hours* (1979), the account of the Rutter study which has had such a profound impact on the effective schools movement. Michael Sterne pointed out that the correlations between some of the factors looked at in the study were not high, in particular those between academic outcomes and behaviour. 'Strikingly,' he said, 'the second best school on the academic measure was the worst for behaviour,' but he comments that we should not be surprised at this result because 'the factors which operate to produce academic success are different from those which operate to produce good behaviour' (Sterne 1979: 198). So it is not adequate to talk about good schools without first asking the question, 'Good in what respect?' Individual schools are likely to be good at some things and not so good at others. Further, one needs to ask who is defining 'goodness' in this context, whose agenda is being served and what devices are being used to judge the extent of 'goodness'.

Ralph and Fennessey (1983), for example, in their survey article about effective schools, propose a 'set of benchmark criteria for what the concept of effective schooling . . . should entail'. Their five criteria are as follows:

• The school 'should produce high achievement in basic academic skills that are not narrowly curriculum specific'
• Those high achievement levels should persist over time; they suggest for at least two consecutive years and with at least two groups of students
• The achievement levels, the school should be able to demonstrate, are 'consistently high for more than a single grade' or year level
• Achievement gains ought to be 'characteristic of the whole school rather than of individual grades'
• All of these characteristics should exist 'even when researchers control carefully for student background'. That is, the achievements need to take note of the socio-economic profile of the student population (Ralph and Fennessey, 1983: 690).

These criteria, of course, focus on academic achievement entirely, but they have the merit that they are in operational terms and are subject to measurement and verification. It is, therefore, incumbent on educators to clarify what an effective or excellent school is according to their criteria, how to produce that kind of school and how to demonstrate objectively that it is such a school.

All of this underlines the importance of clarifying objectives and of basing assessments upon them. School objectives often seem to be vapid, uninteresting, wordy and cumbersome. They seldom have the turn of phrase which can inspire effort or much excitement. They tend also to be treated lightly for two reasons - they seem remote from the realities of the learning processes going on in classrooms with teachers and students; and they are not made the basis for testing. Objectives mean little unless they are accompanied by a regular monitoring of whether the school is achieving them. In short, schools need to get their act together. They need to define their prime objectives, put them into operational terms (that is, what will go on in particular classrooms to give meaning to those objectives) and then regularly assess the school's performances against those objectives, using evaluation methods which are comprehensible to whichever public the school needs to impress.

The Dror model for evaluation of public policy

In his landmark book entitled *Public Policymaking Re-examined* (1973), Dror argues that those who set public policy ought to be able to demonstrate that a policy is in the public interest and is achieving the objectives for which it was brought into being. He admits that this task is very difficult because of the complex nature of much that goes by the name of policy, and the same holds true for education (and education policy). Nevertheless, it is better to 'develop a rigorous approach to analyzing, evaluating, and improving' policy than to leave it as the plaything of 'implicit assumptions, one-sided views, and halo effects we all use for lack of anything better' (Dror, 1973: 25).

Dror's work is valuable because he has been so systematic and programmatic in developing his model to evaluate public policy and performance. He has derived a consistent and relatively simplified pattern after analysing thousands of individual cases of policymaking and evaluation. He therefore provides a logical framework which educators can make use of in evaluating the effectiveness of their schools and school programmes.

To determine quality, he says, it is first necessary to select a criterion or criteria; in effect, these are the categories or topics upon which we choose to make judgements. Then for each of the criteria we must determine a standard, a baseline or yardstick for making the assessment. Criteria can be of two kinds, Dror says, which he labels as primary and secondary criteria.

Primary criteria

In a business firm, for example, which exists primarily to make money, profits become a primary criterion. They can be counted, quantified, measured. In the same way, productivity may be a primary criterion. In this case, the firm calculates what inputs are needed to produce the output; this will include the cost of equipment and materials, power and fuel, rental and interest on loans, advertising and other associated outlays; manpower costs for such items as salaries and overheads will also be included. These production costs will then be subtracted from the returns on output - like sales and income from profits. 'Net output' is the result of income less production costs, and demonstrates the extent to which the company is productive.

In education, as in many areas of public policy, a calculation of 'profits' or 'net output' or 'productivity' along these lines is usually impossible, and it is necessary to invent a more sophisticated assessment, usually based upon secondary criteria.

Secondary criteria

Dror explains that secondary criteria are made the basis for assessment when the primary criteria are too difficult, too complex or too intangible to measure. A secondary criterion, therefore, concentrates on only a part of the desired outcome and it is chosen 'because it is considered . . . to be positively correlated with, and more measurable than, the net output' (Dror, 1973: 26). Secondary criteria can be found for the several parts of any activity, and may be conveniently considered under the four headings:

- Process patterns
- Secondary outputs
- Organisational structures
- Inputs and resources

Let us consider each of these in turn, for they suggest a way for educators to select indicators for school performance when the more intangible objectives of schooling are too elusive to measure.

Process patterns

If it is not possible to assess the primary criteria satisfactorily, then one can examine whether the process delivering the end result is as good as it can be; for process variables will affect the output. Dror suggests eight aspects for examination. First, there should be efficient policy-making machinery and procedures. The policies about making policy (for which Dror coined the terms 'metapolicy') ought to be scrutinised and checked. Secondly, there ought to be formal procedures for receiving feedback and acting upon it. Thirdly, an essential part of policy-making is devising an adequate strategy for its implementation. Fourthly, policy must always be converted into operational terms and someone must always be charged with doing this. Fifthly, every policy decision should be preceded by a search for and consideration of the alternatives. Sixthly, the policy process needs good planning, timetables and cut-off dates. Seventhly, the policy process should be overt and logical, avoiding 'hidden extras'. And finally, every policy has non-rational or extra-rational aspects (i.e. values) which must be considered.

Thus the process of making policies (or setting objectives and carrying them out) will be sound to the extent that these eight considerations are regularly and formally addressed in that process.

Secondary outputs

Dror argues that when the primary output cannot be easily defined or measured, there are at least some secondary outputs which can be identified and assessed. These include the clarity of the policy statement, its internal consistency and whether it can be made operational; the political and economic consequences that will flow from the policy; and the probable social, real-life changes it might cause. These can be identified and assessed and they will give at least some indication of whether the primary objectives are being achieved.

It is easy to convert this criterion into an educational context. We often assess the curriculum by looking at the school programme, the kinds of curriculum packages or materials being used and the appropriateness of the planned content to the children and the social setting of the school. These are nevertheless secondary criteria; they do not tell us what happened to particular children who studied those materials.

Organisational structures

It is a commonplace that, when primary objectives are hard to define or measure, assessors turn their attention to the perceived adequacy or efficiency of the organisational structures which deliver the outputs or the service. Dror comments that those structures are likely to be sound if there is a unit constantly and systematically monitoring them; if the structures include the capacity for long-term and short-term planning; if there is specificity about who makes the policy, who implements it and who 'sells' it to the target audience; if there is clarity about the roles which individuals, small cells and branches play in the processes; and if there is explicit coordinating machinery, 'due processes' and 'proper procedures'. None of these elements should be left to chance in any structure. Is this true of the organisational structures within schools? But good structures do not guarantee good learning; they are secondary criteria for judging effectiveness.

Inputs and resources

In essence, the quality of the end-product will be partly dependent on the adequacy of the resources provided to produce it; and these can be identified, documented and assessed.

None of these four sets of secondary criteria will guarantee the quality of the end-product. The learning outcomes are the primary criteria. But there is a high probability that they will influence either for good or ill the nature of that end-product, and assessing these secondary criteria will give some indication - albeit at times tenuous - of whether the prime objectives are being achieved, or are likely to be.

Standards

Once primary or secondary criteria have been identified for the characteristics or qualities or activities which we want to be evaluated, Dror says, it is necessary to set the standards for the evaluation. In short, each criterion, either primary or secondary, needs a measuring device to be associated with it.

The seven most often used methods of arriving at a standard are then listed by Dror. All of these can be, and indeed are, used in education.

Comparison with the past

Dror calls this the simplest and most widely used standard. We measure where we are now against where we were at some time in the past and then assess whether we are pleased with the progress we have made. It is the typical approach used in research, where the results from a pre-test are compared with those of a post-test to determine the effectiveness of a certain intervention or experimental process. It is also the typical teaching device. The students are tested to see whether they have made learning gains from the beginning of the year, term, or unit to the end of it.

Quality of other systems

In this case, another system 'whose relevant variables are similar enough to permit meaningful comparison' (Dror, 1973: 62) is selected and used as a gauge of progress. In other words, you compare yourselves with something or someone or some organisation like you. This is also a common teaching device; an external or system-wide examination compares students in one year-group with those in the same age-grade cohort elsewhere.

Desired quality

A third way of devising a standard is to make a precise definition of the level you hope to reach or to function at; Dror calls it a 'level of aspiration'. A series of tests over time will then log how closely one's practice comes to reaching that level of performance. This method is implicit in the competency-based curricular approaches.

Professional standards of quality

A fourth method, somewhat similar to the third, is used in areas which are professionalised - such as in medicine, law, education or welfare. Here the 'judgements of highly developed professionals' are sought and they are asked to set a standard they consider satisfactory. This method has been often used in education - professional librarians have defined an appropriate level of resourcing for school libraries; architects and teachers have defined desirable space requirements for school amenities; teachers have defined safety levels for laboratory or workshop use; experts have defined levels of competence needed for skilled work. The evaluations then measure how closely real practice comes to meeting the professionally defined standard.

Survival quality
A fifth device is to define 'the minimum quality . . . needed to achieve a high probability of physical or social survival' (*ibid.*: 64). It is possible to state, for example, that, if a certain level of resourcing is not provided, a programme has no chance of success and should be abandoned or not begun. That level becomes a baseline for the programme. As another example, educators do define what a student needs as a basic level of functional literacy in order to survive as an autonomous citizen in the community or what levels of attainment a student must reach to have a chance of surviving the next grade-level and it is in these contexts that the term 'failure' has real meaning, viz. below the survival level.

Planned quality
In a case where this standard is employed, a target quality is set (even arbitrarily), and a programme or plan is drawn up in an attempt to plot the movement to achieving the goal; it usually includes a timetable which sets deadlines for each step towards that goal. Many curriculum packages and school syllabuses use this programmatic method.

Optimal quality
Dror defines optimal quality as 'how good it could possibly be' (*ibid.*: 67); so it is feasible to use imagined perfection as the yardstick against which real achievement will be measured.

In summary, then, setting standards of this kind and making evaluations based upon them is not new territory for teachers, and they have used these methods to judge the effectiveness of their school, their pupils' performances, and their own.

Sub-optimising

There is a final component to Dror's evaluation model. So far it has included a search for, and then definition of, the criteria upon which the evaluation will be based; when the primary criteria evade adequate analysis, then one needs to select secondary criteria as substitutions. These could include the administrative processes, the organisational structures, the quality of the resources devoted to implementation and nominal, or second-order, outcomes.

For each of the criteria selected there needs to be a standard, a point or scale for comparison. Typical strategies have been to compare with the past, to compare with a similar system elsewhere, to devise a 'level of aspiration', to get an expert to state a desired standard, to draw a minimum threshold below which survival cannot be guaranteed, to plot a pathway and deadlines to a planned point or to compare against perfection, an optimal quality.

But if one evaluated all these things across all the criteria, there could well be no time left to do anything else! Evaluating a policy or practice is after all not the prime objective of the organisation. So, Dror suggests, it is wise to sub-optimise. Put another way, we sample; we cut down the evaluations so that they give us data upon which we can extrapolate or guess at the generalities. And we typically do this in three ways, namely by limiting the evaluation in time, to a small population and to a selected area of activity.

Let us use an example. A school has as one of its prime objectives the development of language skills, a global aim. To give expression to the aim, teachers will define 'language skills' in operational terms (spelling, writing, speaking, reading and so on) and then devise professionally determined levels year by year, grade by grade. If the school (as an entity) wishes to demonstrate that it is making progress with the development of language skills, it becomes a major undertaking to test such progress every day across all criteria or topics and across all students at every grade level. Typically, the school staff will sub-optimise, limiting the evaluation to, say, one criterion like reading aloud, presuming that, if a child can read fluently, there is a strong likelihood that the other language skills have also been acquired. But it is time-consuming even just to run reading tests every day. So the school again sub-optimises and decides to test formally the students for the skills of reading aloud three or four times in the year, at the end of each term, say. Even then, a testing scheme across all grade levels may be unwieldy and hard to handle. So the school sub-optimises again by choosing a smaller sample population - all those in the third and sixth grade-levels, for example. Thus the evaluation is limited by time, area, and population, and one makes judgements about the whole (the whole school, the whole teaching programme, the whole student body) by generalising from sample testing of some parts. The Dror model is summarised in Figure 9.1.

Figure 9.1 The Dror Model for Policy Evaluation

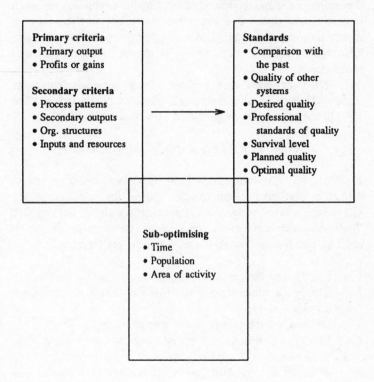

Audience

If schools were as systematic as this over evaluation, it would not be necessary to rely so heavily upon standardised test scores. For example, a school could satisfy its audience or public by having an expert (or a group of parents for that matter) listen to the reading aloud of a group of students and report whether they are at a satisfactory level of performance. In the past, the school inspector performed this role, reporting to an 'audience' at head office about the school's performance. In short, the method of evaluation and the shape of the report stemming from it depend entirely on to whom the report is addressed. Whether the objective is to provide feedback to teachers, a public justification to the client-parents, an audit for head office or as public advertisement of excellence will determine the shape, style and content of the evaluation report. It must not be assumed that one report can satisfy all these requirements. Indeed, a major problem in the past has been that educators have been confused about who was the audience for any one evaluation.

The Dror model, therefore, provides a systematic framework within which to develop the several elements of assessment. The logic of the model can be illustrated by several examples.

Example 1: The Cambridgeshire scheme

In 1984, the Cambridgeshire local education authority implemented a 'performance management system' for its education service which was in many respects consistent with the Dror model. The head office staff was taken through five steps as follows in order to systematise how they would collectively function:

1. Clarify why the organisation exists.
2. Clarify the administrative and managerial structure to deliver that service.
3. Define each job clearly within that structure.
4. Clarify the medium-term policies and objectives for each job and section.
5. Affix the accountability about the delivery of the service on to particular jobs.

Once the 'accountabilities' had been allocated, position by position, administrative unit by unit, the consultants then drew up in cooperation with the role incumbents a set of 'performance measures' which the officers would use to monitor their progress towards fulfilling the tasks for which they had been made responsible. The measures were based upon achievable 'goals' which were made explicit. The officers then drew up their 'action plans', a timetable for the achievement of intermediate goals. Finally, the consultant team built a system of 'performance reviews' whereby every member of the organisation would regularly meet with an ad hoc panel (one member of which was always the officer's supervisor) to discuss the actual progress being made, what revisions should be made, resource deficiencies, performance and so on. The process is represented in Figure 9.2. The intention was to implement a similar scheme in every school but the complications were so great that the scheme could not be made to extend that far. Even so, the example demonstrates how a logical framework can be put in place for monitoring performance and organisational outcomes. But to introduce this scheme across all schools was so large an assignment that it threatened to subvert the prime objectives of the system. Evaluation can become too obtrusive, too time-consuming.

Figure 9.2 Cambridgeshire Scheme, 1984

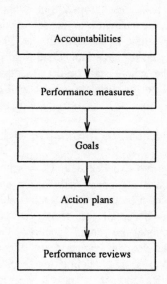

Example II: School resources

For many years the effectiveness of individual schools or school systems was judged upon resources inputs and not on outputs. These input factors could be quantified, of course, and typically included:

• teacher salaries

- staffing levels
- the qualifications and experience of staff
- the number of books in the library
- per pupil expenditures
- the age and quality of buildings
- the extent of provision in special purpose areas like science and craft laboratories

Accreditation procedures still widely adopt this device, on the assumption that the better resourced schools and colleges will produce the better learning outcomes. This assumption was exploded by the Coleman Report in the USA in the mid-1960s, which demonstrated that home background, not school inputs of any kind, was the chief contributor to academic success. Even the longitudinal Rutter study in the UK in the 1970s showed that many of these physical resource inputs had little impact on performance, either of the school staff or the students. The secondary criteria were found not to correlate, or not well enough, with the primary criteria.

Example III: A Nation at Risk

The national study into excellence in USA schools published in 1983 under the title *A Nation at Risk* took a more sophisticated approach. It included a section called 'Indicators of the Risk' listing documentary evidence of the decline in pupil achievement drawn from international test scores, functional literacy tests, average achievement levels over a quarter of a century, Scholastic Aptitude Test (SAT) scores, reading test scores, the extent of remedial mathematics courses in post-school institutions, entry tests for military service and so on. The study group had targeted on competency tests, on measuring outcomes rather than resource inputs (*A Nation at Risk*, 1983: 8-9).

Indicators

It turns out, then, that there are many indicators which could be used as measuring sticks. A study aimed at drawing up suitable methods for use by universities and institutes of higher education in OECD countries (Hufner, 1987) identified hundreds that are currently employed. That study classified them under the four headings of:

1. Internal performance indicators
2. Operating indicators
3. External performance indicators
4. Staff productivity indicators

Figure 9.3 lists some of the devices which fall under these head- ings. The study went on to show that institutions have not been as systematic as one would expect in the way they have used these indicators. There is a tendency, for example, for teachers and lecturers to use indicators which will give them feedback on their students' and their own institution's performance, but they often tend to overlook the need to give their publics, their clients and their trustees (or employers) the kind of feedback which will reas- sure those groups about the enterprise's quality of performance. Supplying these data can be both strategic and prudent, even if such action may not be mandatory.

Mission statements

It is important to note that there is an essential difference between a statement of objectives and a 'mission statement'. Objectives are for an external audience; they tell the outsiders what the institution stands for and hopes to achieve. A mission statement, on the other hand, is for internal use; it defines the particular targets which the insider team has set for itself for the immediate future. The slightly religious overtones of the term are also significant. A mis- sion statement does not have to be limited to bland prose; it ought to contain the metaphors and imagery which build on the symbols that inspire enthusiasm and commitment. A mission statement is short, pithy, sometimes emotively coloured, forceful and pointed. It coheres effort. It sets out to recruit the willing expenditure of energy and drive by those associated with the enterprise.

According to Brown a mission statement is:

> a charter that defines the basic business or businesses in which the enterprise will engage, the types of products it will make or the services it will provide, the markets it will serve, and perhaps how the company will conduct its affairs (Brown, 1984: 44).

It is essentially teleological, a statement about ends and causes, about 'reasons for being'. The mission statement defines not only what the enterprise will attempt to do, but also what it will not do; it focuses the energy of the organisation (or person, since we can have our own mission too) on what can be done well, on what niche it or we will fill.

With these things in mind, Brown gives six principles to bear in mind when one draws up a mission statement. First, it defines what we want to become, rather than what we are doing now. Secondly, it gives 'an appropriate criterion for defining the business', what category of enterprise this attempts to be. Thirdly, the definition must strike a balance between being too broad (and therefore vague) and being too narrow (and therefore too specific). Fourthly, it must not contain chaff, empty phrases and terms. Fifthly, 'all those who will be affected by it in a significant way ought to grasp its implications and be able to live with them.' And finally, the statement must be short, preferably fewer than 25 words (*ibid.*: 51-52). So, Brown counsels, any enterprise which does not have a mission statement ought at least to try to draft one.

A mission statement is like the team's game plan; objectives on the other hand relate to the rules of the game and how to play to win; and accountability concerns the scoreline.

Accountability in context

Let us recapitulate on the argument thus far. We began by pointing out that assessment or evaluation can have several purposes, only one of which may be to demonstrate accountability. We established the need to state objectives before we can develop indicators of whether those targets are being achieved. We then discussed Dror's model for evaluating, which included establishing primary and secondary criteria, standards for each criterion, and how to sub-optimise. We are now in a position to consider the purposes to which an evaluation may be put, bearing in mind that accountability is merely one among several aims. To give a concrete base to the discussion, we take the case of evaluating a teacher's performance (see Beare, 1988).

Teacher appraisal

No professional educator in his or her right mind would advocate that there should be no teacher assessment. Any enterprise or activity needs assessment, review and constant searching for better

Figure 9.3 Taxonomy of Indicators in Higher Education

---

1. INTERNAL PERFORMANCE INDICATORS

> Average length of study
> Success rates : graduation rates
> Distribution of students
> Market share of applicants
> Teaching performance
> Student learning outcomes

2. OPERATING INDICATORS

> Class sizes
> Staff : student ratios
> Student work loads
> Resource usage
> Space usage
> Assets & equipment

3. EXTERNAL PERFORMANCE INDICATORS

> Acceptability of graduates
> Destination of graduates
> Employer/community feedback
> Awards & honours

4. STAFF PRODUCTIVITY INDICATORS

> Publications
> Contracts
> Invitations
> Citations & qualifications
> Membership in professional bodies

---

practices; any professional operator needs that kind of informed feedback too. The problem has always been that several incompatible purposes tend to become entangled in the one practice and thereby destroy its effectiveness. Teacher assessment is one such area.

In considering the question of teacher assessment, then, it behoves the educator community to make its ground rules conceptually clear and fully understandable. The architectural dictum 'form follows function' applies as strongly to teacher assessment as it does to the shape of buildings. Two prior questions largely determine the nature and the mode of the assessment adopted:

- The first question is 'Why is this assessment being carried out?'
- The second is 'What audience do we have in mind to read the findings?'

In consequence, the prime purpose and the proposed audience need to be made manifest before the assessment exercise begins.

There are five often-used purposes behind teacher evaluation, and we cannot presume that an evaluation carried out for one purpose will produce results usable for another purpose. The five common assessment purposes are as follows:

1. Assessment of the teacher for professional improvement
2. Assessment to determine the teacher's fitness for promotion
3. Assessing the teacher in order to improve the school
4. Assessment in connection with accountability
5. Assessment of the teacher's performance in order to improve learning outcomes; put simply, this is research-oriented assessment.

Consider each of these purposes in turn, and how the focus, method and assessor change as the purpose changes.

1. *For teacher improvement*

When a teacher's performance is assessed with the idea of improving his or her practice, the exercise is akin to coaching. The teacher is a willing partner who will gain from the exercise. The person carrying out the evaluation will be regarded as a skilled mentor, trusted and respected by the person being evaluated. To ensure that full value is gained from the process, the teacher will be concerned to reveal to the mentor all those

218

areas where his or her practice is not as skilled as the teacher wants them to be, for in this context there exists an opportunity to become a champion instead of an also-ran. The audience for the assessment is the person undergoing the review; and the direct feedback allows the recipient to improve his or her practice. It is usually confidential feedback; the findings need be shared only by the reviewer and the one being reviewed.

In past years, the inspector often undertook this task of coaching and advising teachers to help them improve in their teaching role. If there is no inspector, then someone else needs to be chosen, formally or informally, for the task. In fact teachers may well make the choice, selecting one of their peers or a trusted colleague.

2. *For promotion purposes*

Teaching performance must at times be evaluated to determine whether the teacher is ready for promotion, or to grade the teacher so that an employing authority will know which teacher to appoint to a position for which there are several contenders. In this context, it is likely that the teacher being evaluated will be at pains to hide from the evaluators any inadequacy in his or her teaching practice and will attempt to highlight all the strong points in his or her performance. It is a situation completely opposite to the one where the assessment is for coaching purposes. In the one, weaknesses are examined and indicated; in the second, strengths are emphasised and weaknesses concealed. If the same assessor attempts to undertake both tasks, the one being assessed will no doubt play safe and keep hidden any weaknesses, just in case they will be brought to light in the promotion assessment. So the assessor-for-promotion-purposes, no matter what his or her skills may be, must be an inadequate coach, since information secured in one context may be applied detrimentally in the other context. In this model, the assessor is an agent of the employing authority and the audience for the evaluation report is the authority with the power to promote or to select.

In recent years, there has been intense lobbying to ensure that the one assessed has access to the same assessment findings as the prime audience - the superordinate authority. This access has been pressed for to ensure fairness to the person being assessed, to put that person on an equal footing in any appeals arena and in any situation where inaccurate or biased information could be used as the basis for judging the relative merits of several candidates, in short, to ensure openness.

3. *Evaluation for school improvement*

If the evaluation is carried out for school improvement, and especially if the exercise concentrates on the school's prime task (the stimulation of children's learning), then the performance of the teachers may be a crucial part of the assessment. In this model, however, it is as though the whole teaching team is being coached rather than just one player (as was the case with the first model we discussed). Inspectors and HMIs have carried out 'inspections' for this purpose for many decades; the object of the exercise is not to assess individual teachers but rather to determine how well they combine to produce a fully functioning institution. A perceptive reader of the school appraisal report can distinguish between the lines those areas and teachers which enhance or detract from the school's effectiveness.

In this model, the assessor or assessing team are agents of the authority responsible for running the school, or of the school itself, or of both, and their report would be written for that audience. The report could become an action plan to enable the school to improve its own operations, or the report could be used by management to redistribute resources, to provide more support or to vary staffing and staffing structures. An assessment for school improvement, in other words, should lead to some change and the report would recommend in those terms.

4. *Evaluation for accountability*

Teachers - and schools - may also be assessed in the name of accountability. In simple terms, evaluation for accountability is an audit. This kind of assessment can be fairly routine and is sometimes entirely statistical. It is likely to be driven, quite legitimately, by an economic and a political imperative. Any authority which provides resources, including finance, is likely to ask that some account be given about how those resources were used, whether they were committed to the purposes for which they were provided, whether they were efficiently spent and what profits they produced. It is increasingly likely that performance indicators and productivity measures would be used. In fact, the receivers of the resources could be regarded as derelict in their duty if they did not provide some account of their stewardship.

The assessor in this case acts for the resource providers or for management, and the audit report is addressed to that audience. It will obviously influence the future allocation and size of resources, and will be the basis for policy and resource planning. A bad assessment can, therefore, lead to penalties - perhaps a rearrangement of resources, some disciplinary action against operators who do not conform with management targets and priorities or a reshaping of the programme and its budget. Less often, an audit report can lead to incentive payments and rewards, either tangible or intangible.

5. *Assessment for research purposes*
A fifth purpose of assessment is to provide feedback so that those associated with the professional field can develop new insights about the learning process or can extend the frontiers of knowledge by looking at causes and effects or by testing plausible hypotheses and so on. Evaluation for research purposes is aimed at refining professional practices. In this case, the assessor is an expert of some kind, and the report from the evaluation is likely to be addressed to an expert community, the guild of people knowledgeable about that specialist field. Ideally, an evaluation process of this kind should be a threat to no one, should be done with scholarly objectivity and should assume complete cooperation of the people involved in the exercise.

There is a logic, therefore, about each of these five evaluation processes, and they constitute in different ways the nature and role of the assessed, of the assessor, of the report, of the audience for the report and of the action which stems from the assessment. In several instances, as in Modes 1 and 2, there are basic incompatibilities in several of these dimensions, and it cannot be assumed that an evaluation carried out for one purpose will furnish reliable or usable data for an assessment with another purpose. Table 9.1 represents a map of the terrain usually traversed in one mode or another by any teacher appraisal programme.

This survey has tried to set accountability in its context. Assessment for that purpose cannot be legitimately carried out simultaneously with assessments for other purposes.

A theme running through this chapter has been the difficulty of defining the objectives of education. In spite of the logic for evaluation which has been outlined, it is not easy to make education fit into this Procrustean bed. Yet accountability is an insistent, and often a legal, requirement. In consequence, educators are sometimes forced into practices which appear concurrently to satisfy and subvert the demand for accountability. Consider two of

Table 9.1 Rationales for Teacher Assessment

Objective	MODE: 1 Teacher Improvement	MODE: 2 Teacher Promotion	MODE: 3 School Improvement	MODE: 4 Accountability	MODE: 5 Research or Prof. Feedback
Specific Purpose	To improve teaching performance	To rank and compare teachers	To improve team skills	Efficient and effective use of resources	To improve student performance and learnings
Audience	The teacher	The employer	The team or manager	The patron or owner of the enterprise	The profession
The assessor	A mentor or professional coach	An external assessor	An agent of the team	An 'auditor'	A professionally expert analyst
Nature of assessment	Advice to the assessed	Formal grading; advice to employer	A report to the team	A productivity audit, including efficiency measures of some kind	A research report, including targeted data and their analysis

the strategies which educators may need to adopt, namely loose coupling and assessment facades.

The consequences of loose coupling in educational organisations

The application of economic models and rational indicators to the performance of educational organisations and to teacher activity runs into one of the most problematical aspects of education. In their thesis about university administration, March and Olsen (1976) coined the term 'organised anarchy' to explain the logic of the way such institutions actually operate. No blame was implied in their description; rather it was an endeavour to represent what really occurs in an organisation where its most significant operations are less easily articulated than is the case in a business enterprise where the objectives are relatively obvious and straightforward. Organised anarchy occurs when:

• The technologies are unclear; that is, the procedures, the ways of getting things done, are difficult to systematise or to keep in a set pattern

• The goals are ambiguous; at least they are not easy to define in simple, straightforward terms which lead to uncomplicated testing

• Participation is fluid; that is, one cannot be certain that the same people or the same office-holders will be consistently involved with any issue.

Weick (1976), as we have shown in an earlier chapter, pointed out that organisational loose coupling is particularly characteristic of education. Systemic restructuring, for example, can often have little impact on the way particular schools or classrooms function. Even inside a school, what goes on in particular interchanges between teachers and children can be relatively unaffected by turbulent classrooms elsewhere in the same school. Children's learning programmes can flourish largely independent of what organisational patterns exist among the staff. If education is so loosely connected in its organisational parts, it is simply not possible for those in status or supervisory positions to make unequivocal claims about the functioning of the several parts of the whole. Or to be more particular, there are literally thousands of interchanges which occur between teacher and taught behind the doors of any one classroom in any one week. Most of those interchanges are never supervised, or programmed, or recorded, or even assessed; yet the quality of life in that classroom depends directly on the quality of those interchanges. No principal, no supervising teacher, no head of department can be so closely coupled with the activities of every classroom to be in a position to make definitive judgements about the nature of instruction and learning in the school. The school is loosely coupled in one of its most important activities, the teaching of children. To impose tight coupling could well vitiate, by an oppressive inquisition, the delicate fragility of real learning, while making easier the task of giving an account of oneself, as a teacher or a teaching institution.

What principals and senior staff, therefore, tend to do is to buffer. They become, as it were, gatekeepers, allowing scrutiny of operations only to the extent that the tender growth of learning within the classroom remains protected. The school and the principal need to take soundings to be satisfied that real learning and a wholesome atmosphere prevail within the school and in every place where learning is to be sponsored and enhanced;

experienced educators do this by collecting a myriad of incidental indicators. But once their sensibilities as professional educators have been satisfied, they then act as the protector of that enterprise, standing at the gate to ensure that what passes through from the outside (including those seeking accountability) will enhance and not destroy.

And those who ask for accountability must also understand the nature of loose coupling in the education organisation, even in the educational act. It is endemic to the act of teaching, a strength as much as a weakness. They too should ask for the indicators which will satisfy their need for feedback, but which will not be so oppressive or obtrusive as to get in the way of the real business of education.

Assessment facades

In their article (subtitled 'Formal structure as myth and ceremony') Meyer and Rowan (1977) argue that many organisations are incapable of giving an adequate account of themselves, but that their public is satisfied if they are seen to be conforming with culturally condoned behaviour. They say that most organisations are de-coupled in some of their activities, but there are 'highly rationalised myths' about the way organisations operate. So if an organisation has a good organisation chart, if its offices are appropriately listed and labelled, if its programmes and formal activities are suitably tabulated, they construct a reality of efficiency which the surrounding culture accepts.

Elsewhere this is called an organisational facade. If the part of the organisation which the outside world sees sends the right signals, looks appropriate, has what appears to be acceptable rituals and behaviours, the public will accept it for what it tries to be. Those signals will confirm a 'socially constructed reality'. People will make the assumption that things are as they seem. When that occurs, the organisation and its members can carry on with their activities largely unburdened from stifling scrutiny.

In general, then, the accountability issue poses three fairly fundamental questions:

• Are there some primary objectives about education and learning which can and should be regularly assessed? How can that assessment be done? And who should be the audience for that assessment?

• Given that many of the most significant aspects of education and schooling are either difficult to define or are incapable of formal assessment and supervision, what indicators will give a relatively reliable gauge of whether the school is doing a satisfactory job? How often do these indicators need to be used? And to what group or groups does the school staff need to give regular account of performance?

• Given that many of the aspects on which the public judge a school, its teachers and its students are formalised facades, ritualistic and ceremonial behaviours, what should the school and its staff do regularly to retain public confidence in what it is doing or attempting to do?

This chapter has attempted to show that there are systematic frameworks within which schools and teachers can attempt to answer those questions both with credibility and conviction.

10

Projecting a Public Image
About the School

In a previous chapter we discussed the way we image organisations; we tend to favour some metaphors more than others to describe how the organisation or school works, and then that recurrent imagery becomes tangible in many incidental aspects of the institution's life and functions. If the leading images are satisfying and suitably expressive of what the school stands for, they ought to be projected, and can be evocative, uplifting, transforming, becoming a picture which conveys meanings more powerfully than many words. These metaphors ought to be the basis for formulating the view about the school or organisation which its public as well as its own members hold. This chapter explores ways in which this act of creation might be carried out.

The public face which schools and school systems present to the world has been left for too long to agencies outside the schools. Indeed, one gets the impression that a bad name for education is often consciously cultivated, not the least by bad media publicity, and by influential citizens, parents, politicians and industries. The litany of sins listed by those in the marketplace has included accusations that:

- Teachers are always on strike; they are selfishly concerned about their own conditions, not about the welfare of children
- Schools are badly equipped, understaffed and badly housed
- School discipline is bad
- Students are unable to read, write or calculate at acceptable levels of proficiency
- Schools prepare their students poorly for the job market
- Government schools are so bad that people are now putting their children into private schools

226

• Educational administration is characterised by red tape, bureaucracy and over-regulation

• School principals are reactionary, opposed to good ideas, not very competent and resistant to community involvement

and so on, and so on. The assertions are generally unproven, except by anecdotal evidence or generalisations derived from one or two examples, and an educator would probably say they are generally wrong. Yet, in this context, it is not a question of what is right or wrong; it is a question of what people believe or are made to believe, and those beliefs can be manipulated, controlled or changed. It is largely a question of image-building and of those to whom educators entrust this task. In private enterprise, since profits and economic survival depend on it, image-building is not left to others or to chance. You buy image-makers, you advertise and you mould others' opinions about yourself and your organisation.

It is fairly easy to understand why education is criticised when economic conditions are adverse. Consider three aspects of the way these negative attitudes form. In the private sector, high inflation or high costs cut into profits. Lower profits decrease industry's operating margins. So industry pulls in the belt, cuts salary costs and reduces the number of people employed. In addition, using technology to save on overheads helps rekindle profitability. Why employ four or five typists, for example, if a word processing machine will do the same work for lower costs? Accordingly, the job market shrinks, comparatively speaking. Since in this context a secondary school education or a diploma course no longer ensures a job, at least in the way they did in the past, people assume that there must be something wrong with the secondary school education or the diploma course. The standards must have slipped: education gets the blame.

Secondly, in the public sector, a similar kind of scenario takes place. When the government experiences high inflation or a recession or spiralling costs, it has the alternatives of increasing taxation to cover the costs of public services or else of cutting back those services. Since it is clearly counter-productive to cut services which produce revenue, the brakes are applied first to those which produce no revenue, at least, directly. So the pruning hook usually falls first of all on health, education and welfare. It helps, of course, if the government can argue that education or health services or welfare are inefficient, not delivering adequate services and therefore deserving of the cutbacks and a shake-up. If public opinion can be so moulded, then the government can escape political odium in making the cuts. Furthermore, just as in the private sector, since higher productivity and efficiency can possibly be gained if more work can be done by fewer people, the numbers of public employees are reduced. Those with a previously acceptable level of education who were once employable in public service positions are now passed over in favour of the better qualified, so the public assumes that the education of the former must somehow be at fault. In addition, since productivity and efficiency are the targets, then quantification - mathematical measures - are used to demonstrate the extent of productivity. Education, which has always been soft on such measures, is thereby highly vulnerable. Indeed, inappropriate measures will be used when no others are available; hence SAT scores, literacy/numeracy tests, reading test scores and examination mark aggregates can all be used inappropriately as productivity measures. In a situation the root cause of which is economic, they look like economic indicators.

The 'taxpayer's revolt' produces a third scenario. High inflation means that government services cost more. When taxes are increased to meet these costs, the taxpayer sees more money being spent with no visible improvement or increase in the services. For example, higher salaries for teachers may bring no increase in teacher numbers, or in the level or quality of the teaching service. So the taxpayers become vocal if not politically militant. They object to higher taxes and they become critical of the services provided by government. The service closest to hand feels the heat first. Thus the locally delivered services, and those with which the public has most of its involvement - health, education and welfare - again take the brunt of the public anger.

In this context two disabling, even destructive, responses can occur in the public services. First, the agencies set up to serve the public may begin to fight amongst themselves in a selfish scramble for a bigger slice of a smaller cake. Their self-regarding actions and apparent lack of concern about the public they are supposed to be serving further sours public opinion. Secondly, the degenerating economic situation can sour the people who deliver the service to the public, making them bitter and inclined to retaliate in strike action or in working to regulations or in giving a less effective service. Both reactions are understandable but are in the long term counter-productive. Rather, creative but hard-nosed responses to the new conditions are needed, new strategies, new configurations for the limited resources and clear priorities for action.

We need to admit first of all that there are not likely to be massive increases in spending on education, except perhaps in those areas which produce short-term effects in national productivity and which improve competitiveness in the international markets. So, in specific terms, money to employ comparatively more people in the education industry is not likely to be a viable option, and if educators or policy-makers want to sponsor reforms which require additional manpower, then trade-offs will have to be offered up from elsewhere in the education budget. The education industry will not have the resources to buy everything on its shopping list, and improvements based upon simplistic educational arguments will simply not be funded. Indeed, educators may have to contend against a new 'cult of efficiency' in education, to use Raymond Callahan's term (1962), and it will influence how educators grade and document pupil achievement, how the education tax dollar is spent and accounted for and how the educational workforce is deployed.

This state of affairs, then, has introduced a kind of free market to education, which means that no school can assume it has a monopoly over any group of students, or over resources. As in industry and commerce, the school with a bad track record over industrial stoppages, or over productivity, or over customer satisfaction will quite simply lose clients and thereby some of its funding, its staff and its per capita resources.

In short, then, the image which individual schools project has now become a matter of survival. So if your school wants customers and resources in the next few years, it had best proclaim how good it is, how competitive are its services, how excellent its staff; it should parade its strengths rather than its deficiencies. It should use its resources - capital, monetary, personnel - in ways that will maximise its priorities. Only successful, positive, confident, client-oriented schools will have a right to survive or be rewarded with improved resources.

In summary, then, difficult economic times and the market economy mentality in education could produce in the next few years:

• Increasing independence for all schools

229

• Increasing exercise of parental choice, with parents shopping around among all schools, public and private
• Increasing diversity among schools, with a continuing trend for parents to sponsor new schools which have a clearly defined values framework within which to operate; schools, that is, will become sensitive to the expressed expectations of its client population.

Defining the terms

Pursuing the question of improving education's image beyond a cute analogy into the realm of deliberate action leads to a substantial literature and some very interesting experience in the private sector. For the analysis, we must clarify some of the terms now being used, in particular 'corporate personality', 'corporate identity' and 'corporate image'. In our definitions, we lean heavily on Olins' book entitled *The Corporate Personality* (1978).

The term 'corporate personality' refers to the character or the culture of the organisation, the style of life or mode which a group of people develop as they create an organisation. Such a culture can be deliberately changed or fostered; but whether it develops by plan or by chance, there is such a culture as soon as an organisation comes into existence. 'Corporate identity' is different from 'corporate personality'. There are some physical features, some observable characteristics which allow us to identify one person from another: the way they speak, what they characteristically wear, the colour of their eyes and hair, even their handwriting or their style of expression. One's own identity is built up by a collection of identifiers or 'descriptors', the outward manifestations of the inward character. Increasingly business firms are realising that their identity is something which they can influence and remodel. So businesses develop:

• a logo, a visual symbol which is easily recognisable as the firm's trade mark
• a house style, a format which consistently runs across the firm's stationery, its letter heads, its directional signs, its furnishings, and its advertisements
• a livery, that is, a colour code which determines how its delivery vehicles are painted, the colour of its advertisements, the clothes and uniforms of employees, its sales promotion materials, its packaging designs and so on

• work codes, a set of behaviours and dress which employees are required to adopt: for example, the pervasive use of uniforms, and the consistent style of places like Macdonalds, Electrolux, IBM and Telecom
• an appropriate name, especially a brand name: a great amount of care, thought and intricate planning goes into what a business house calls itself and its products.

'Corporate image', therefore, is how you and I read the company, what we think about it, how well we regard it. One could say that:

• corporate personality is the culture created by the people who make up an organisation
• corporate identity is that collection of actions and materials which signify what the company is like. Corporate identity is the outward manifestation of corporate personality
• corporate image is the perception which others form, from the combined impact of company personality and company identity.

The image issue is much more complicated for schools and education than it is for a single industrial or business enterprise:

• Each school has its own image and style. Principals and teachers are aware that the school is the most elementary unit in the education industry and they have a good record in projecting a satisfactory image of it. But the milieu in which a school operates and its image are heavily dependent on more global and less local considerations
• The schools in a town or area tend to project a collective image. Thus people may say: 'the schools in (a particular town) are energetic and innovative' or 'the schools in (these particular suburbs) are middle class'
• The school system within a state, province or county also projects a collective image; and people also carry an image about a particular country. Consider the way we compare 'schools' (a huge generality!) in the USA, Canada, France or Sweden
• There is also an international image about education, at least for the Western World. So people talk in general terms about problems of literacy and numeracy, or youth unemployment, or falling rolls.

If that were not enough, the cake may be cut other ways; people may generalise about primary education in comparison with secondary education, for example. So educators are faced with multiple educational cells, each of which can be treated separately, or in layers or in collectivities; and the whole makes up an organic mass which may be called The Education Industry, which sometimes behaves like a multinational conglomerate, which has a collective image and whose several parts also each project their own images. But the complexity of the task should not deter educators from attempting some positive action, in the interests of their schools and their students.

Identifiers of image

Projecting a positive, constructive image of the school can best begin by asking the questions, 'What characteristics does this school have which make it different from any other school?' and 'What characteristics will identify this particular school, so that when I plumb my memory I shall be able to say "Oh yes, that's the school which has or does such and such"?' Apparently it has not occurred to many educators not only that each school ought to be distinctive and different, but that each one is - and sometimes in ways that are anything but flattering. It is thus a serious question to ask how well a particular school's image has been fostered, for an image is built up in many, incidental ways. Some of the school's characteristics which are creating a strongly negative impact could, with very little care, be turned to strong advantage, or be remade.

Let us take a particular example. A certain school has a school hymn, 'We build our school on Thee, O Lord', written by Rudyard Kipling. The facts that it does have a hymn, and that it is a hymn rather than a song, are significant as indicators. That it was written by Kipling, whose writings are associated with the height of the British Empire, is also important for the school. The hymn has a refrain which goes:

> Dear Lord, we pray, Thy Spirit may
> Be present in our school alway.

The problem is that the verse was palpably untrue, at least in the sense the ordinary person would read it. The Christian ethos and spirit were not always evident in the way the school operated. It did not pervade the way every teacher related to every student, it was not an overriding concern in every school rule, or in the way the school set its examinations, or in the attitudes which the school inculcated wittingly or unwittingly in its student body. Indeed, much of the institutional in schools is antithetical to such a posture. And, of course, that is part of the problem, for if one makes a deliberate attempt to build an image for a particular school, the image must ring true. Its clients will very soon see through hypocrisy. This is not an argument against the image-building notion; it is rather an argument for genuineness, for honesty, and most of all for an act of will. The image-building exercise assumes that the members of the school community will collectively say, 'This is what we want our school to be, and we strive to make it so, even though we may often fall short of our mark.'

What might educators do to build a strong image for a school or system? Here is a check list of questions to ask:

● What particular, identifiable organisational style does this school now have, and what do I want it to be?
● What documents, already in existence, put it most clearly into words? Are they constantly referred to, consulted, quoted, used as a starting point for planning?
● Who established that style? (That will reveal something about organisational style!)
● Which characteristics best highlight the nature of the school?
● Can the school guarantee that the behaviours and style of all staff conform with the desired ethos of the school?
● What impression does the school building create from the street? (Get someone you know and trust to stand on the footpath and describe aloud what impressions are formed when facing the building.)
● What face does this school show its visitors? What first impresses my attention as I walk through the front door? What do I see? How inviting, off-putting, or confusing are the directional signs? To whom does the visitor first speak? What about that person's manner?
● How easy is it to phone the school? Who answers the phone and what impression does her voice convey?
● What impression is created by the way the staff dress, or talk, or speak to children?

233

- What visual symbols (logo, motto, monogram, colour scheme) identify the school? What organisational style and what ethos do they convey?
- Is there a consistent livery or house colour and style adopted for the school?
- What impression is created by:
  - the principal's office, including its decor and arrangement of furniture?
  - the classrooms?
  - the staff rooms?
- Look collectively at the documents which have been sent out to parents over the past month or term. Are they first class productions? How many have there been? (That will tell you something about the organisation.) Who sent them? (That will also say something about the organisation.) What impressions, especially subliminal ones, are conveyed by the wording, the expression, the subject matter? For example, do a spot survey to identify how much of the content deals with such items as money matters or organisation, and how much deals directly with education and learning.
- What regular ways does the school use to speak on TV and radio, or to appear in the press? And what items are dealt with? And if they have dealt with teaching and learning, how interesting, or lively, or dynamic, or gimmicky, or deadpan, or conventional do they seem?
- What ceremonials and ceremonies are regularly conducted at the school: assemblies, chapel services, speech days, and the like. Analyse their format and their 'message'; is that what the school intends to convey about itself?
- Take another look at the wording of the school hymn, school song, the war cry, and consider the message and its quality.
- How often, how well, and in how much detail does the school report to each parent on the progress of his/her child?
- Consider the mode of reporting. What does that say to the parent about the part the parent plays in the school, or in the education of her child?
- Is the school's annual report to its community or, if a verbal presentation, a first class, readable, informative document that highlights education, learning and children?
- How much money is the school prepared to pay on school publicity, on advertising itself? What budget has been set aside from school funds for this item this year?

All these factors contribute to the school's style, help to create its atmosphere and tone and as a collectivity fashion the school's public image. What is more, this activity of image-building is a worthy one, for the students served by the school or system are the ultimate beneficiaries. Consider three aspects.

First, image has a powerful impact on how well the child learns, because the parent's attitudes to the school have a direct impact on the child. Image is an important factor influencing the slippage of enrolments among the sectors, and the educator who is serious about the wellbeing of his or her students needs to be serious about how the school is perceived among parents.

Secondly, a large number of teachers do not seem to appreciate that the school is only one element in a much larger educational enterprise, and that how any one management unit (or school) and any one employee (or teacher) behaves affects education's total image - and often in unfortunate ways. Teachers - of all those in the so-called professions - seem prone to criticise their own colleagues publicly, thereby breaking one of the basic tenets of professionalism, and to criticise the educational practices of other teachers and of other schools. Perhaps just as damaging, they speak cynically and destructively about their professional colleagues in management positions and often disparage in public the reputation of the system of schools to which they belong and of which they are essential parts. It is no wonder that the image of the education industry is bad when its own members are unthinking about its public standing. When, for example, did you last hear a principal or a school board/school council/governing body chairperson or county councillor praise the practices of another school (especially of a neighbouring school) and advertise its excellence?

The third point is related, and concerns the political implications. Image begets public esteem; esteem creates public support; public support begets political attention; and political influence begets finance and staff numbers and governmental priority. There is no magic in the formula. Education can win tangible public support and finance when respect for its operations and output are high, but kill community regard and in the same process one kills the supply of resources. Thus a common pattern emerges out of surveys conducted into parental attitudes to schools. When asked, many parents tend to say that the school which their children attend is very good, but that something is wrong with education generally. They believe that all the other schools must be at fault; but theirs is exceptional.

The implications deserve comment. It is the overall image which determines political support and therefore resource levels. Happy parents associated with one local school hardly constitute a lobby powerful enough to influence the funding priorities of a state, provincial or national government. But when parents do unite, they usually seem to attack politicians over what is wrong in education, over what is deficient and over what is not being done. Rarely do they project the image of a group firmly committed to excellence in the system and determined to highlight the best and most admirable practices within it. What transformations would occur if such a positive approach were to be adopted by educators and parents?

If one fosters hatred or ill-will inside any living system, it spreads like a cancer creating sourness, an internal festering and ill-health. To be specific, if people keep sponsoring antagonisms, anger, a cynicism about other people and their motives, if they keep pointing to the things that are wrong in education, it is quite likely to cause to grow in the young clients of the system metaphorical tumours. On the other hand, a school or system which encourages well-being, absolute honesty, love and not hate, and a belief in the fidelity and trustworthiness of other people will reap a harvest which it is impossible to predict. By many incidental means we create the feelings about and within a system. The fact is that the things to which you choose repeatedly to draw attention and the matters which collectively you put before your friends and the community reveal very clearly what your motives are, what you consider important and in what you are prepared to invest your time and your enthusiasms; those repeated sayings then influence your actions and those of other people.

What would happen, we wonder, if a set of people like educators for a whole year refused to be drawn into any public debate on education which did not focus on how children learn? Would it not be refreshing, if, for a whole year, they kept out of the public media any dissensions which related to working conditions, pay scales, teacher promotions or industrial matters, if these were matters treated away from the public press? What new image about education would emerge if educational spokespersons always spoke on educational matters, about children and learning, about the competence and excellence of educational colleagues? We are not arguing that educators should hide their problems, conceal bad practices or remain passive about issues that are important; but must they speak so constantly about bad practices, about things that seem to be wrong? Why do they undermine the public standing of their committed colleagues, criticise the enterprise's managers, raise doubts in parents' minds about the wellbeing of their children who are in the community's schools, and weaken educators' and their own credibility? Could educators sponsor positive trust, poise, confidence and ecological harmony around the learning child? And think what such a spirit could do in terms of image, support and public respect if it were breathed into education throughout the land.

To demonstrate what a school can do to foster public goodwill and confidence in its operation, and to build a strong public image, we consider now ten aspects of the matter which ought to be addressed.

Consistent professional behaviour

A spate of books, published in recent years, has attempted to explain why some firms have been able to maintain market leadership and reputation for excellence. Corporate culture is a common feature of all the formulae. Put another way, every excellent firm apparently goes to considerable expense and planned effort to ensure that there is an identifiable, externally respected and internally honoured pattern of behaviours and attitudes held by those people employed by the firm. Olins (1976: 28) puts it this way:

All the organisations we have looked at try to inculcate a permanent attitude and set of standards in those who belong. Second, they have an opportunity to do this because they influence the manner and style in which the group behaves, and the environment in which it lives. Third, they are thorough in the use of the opportunities available to them. Fourth, they are anxious to impress the world outside with their homogeneity and strength.

It is important for those associated with schools to recognise that if the analogy with business firms is to be preserved, this consistency should characterise the teaching and administrative staff, not the students who are the clients of the school or system. There needs to be, in short, a code which governs the behaviour of those who provide the educational service. That being so, how do educators shape up to the Olins prescription? Could we say of

237

educators that they are careful about the attitudes of their colleagues; that they insist on high standards in themselves and in
other teachers; that they demand a positive style in their group
behaviour; that they use the school environment, the physical shell
of the school, to emphasise that style; that teachers are thorough
in policing their own professional behaviours; and that they are
anxious to impress their publics with their consistent excellence
and strength?

It is obvious that in the well regarded organisations these
behaviours are not left to chance. Anyone who breaks the pattern
faces discipline or dismissal, for the company's market niche can
be maintained only by deserving confidence and customer satisfaction. Olins cites IBM to demonstrate the point about consistent
excellence of performance. He argues that 'the most striking
characteristic about IBM style is its ubiquity . . . Whatever it's
doing, IBM wants to be top' (*ibid.*: 30). Anyone who represents
IBM 'has the whole crushing burden of IBM's imagery sitting on
his head'. The person is expected to arrive on time, be dressed
appropriately, be polite and to conduct the business with crisp
competence. He comments that the IBM style is based upon the
premises:

> set the highest standards, demand the highest levels of perfor-
> mance, create an atmosphere in which people think they are
> better than anyone else and they will believe it and perform
> accordingly. (*ibid.*: 102)

One essential component determines whether such a style will survive. This culture develops only if it is managed from the top.
The chief executive (or executives) must demand it, and they
probably need to have a formal corporate strategy - or a master
plan - to make it work (*ibid.*: 173). Does education have that kind
of competency, leadership and planning? It would need the principal and the staff to negotiate amongst themselves what the professional code of behaviour is, and then very seriously to require it
of all who join the school staff.

Institutional training

Consistency of behaviour, of performance and of image rarely
comes by accident. It is usually developed by means of a sustained training programme, beginning with a careful induction

process. Olins cites the case of Unilever, an international company with a 'very powerful corporate identity'. Unilever's great strength (he says) is in its training systems. It teaches people not only how to be good at marketing and other specialised techniques, but also how to be good Unilever people. There is a Unilever way of behaving, a Unilever way of getting on with other people and a Unilever style of doing business that anybody who has ever dealt with Unilever recognises. The company can ensure this homogeneity across national frontiers and among different cultures only by having 'powerful internal disciplines and predictable behaviour patterns' (*ibid.*: 30).

Educators as a profession have an enviable record for professional development activity. In most developed countries there are extensive inservice education programmes available, they are well patronised, are well organised and led usually by members of the profession. There are many energetic professional associations to which educators belong. Teachers frequently attend conferences - local, national, international. And as a group they are among the best users of the formal, continuing education facilities. A fifth of the postgraduate students in Australian Universities and Colleges of Advanced Education are teachers, a large proportion of whom are taking higher degrees or diplomas through part-time, after-hours study. The largest single group of Open University diploma and degree course students in the UK comes from the teaching profession. Indeed, the way the teaching profession has raised itself virtually to a graduate service in several countries inside about three decades is impressive by any criterion. So the teacher record of professional training makes a strong, positive story - one worth talking about and publishing.

Adding the next dimension of induction programmes for particular schools or units, of conducting regular in-house programmes and developmental activities (and they can be of many kinds), and of building acceptance about appropriate collective professional behaviours, that is the point at which an 'emerging profession' usually crosses the boundary and becomes accepted widely and publicly as a profession. It needs to be noted, too, that a profession can slip back across that boundary of public esteem, as both the medical and nursing professions in some countries have discovered following militant industrial action by their unions.

How does the educator group and the staff of a school compare against such a criterion? Do educators concentrate on learning about the craft of education and give too little attention to appropriate professional behaviours? (One needs to consult any list of inservice education offerings before one answers that question.) Does the teaching profession have 'powerful internal disciplines' and who imposes them - industrialised teacher unions, or head office controls, or a shared professional ethos? Do teachers have 'predictable behaviour patterns'? (What response would one get from a person in the street if asked to state what teacher actions are predictable?) Are educators overtly dedicated to excellence of learning outcomes? And how can they best communicate that dedication?

In summary, then, strong public regard and support are likely to be by-products if educators as a group - or as a school staff - ensure that there is a coherent, continuing and comprehensive training programme for all the staff on a school site. Training ought not to be the sole responsibility of the individual teacher.

Product diversity and customer choice

The educator community could learn from one of the oddities evident in the commercial marketplace. In many commodity areas complexity, diversity and the impression that the customer has multiple choices are cultivated by the advertisers. Are you aware, for example, how many brand names the cigarette giant W.D. & H.O. Wills markets? The same is true in the detergent, toothpaste, soaps and toiletries fields. Is it not curious to discover the one firm conducting an advertising war against itself by sponsoring competition among its own brand names? There are several reasons why. A detergent is not merely a substance that makes water frothy and breaks surface tension. It can be a powder or a liquid; it can have a lemon tang or a blue rinse; it can be different for dishes and for clothing (no longer will just soap do!); it can be biodegradable; it affects your hands differently; it creates degrees of whiteness, or sparkle, or smell; it can come in economy size, king-size, or dwarf-size; each brand is different. The customers have choices to suit their sense of smell, their budget, self-esteem, values or morality.

Marketers know that a single scale of excellence is an advantage for only one group: those at the top of that scale. The secret of winning a share of the market is to admit, usually by advertising in its many forms, that there are multiple lists of excellence, and to argue that this product sits at the top of the list you, the customer favour. There can be many winners if there are multiple contests. It is by adroit manoeuvres that any one product gains its place in the sun, its market niche.

Much of this diversity in product or services may appear to be manipulated and sometimes rather hollow. But in the realm of education, diversity is endemic and, indeed, one of its strengths. The education profession should be able to demonstrate with intellectual validity and without compromising truth or morality in any degree that there are many categories of excellence in education - indeed in educational achievement - and that even the same excellence of learning outcome can be achieved by quite different methods and out of clearly different milieus. Healthy competition, product diversity and differential excellences are desirable factors - in education no less than in the toothpaste industry. Why are educators so coy about exploiting an aspect of their craft which is so obviously a strength about schooling?

Since advertising must be honest and must not deliberately mislead, the provider must pose as the first question, 'What is the most distinctive feature of my product or service?' The provider must define exactly the quality which distinguishes this particular product or service from all of its competitors. It is not an exercise which educators are particularly good at doing, for it requires of them these considerations:

• What makes my classroom or my lessons unique, different from any others conducted anywhere else in this school or in this country or in the world? In what respects am I literally a world-beater?
• What characteristics or features make this school different from any other, anywhere in this region, state or country?
• What pattern or 'trade mark', recognisable by the world, do the members of this school community carry about with them? (Some schools, of course, take the easy answer to the hard question by simply making their school uniform the identifier.)

And so on. Once a teacher, a school, a region, and a system ask questions of this kind, there can be only one outcome: a vigorous search for excellence, or rather for diverse excellences, and a relentless drive to highlight the particular excellence of which each unit is capable. Frankly, until the educational fraternity is prepared to take this approach, the judgements about excellence will continue to be taken for them. The people at the top of the extant list - that one, accepted, established (but questionable) pecking order - will reassert the validity of that one scale and, in the process, corner the best part of the market: the most money, the best support, the most desired students, and the power to choose the measuring devices which most favour their cause.

One further aspect of this legitimate sense of competition within an industry should be noted. On first thoughts it may appear wasteful if not pointless for the detergent manufacturers to wage what appears to be a specious advertising campaign amongst themselves. What the campaign achieves, however, is a heightened public awareness of detergents as a whole; in short, the gross sales of all detergents rise. How many people now wash their dishes with common soap (if that product now even exists)? Only rarely would anyone consider using dishwashing powder for the laundry, or laundry detergent on dishes. If we extend the analogy to education, then, we could achieve a most desirable outcome, namely a more widespread awareness of the colour, variety and possibilities in education, more informed, less biased and less simplistic judgements about schools and about students, and much more sophistication in the public discussions about education.

So one important technique which education and particular schools might use is to break up the stereotypes, to diversify public awareness and to sponsor a variety of educational excellences. There is not 'one best way' in education.

Capitalising on the privatisation rhetoric

There is a further aspect to the diversity factor which educators could capitalise upon in order to build a strong public image for their school. In several western countries - including Great Britain, the USA and Australia - there has been extensive discussion about privatisation of schooling, including the so-called flight from public to private schools. To give their arguments some empirical validity, the proponents for and against public schools have engaged in an exchange of statistics, including the claims that one set of schools has long waiting lists, yet the facts affect the situation only marginally, for in the matter of public image we are dealing with what people believe and we must confront those perceptions. If people believe that there is flight to non-government schools, then it becomes a self-confirming prophecy; people will act upon it. Schools have taken a long time to comprehend this point.

An interesting case was cited in the Australian capital, Canberra, where there are excellent public sector schools. One perceptive government school principal, on being told by a Catholic
parent that there was a waiting list at the local parish school,
deflated the parent by replying, 'Yes, I know the problem. I have
a waiting list at my school too.' He realised that there is a mythol-
ogy at work here. Does it matter how many are on those waiting
lists? Merely claiming to have a waiting list says something about
how desirable my school is.

What lies behind the privatisation movement and what
seems to make it so popular? First, people dislike bigness, remote-
ness, and regulation from afar, and teacher unions (indeed, any
large unions) can be among the chief offenders. Any centrally
determined prescription which must apply across the board is usually unnecessary and it takes away from the local people, whom
we tend to trust, the power to take action which is clearly tailored
to our wishes and is clearly aimed at our advantage. Wherever
there is prescription from afar, people tend to 'go local' and priva-
tise, if necessary by deliberately stepping outside the system
which imposes the prescriptions.

Second, most people value the power of self-determination,
especially over affairs which affect them directly - and the welfare
of their children is such an affair. Increasingly, then, parents seek
to exercise choice over schooling, demand some voice in their
local schools and support local authorities over central authorities.
The more educated the population becomes, the more sophisticated are the demands and the stronger run the trends towards
localisation and privatisation. Indeed, any central agency - bureaucracy, government, large business, union - which tries to stem the
flood could be inundated by such a stream of locally oriented
administrivia that the centre will be in danger of collapse from
overload. Decentralisation is therefore tending to become a coping
reaction.

If privatisation aims to give schools more initiative, to allow
parents more genuine engagement with the place where their children are being schooled, and to give the teaching staff a more professional and responsible climate to work in, then all kinds of
schools can and should share in it. It must not be allowed to
become a new means to perpetrate social injustices or inequities.
Public sector schools can begin to win a better public reputation if
they are allowed to develop their differences; if excellence within
this variety is demanded; if parents and the local community are

welcomed into the affairs of the school; if it can be openly demonstrated how well the students are achieving; and if good, simple, and strong messages are fed back to the local client community. Many public sector schools are now beginning to resemble some independent schools, many with their own governing boards, with a discretionary budget, many with reasonable involvement in selecting their staff, and with considerable powers to use - even to lease - their own buildings and equipment. Whilst there is some variation between North America, Australia and the UK in these matters, in short, most schools have the power to take initiatives to lift their reputations.

Networking, or using the grapevine

Education by its very nature touches a high proportion of the population. Most other organisations have far less contact with their publics or their clients/customers. In consequence, those organisations do not cope (as educational enterprises do) with the natural human propensity to trade in gossip. This characteristic of education systems is one which teachers have not yet come to grips with. Education everywhere spawns a network of informal communications, in short, a grapevine. Whenever people talk to other people they produce a network of idea sharing, sometimes formal but more frequently informal.

The term 'grapevine' originated during the American Civil War. The telephone was in its infancy and to enable officer to talk to officer, wires had to be strung out across trees, crisscrossing here and there like vines to the places where the key people were. The possibilities of poor reception and crossed wires were enormous; and hence the grapevine acquired the reputation both of rendering inaccurate, garbled messages and of acquiring a legion of eavesdroppers.

In fact, the accuracy of the grapevine's messages has been fairly well researched, and the results are impressive. By the mid-1970s, Goldhaber (1974: 123-124) could summarise the findings as follows:

• The grapevine is generally fast. It far outspeeds any formal networks where niceties of protocol have to be observed. Walton in his 1961 study concluded that the grapevine was 'the speediest channel for spreading messages among employees'

• Second and perhaps surprisingly, the grapevine is accurate. A cluster of studies carried out during the 1970s showed that the grapevine's information was correct about 80 per cent of the time

• The grapevine clothes the information in ways that will be heard and in which the significance will be understood. People in managerial positions could learn a great deal both about their organisation and their environment by analysing the transformations which the grapevine makes to official information. An organisational and social style begins to appear

• And lastly, the grapevine is not like a telegraph wire on which the message travels in a linear fashion. The grapevine in fact sprouts like a vine, sending the message out in clusters simultaneously and in a non-linear fashion.

Why is this all so important in the context of education's public image? The positive advantage of 'networking', as it is now called in the literature, could be more actively explored in the interests of education's public reputation.

We are aware, for example, of a system where the principals have constructed their own formal grapevine for communicating important information; the system operates on having about six key persons (the primal nodes) who are then given six colleagues to whom they phone information; they have further contacts. The alerting system can spread a message throughout the school system within two hours. Other principals have used the same device with parents, formally linking them into a branching set of telephone and street contacts; he can receive quick feedback on any issue by using the same network.

Market research

Now that school-based decision-making is so widely practised many of the actions which in the past may have been initiated from head office are now falling to individual schools and to regions. Let it be clearly understood what this means in a formalised school system. Initiatives taken in a school or region may be heard about in the head office at second- or third-hand, but the public sees the action nevertheless and imputes it quite rightly to the system. In short, schools and regions are part of the system, indeed fundamentally important and very active parts of it. The local initiators of actions must therefore now take it upon themselves to attend to all the consequences of their actions in the same way as the Head Office once did. The initiators have to address the questions of public information giving, of appeasing the opponents of an action, of building coalitions and support, of handling the public media, of analysing ahead of time the impact of new policy and so on. Schools must become 'miniature Ministries', and public image is as much the school's job as it is anyone else's in the education system.

Political parties and business firms regularly use public opinion polls to guide them in their corporate strategies. It has been suggested that in the fairly near future formal mechanisms will be set up so that governments can sample public attitudes to proposed legislation or government policy, and determine whether the majority would support the idea behind a new initiative before action is taken on it.

Whatever the developments, however, the fact is that those in decision-making positions need to know how the public views a particular issue. Since privately commissioned opinion polls have now become a domestic industry, it would be prudent for the managers of schools to ensure that they have available the means to find out the level of support the community will give to particular educational policies or enterprises. The machinery should include:

- Formal feedback from parents and students
- Carefully worked out and tested 'indicators of unrest'
- Machinery for picking up 'weak signals' coming from the community, those tentative and somewhat muted noises which are harbingers of more significant things to come.

The school should have readily available the means to conduct opinion polls among a sample of its own client community.

We are aware that some schools, or clusters of schools, are now developing a kind of 'electoral college' for their community so that they have available a really representative body of opinion on particular issues. The members need not ever be assembled physically in one place. The information can be mailed to the electoral college members, and they record their votes by mail or by telephone. Another imaginative proposal from a Canberra school was that membership on the school's governing board should be determined by a kind of jury system. Instead of having elections for the positions on the council, the parent and teacher members would be chosen in the same way as a jury is assembled; every parent and every teacher associated with the school could be called up for 'jury service', either for a set term of office or to form a committee on a particular issue. The self-selection which too often characterises school board or parent association elections would no longer prevail.

School managers, at whatever location they operate, have in the past been rather unimaginative in the way they have tried to involve the interested public. The standard strategy has been to call a meeting of all parents (and to be satisfied with an attendance of a few dozen) or to call a public meeting (and create an arena for the demagogue). Neither device is particularly good for rational debate or for a representative polling of the community's wishes. And if schools were more confident that the public was behind them and intelligently informed about the issues, how much more confident could their actions and practices be? And if the parents and the public knew their opinions were so highly valued that there existed a formal and regularly used means of consulting their opinion before action was taken, how much more credible and cohesive would be the public support for the education enterprise?

Using the media; and education's own printing press

One tends to think of newspapers, radio, television and magazines as the media to carry paid advertising and comments on news and events. But an alternative is available to educators.

The education industry is well equipped to handle much of its own image-building, for it has natural and ready access to its most important public, the parents, and can use those access channels without any recourse to the public media. Furthermore, schools collectively own probably the largest corporate printing works in the country - in the form of photocopy machines, duplicators, word processors and desktop copiers located in thousands of schools and education units. It already has in existence, albeit in an uncoordinated mass, a bewildering set of newsletters, school magazines, journals and official magazines. If educators, particular schools and educational editors were less amateurish, more knowledgeable about impact, style and readability, and were more inclined to put forward a positive, altruistic and consistent message, they would discover that the power to project a new collective image for education is within their own hands, at almost no additional cost.

In any case, it is important for a school's managers to attend to their own productions. They need to be carefully edited and in a professional manner, they need to be coordinated in terms of livery, layout and content, and the productions should be geared to their target audience (especially in such basic areas as reading levels, vocabulary, avoidance of jargon and acronyms, reader motivation and subject matter). The spoken, written and media presentations from the school ought not to be haphazard, unplanned or below professionally established standards.

The symbolic aspects of policy

Thomas Dye (1978: 311-316) has argued that the symbolic aspects of a policy can be more significant than what the policy programme actually achieves. The policy impact may be more influential than the policy's real effects: the policy may seem to achieve very little but if it convinces people that the government or the organisation is at least trying to do something, it may be successful as a policy. So, Dye (1978: 316) says:

> the policies of government may tell us more about the aspirations of a society and its leadership than about actual conditions ... For example, a government 'war on poverty' may not have any significant impact on the poor, but it reassures moral men ... that government 'cares' about poverty. Whatever the failures of the antipoverty programme in tangible respects, its symbolic value may be more than redeeming.

Dye comments that television has made the image as important as the reality, and that what governments say is now as important as what governments do.

In the interests of the good standing of the school, then, educators - and especially the principal and senior staff - must be conscious of symbolism, of what they associate the school with and in what way they do it. And even when there seems to be no final, obvious or definitive way to solve a problem, some action, some gesture which indicates the educators' concerns, can project an image of a genuinely caring school.

Names and titles

Naming the company, selecting the titles for its office holders, and labelling the merchandise is one of the devices private industries use in image-building. Names (whether of the product or of the company) can go out of date, sometimes so badly that the name begins to limit sales. Some corporations in recent decades have had to drop quietly from their company names and terms like 'Colonial' and 'Imperial'. Sometimes it can be disguised by using initials, as with ICI (Imperial Chemical Industries) or CSR (Colonial Sugar Refineries). A national description like 'US' can be a disability too, especially in multinational companies. Thus, US Rubber changed its name to 'Uniroyal'. To cast a different image, the G.J. Coles emporia were renamed 'Coles New World'. Company mergers produce double-barrelled names like Rank Xerox to preserve the proud traditions of both companies. One company may go by several names, as in the car, soap and tobacco industries. And some companies, even in the public sector, have invented elisions like Telecom, Australia Post, or Britrail, and Amtrak.

By comparison, educators appear amateurish in their selection of suitable nomenclature. What impressions do we perpetrate by using terms like 'Director', 'Director-General', 'Inspector', 'Head Master', 'Principal', and now increasingly 'Chief Executive' and 'General Manager'? What activates educators' motives when they choose names for particular schools or educational services or for parts of a school?

> There are . . . quite different impressions conveyed about the school if the place where the chief educator works is called -
>
> > The Principal's Office, or
> > The Head Master's Room, or
> > The Chief Executive's suite.
>
> Each title implies a different attitude towards the organisation and its members, a different vision about relationships, a different picture about that world of people (Beare, 1987: 17).

Educators need to use as much care and sophistication as do other enterprises over position titles, the names of buildings and parts of buildings, the title of the school (especially if it amalgamates elements which have strong traditions), and the names given to services, subjects, curricula and regular activities. They are all powerful carriers of image.

Education's public face

What educators and schools say to the public and who says it are important. Educators should avoid the convention, 'A spokesman for the Education Department said today . . .'; since education is itself so personal, the profession should use identifiable people, give their names and personalise the service. It should give kudos and public visibility to the people who are respected for their skills and who deserve praise. In the education business, however, who makes the regular statements to the Press? Whose face and whose voice do the public regularly identify with education?

The education industry tends to use the wrong people to carry its image. In the private sector the general manager or the chief executive features in company advertisements only when the situation warrants it; almost never does the shop steward or the union boss feature and frequently the company highlights an ordinary member of the firm, or, more frequently, a satisfied client. So if the regular spokesperson for education is a politician, then education will be seen to be political. If a union official is regularly seen on the public media talking about schools, then education will be viewed predominantly in terms of industrial relations. If the Chief Education Officer is the regular spokesperson, then education may appear centralist, office-bound and authoritarian. Whose smiling face should be chosen? And what regular message should the public be hearing about education?

Educators need to give careful consideration, then, to the question of who is allowed to be the educators' voice, what faces continually and regularly appear on television and in the papers representing the education community, and what topics are treated. Do we need to change the actors and the image?

Conclusion

We have listed here ten areas which influence the way education is imaged by the public. We have deliberately not listed the many specific techniques which educators could use, for educators are essentially communicators and they have a good track record in inventing appropriate methods to meet particular teaching situations. Educating their publics about education is one requirement of their field; and we have therefore in this chapter itemised some of the domains which educators need to address. It will also be obvious by now that projecting an image is just a part of the more important, more embracing topic of building an ennobling culture within which learning can be sponsored and can thrive. Without such a motive on the part of educators, the act of public image-making can seem a hollow exercise; with the right motive, however, it becomes a task of huge significance for the learning enterprise.

11

Excellent Schools:
Putting it All Together

Let us now summarise the new management techniques for creating excellent schools. We have tried in this book to give a clear enunciation of the actions which will assist schools and school systems to come closer to creating genuinely excellent educational environments for students and teachers. You should now be able to answer the fundamental questions underlying the content of this book, namely

- What constitutes an excellent school?
- In what ways can school principals and school communities act to enhance the learning environments of students?
- What responsibilities belong to system administrators and to governments?
- What qualities, attitudes and values are necessary in principals and headteachers?
- What operational mechanisms and procedures can be adopted by schools to increase excellence in ways which are pertinent and appropriate for individual students and families?

The initial chapter surveyed the recent interest in school effectiveness and excellent schools, and the extent to which these have been in response to, or influenced by, political agendas. The two most notable commentaries have been those of Coleman (1966), in which he argued that the school environment made relatively little difference to the quality of student's learning, and that of Edmonds (1982) who stated that the quality of the school environment made a significant difference to a student's academic achievement. Other reports of the period - the Crowther and Robbins reports in Great Britain, for example - placed importance on

the occupational characteristics of parents. The Australian 'generation study' also confirmed the finding that parents are critical figures within the child's educational environment. Thus it is reasonable to argue that parents play an important place in the school's
milieu, and that their involvement should be fostered.

It has been an era which both encouraged and legislated for
greater involvement of parents in the processes of schooling - particularly pertaining to their representation on school councils - in
an endeavour to help achieve greater degrees of school-based
decision-making in matters of curriculum detail and school organisation. Some of these experiments have been more successful than
others in attempting to achieve, or to account for, greater quality
and relevance in schooling. What we do know is that, within the
school effectiveness movement, the best schools developed certain
characteristics which placed them apart from others. Notably, they
espoused effectiveness but within existing structures and frameworks; they required the existence of outcome measures, and an
accompanying set of accountability criteria, but in many respects
these were too narrowly conceived; there was concern about the
possible affirmation of social status among schools; there was concern about entrenching domination and power distributions; and
there was concern about the inability to be flexible enough in
adapting to rapid change. These were all thoroughly constructive
beginnings, but their potential, and in some respects their realisation, were constrained by inflexibilities in both thinking and
action.

The more recent theoretical writings on the effectiveness of
schooling have given more emphasis to the qualitative aspects of
the enterprise. A major impact on consideration of qualitative elements was made by Greenfield in 1974. Reference to these less
tangible elements which pertain to organisational culture in
schools were addressed in subsequent chapters. This amounts to a
cultus corporis about the myriad of influences upon children's
learning patterns. We concluded the first chapter by making reference to the rich body of literature on organisational cultures - both
that pertaining to organisations in general as well as to educational
enterprises in particular.

Chapter 2 comprised a review of the literature on developments in educational administration, with particular reference to
influences since 1975, the date of the challenge to the positivistic
domination of the earlier era. It has been described as an era of
'intellectual turmoil' and 'an awakening of criticism'. The

approaches which have blossomed since that date reveal new para-
digmatic ways of conceptualising schools in particular, and education in general. New terminology has also entered the field, some
of which relates to paradigms which place strong economic and
political emphases within the educational domain. However, the
terms which have had a strong impact upon educational thinking
and system restructuring in recent years include: loose coupling,
culture, corporate planning, programme budgeting, and policy
analysis. Changes to school and system management associated
with these conceptualisations have resulted in the development of
school councils, decentralisation and devolution of powers and
responsibilities, and associated with these are the new emphases
directed at the role of the principal, and of leadership in schools.
Educational managers must have a clear understanding of these
concepts if they are to survive the complexities of the current era.

We followed this with a chapter entitled 'Reconceptualising
the School' in which we raised questions about our common
understandings of the role of schools and of education. We raised
the questions: What is the difference between schooling and education? What are society's expectations for schools and for school
teachers? Can the school meet its own stated aims and objectives
for the students they teach? Have schools over-stated their capacities, or are they being constrained by unsympathetic structures and
attitudes? The underlying thesis in this chapter was that schooling
must be re-conceived of as being the responsibility of the whole
of society, rather than just that of a government Ministry of Education. Expectations for schools and schooling have changed in
the light of increasing societal pressure on negotiable outcomes
and subsequent applications for further study and the world of
work. Some of the operational constraints to the achievement of
excellence in schooling were enunciated. These included the
length of the school day, the increased involvement of teacher
unions in all aspects of school operation and the diminution for
many students of family and social support structures, which have
in turn placed pressures for additional personal support on teachers, over and beyond formal teaching. There has developed a curious tension between the rhetoric of increased devolution of
responsibility and decision-making, and the requirement for
greater accountability.

In terms of schools' stated aims and objectives, we asked
whether we are aiming too high in our expectations for schools.
Can we expect the school to educate the 'whole' child, and to take

on the responsibilities which were hitherto those of the wider community? Is society in general, and end-user groups in particular, expecting our students to have skills and qualities which are beyond the scope and capacity of the school to provide? Or are we maintaining impediments to this greater development?

We posed six major items for consideration which we believe would increase excellence in schooling. Mastery learning is an approach to formal education which permits every student to progress at his/her own rate whilst attaining mastery over curricular content. Vertical curriculum is the mechanism whereby this individualised progress is made possible. Students are no longer artificially grouped but may extend or restrain their progress in any subject within reasonable limits according to their needs or abilities. Teachers instruct each student on a more individualised basis and monitor their progress within a balanced choice of studies. A more flexible school day and school week increase the opportunity for variation within the general curriculum, whilst also acknowledging the uniqueness of needs of every individual school and school community. The corollary is the need for flexitime employment of school staff. This permits greater opportunity for personal and professional growth. Schools need to make greater use of the professional expertise available within their particular communities. There are many circumstances in which other qualified and skilled adults can assist with the formal education of students. Finally, schools need to reconsider the extent to which they can meet their own stated aims and objectives. To what extent can, or should, schools educate the 'whole' child? Most address only some the student's developmental needs. Clearly, schools are not presently organised in a way that enables them to educate the whole child. Predictably schools have therefore concentrated their efforts on intellectual teaching and learning as their *raison d'être*.

In the fourth chapter we addressed the issue of what constitutes appropriate administrative structures for schools. The Coalition of Essential Schools listed nine principles as representing the essence of schooling. These were as follows:

- Schools have an intellectual focus
- The school's goals should be simple
- The school's goals should apply to all
- The governing metaphor is the student-as-worker
- Student exhibitions are required

- Attitudes are important
- Staff are generalists first, and specialists second
- Education is personalised learning
- The budget demonstrates priorities

Within this set of criteria the instructional programme remains the dominant thread, and within this, the effective school will have a clearly articulated instructional focus, will use systematic evaluation and assessment, will have an expectation that all students will learn well, has an orderly and safe learning environment which encourages high quality teaching and learning, and the principal will be first and foremost a strong educational leader.

The newer organisational principles being adopted worldwide include corporate management structures. Handy (1978) specifies a number of factors reflected in this new order: greater professionalism in work; management by consent; productivity as the basis for remuneration; smaller 'organisational villages' rather than larger institutions; and harnessed technology. Work environments will be more collegial, status will be more fluid, authority will come from peer recognition, and stake-holders will be the decision-makers. People are seen as assets, capable of development and commitment, and organisation members are shareholders in every sense of the concept. The above dicta constitute a major shift in attitudes and practices when applied to most schools and school systems.

Toffler (1985) argues for a major shedding of functions away from the centre to the subsidiary units, along with a reconceptualising of roles. Teachers should be seen as the providers of a highly specialised service rather than as mere employees of a major organisation. The autonomy of the individual school and its professional personnel become of paramount importance in the approach to excellence in schooling. Deal and Kennedy (1982) call for an 'atomised organisation' which is characterised by smallness, member-ownership, lean middle-management, and a corporate culture. Naisbitt and Aburdene (1986) list ten features of the re-invented corporation. These characteristics apply particularly well to schools, and refer to things like quality, intuitive thinking, visionary leadership, adaptability, and productivity rewards.

In building a unique culture, the four domains of the structural overlays model more appropriately address the peculiar characteristics and needs of human service organisations. These are: bureaucratic; matrix; collegial; and political. The bureaucratic domain is excellent for rationally dealing with the routine, and where the exceptional is not a factor. The matrix mode is especially appropriate for contrasting yet interacting operations in which different controls and time-lines are necessary, for example the use of task-forces. The collegial mode grants significant autonomy to professionals and largely removes the constraints of hierarchial interference. The political mode takes account of social and environmental changes and pressures as these impact upon the organisation. All four modes are necessary and school leaders need to ensure that they use the appropriate mode for the particular task. The other very attractive concept which has been readily applied when considering educational organisations is that of loose coupling. However, Peters and Waterman (1982) describe a more appropriate concept as 'loose-tight' structure, one which maintains tight controls over inanimate and technological elements of organisations but permits greater freedom (looseness) for professional expression. Appropriately managed corporate structures can effectively supplant the traditional and inappropriate bureaucratic structures which bedevil most educational organisations. Functional designs, parallel structures and loose-tight coupling are all compatible within the new modes for school and school-system operations. School leaders must become multi-modal.

Following the discussion of re-conceptualising the school and system structures, the issue of leadership in excellent schools was next addressed. The older conceptions of leadership were far too narrow and failed to incorporate the need for values and vision. Leadership is a *gestalt* phenomenon, and needs to be conceived of as transforming, being concerned with organisational and operational potential and with motivating followers. It is proactive rather than reactive; it is constructive rather than merely responsive. We presented ten thrusts associated with transforming leadership. These include: a vision for the organisation, and its communication to the members in a way which engenders commitment; the development of a strongly symbolic culture; and a critical mix of both sensitivity and caring on the one hand, and healthy competitiveness on the other. This concept of transforming leadership greatly surpasses the earlier bi-polar approaches of task and relationships, and even the more sophisticated contingency models. Leadership includes human, technical, symbolic, educational, and cultural forces.

The translation of transforming leadership into actual practice requires a management model. In Chapter 6 we discussed the guidelines necessary for bringing such vision to reality by incorporating a number of aspects of leadership, notably: purposing, values, clarity, consensus and commitment of purpose, the unification of people around the espoused values, autonomy and authority at the school level, school-site management and collaborative decision-making, 'leadership density', and the institutionalising of vision.

We have referred to the Project on Improving Urban High Schools undertaken in the United States as being a useful guide for the management of change. Miles (1987) has depicted the relationships of preconditions and factors as presented in Figures 6.1 and 6.2. Our model presented for collaborative school management was developed by Caldwell and Spinks (1988) and is included as Figure 6.3. We have discussed in some detail the various components within the major sections of the model: the goal-setting and need identification; policy-making; and initial evaluation of the policy group (above the diagonal); and the planning, budgeting, implementation, and evaluation of the programme teams (below the diagonal). As indicated, this model has been successfully introduced into hundreds of schools in Victoria, though three to five years need to be set aside for comprehensive adoption, consistent with the time-line for the change model suggested by Miles. The model needs to be aligned with the outstanding leadership styles as presented in Chapter 5.

In Chapter 7 our focus was on learning and teaching as the primary determinants of excellence in schooling. We provided an overview of the most recent trends in this area in western countries, followed by some guidelines for the design and delivery of programmes for school level utilisation. A scenario pertinent to the twenty-first century provides some futures focus to the way schools may very well develop over the next 10-15 years.

We cited six fundamental qualities for excellence in teaching:

- Diagnosis of student learning needs
- Selection of appropriate learning and assessment procedures
- Clear communication of achievement expectations
- Maintenance of an orderly learning environment
- Continuous monitoring of student progress

258

• Living the values which reflect respect, acceptance, support and recognition.

The provision of these by classroom teachers requires suitable pre-service and in-service support. Duke (1987) isolated seven 'key situations' gleaned from effective schools research. These were:

• Teacher supervision and development - flexibility to enhance individual potential
• Teacher evaluation - in line with espoused policies
• Instructional management and support - within a climate of excellence
• Resource management - in keeping with policies, priorities, and needs
• Quality control - continuous programme evaluation
• Coordination - matrix supervision
• Trouble shooting - anticipation and resolution of potential difficulties.

Fantini's (1986) state-of-the-art concepts pertaining to learning and teaching have implications for reforms in the present approach to, and provision of, education. There needs to be an unqualified acceptance of the principle that all people can learn under the appropriate conditions; that choice and the provision of alternatives and options both within and among schools are necessary; that school organisation must be vastly different to accommodate the multiple areas of personal intelligence (Gardner's seven areas); that the accelerating technological revolution must be acknowledged and accommodated; that school-based and non-school-based formal and non-formal learning modes will become the norm; and that education must be accepted by all as a life-long process.

  These considerations led us naturally to the issue of culture, and its application to schools. A conceptual framework was presented which incorporates the two operational interpretations of culture: the anthropological (social/ethnic) on the one hand, and the literati (creative expertise/appreciation) on the other. From this broadened definition we outlined a set of relationships pertaining to all aspects of a school's operation. These were subdivided into the intangible foundations (values, philosophy and ideology) and their more tangible and symbolic expressions, further subdivided into conceptual/written/verbal symbolism, visual/material expressions and symbolism, and behavioural expressions. We provided interpretational definitions of these elements to show the ways in which each interacts with the others, and with the wider school community. The extent to which this culture is shared by the school community, and can interact freely with the wider constituency, is essential to its successful development and maintenance. Once again, the role of the leader is crucial in the development of culture and its contribution towards achieving excellence in school practice.

In Chapter 9 we addressed the issues of performance indicators and accountability. How do we know if we have an excellent school? Or alternatively, how do we know to what extent, and in what ways, we may be falling short of achieving excellence? The criteria which Ralph and Fennessey (1983) believe pertain to excellent schools includes high academic achievement as an ongoing quality throughout the school, and after controlling for background variables. For the purpose of establishing the presence of such qualities, we have utilised Dror's (1973) model for policy analysis. To determine quality, it is necessary to establish criteria, and for each criterion there must be established standards. In education, the primary criteria are more difficult to calculate than they are in a business firm, and thus secondary criteria must be established: process patterns, output, organisational structures, and input. Once these are established, standards must be set for evaluation. Dror lists seven such standards

- comparison with the past
- quality of other systems
- desired quality
- professional standards of quality
- survival quality
- planned quality
- optimal quality.

The final component in Dror's evaluation model is sub-optimising, that is, compartmentalising into manageable bits, and typically these relate to time-frames, populations, and selected activities. Were schools to adopt the Dror model, the task of determining productivity would be very much easier. These productivity measures constitute performance indicators, and those used in OECD countries are classified into four main categories:

- internal performance indicators
- operating indicators
- external performance indicators
- staff productivity.

We need to bear in mind that accountability is only one of several aims. For example, the five common assessment purposes for teacher appraisal are as follows:

- for teacher professional improvement
- to determine fitness for promotion
- for school improvement
- for accountability
- to improve learning outcomes.

In general, there are three fundamental questions which underlie all teacher and/or school accountability: What should be assessed? How often should assessment be undertaken? What public needs the report?

In the final substantive chapter, we discussed the issue of how schools project a public image. The first point to be made is that image-building should be a conscious and purposeful activity undertaken by the school, not by others on behalf of the school. Secondly, the measures adopted should be relevant: economic indicators will measure economic efficiency but not necessarily educational quality or effectiveness. The difficult times confronting most western societies are likely to produce the following results in the immediate future: increasing independence for all schools; increasing exercise of parental choice; and increasing diversity among schools, with increasing sensitivity to the school's espoused values.

We discussed the terminology used in image building. There are subtle but important differences between the terms 'corporate identity' (the external public face of the school), 'corporate personality' (the internal culture created by the members) and 'corporate image' (the subjective perceptions which others form about the school on the basis of corporate identity and personality). However, schools and educational enterprises in general are much more complex than their corporate cousins when it comes to image-building and marketing. To assist in this task we have provided an extensive check list of questions schools should ask of themselves. Such questioning needs to be comprehensive, wide-ranging, and honest. We have followed this with ten aspects pertaining to image. These are:

• Consistent professional behaviour by the school's principal and teachers
• Institutional training - that is, professional development for the school's personnel (both formal and informal induction and in-service)
• Product diversity and customer/client choice - we need to capitalise on the fact of difference and uniqueness to generate excellence
• Capitalising on the privatisation rhetoric - act to create greater local autonomy, and with it greater excellence of operation
• Networking, or grape-vining - teachers need to utilise these potentially constructive mechanisms for their professional advantage and their students' benefit
• Market research - schools must seek information about client needs, and the relevance of the school's response
• Using the media, as well as your own publicity - become professional about news-making and news-casting
• The symbolic aspects of policy - illusion can be as important as reality
• Names and titles - since words carry images, educators must choose their words carefully
• Education's public face - educators must be careful about who act as their spokespersons.

The education of the young is one of the most noble enterprises in which mankind is destined to engage. Our entire existence rests on our ability to do it well. Our past, our present, and our future has been, is, and will be, shaped by the quality of our educational activity. So teachers have an awesome responsibility in the nurture of future generations. Teaching is not a trade, it is a calling. It is not just a job, it is a profession. It is not something in which one engages merely for self-seeking rewards, but rather for the service which one can give to those who need and seek knowledge and skills. Anything short of excellence either in terms of the input by teachers or the output of educated people will prove to be nationally costly, economically inefficient, and philosophically philistine.

This text has been about schools, principals, teachers, students and communities. Each school has a unique culture; each principal has a distinctive style; each teacher operates in an individualistic way; every single student is both unique and precious; every community creates an idiosyncratic environment for learning. So excellence anywhere grows from elements that are both peculiar and particular. We have tried to give a guide for improving the process of schooling. Excellence in schooling quite literally means excellence in every facet of the school's operation. Our students are our future, and schools build their future. The immediate responsibility to make these places excellent is ours.

Bibliography

Acheson, K. A. and Gall, M. D.   (1980)
Techniques in the Clinical Supervision of Teachers. New York
and London: Longman.
Ackoff, R. L.   (1981)
Creating the Corporate Future: Plan or be Planned For. New
York: John Wiley & Sons.
Adler, M. J.   (1984)
The Paideia Proposal. New York: Macmillan.
Allen, R. F. and Silverzweig, S.   (1977)
'Changing Community and Organizational Cultures'. *Training
and Development Journal.* July.
Argyris, C. and Schön, D.   (1978)
Organizational Learning. Reading, Mass.: Addison-Wesley.
Arnold, M.   (1982)
Culture and Anarchy. Wilson, J. D. (Ed.). Cambridge: Cam-
bridge University Press.
Austin, G. R.   (1978)
Process Evaluation: a Comprehensive Study of Outliers. Mary-
land: Centre for Educational Research and Development,
University of Maryland. February.
Austin, G. R.   (1979)
'Exemplary Schools and the Search for Effectiveness'. *Educa-
tional Leadership.* October.
Barnard, C. I.   (1938)
The Functions of the Executive. Cambridge, Mass.: Harvard
University Press.
Bates, R. J.   (1982)
'Towards a Critical Practice of Educational Administration'.
Studies in Educational Administration. No. 27. Armidale, NSW:
Commonwealth Council for Educational Administration. Sep-
tember.
Beare, H.   (1974)
'Is your School Achieving? Why not an Independent Review of
its Accomplishments?' *Developing Education.* August.
Beare, H.   (1981)
'Educational Administration, Power and Politics'. *ACEA Bul-
letin.* No. 22. December.

Bibliography

Beare, H. (1982)
'The Image of Education: Coming to Terms with the New Marketplace'. *The Tasmanian Teacher*. No. 3.

Beare, H. (1982)
'Education's Corporate Image'. *Unicorn*. Vol. 8. No. 1. February.

Beare, H. (1984)
'Effective Learning: the Recognition and Promotion of Effective Schools'. *Western Australian Primary Principal*. Perth, Australia. June.

Beare, H. (1984)
'The School's Subculture as a Learning Habitat'. *Western Australian Primary Principal*. Perth, Australia. September.

Beare, H. (1985)
'The Canute Principle of Executive Effectiveness or Are Good Heads Really Successful or Just Plain Lucky?' *Educational Administration Review*. Vol. 3. No. 2. Spring.

Beare, H. (1987)
Shared Meanings about Education: the Economic Paradigm Considered (the Buntine Oration). Carlton, Victoria: Australian College of Education.

Beare, H. (1988)
'The Purposes of Teacher Appraisal' in Lokan, J. and McKenzie, P. (Eds) *Teacher Appraisal: Major Issues and Approaches*. Australian Education Review series. Hawthorn, Vic.: Australian Council for Educational Research.

Beare, H. and Millikan, R. H. (1982)
'Educational Administration: Past, Present and Future'. Second National Conference of Lecturers in Educational Administration in Australia: Macquarie University (unpublished paper). University of Melbourne. August.

Beare, H. and Millikan, R. H. (1983)
'Change Strategies: A Framework for Systematic Discussion and Planning' in Harman, G. S. (Ed.) *Managing Structural Change in Education in Asia and the Pacific: A Blueprint for Action*. Canberra, ACT: Australian National Commission for UNESCO.

Bennis, W. and Nanus, B. (1985)
Leaders. New York: Harper & Row.

Biggs, J. B. and Telfer, R. (1987)
The Process of Learning (Second Edition). Sydney: Prentice-Hall.

Bloom, B. S. (1968)
'Learning for Mastery'. *Evaluation Comment*. Vols 1 and 2.

Brady, L. (1985)
Models and Methods of Teaching. Sydney: Prentice-Hall.

Brandt, R. (1982)
'The New Catechism for Effective Schools'. *Educational Leadership*. December.

Brookover, W. B. (1978)
'Elementary School Social Climate and School Achievement'. *American Educational Research Journal*. Spring.

Brookover, W. B. (1979)
School Social Systems and Student Achievement: Schools Can Make a Difference. New York: Praeger.

Brookover, W. B. and Lezotte, L. W. (1977)
Changes in School Characteristics Coincident with Changes in Student Achievement. East Lansing: Michigan State University, College of Urban Development.

Brown, J. K. (1984)
'Corporate Soul-Searching: the Power of Mission Statements'. *Across the Board*. March.

Burns, J. M. (1978)
Leadership. New York: Harper & Row.

Burrell, G. and Morgan, G. (1980)
Sociological Paradigms and Organizational Analysis. London: Heinemann.

Caldwell, B. J. (1983)
'Teaching Educational Administration: A Recapitulation of the Macquarie Position'. Third National Conference of Lecturers in Educational Administration in Australia (unpublished paper). Brisbane: Bardon Professional Development Centre. June.

Caldwell, B. J. (1983)
'New Approaches to Planning in Tasmania: A Critical Appraisal of Corporate Planning and Program Budgeting'. Winter Lecture Series (unpublished paper). University of Tasmania. June.

Caldwell, B. J. (1983)
'Teaching Educational Administration: A Recapitulation of the Macquarie Position'. Paper presented at the Third National Conference of Lecturers in Educational Administration in Australia. Brisbane: Bardon Professional Development Centre. June.

Caldwell, B. J. (1987)
The Promise of Self-Management for Schools: An International Perspective. London: Institute of Economic Affairs (Education Unit).

Caldwell, B. J. and Misko, J. (1968)
The Report of the Effective Resource Allocation in Schools Project. Hobart, Tasmania: Centre for Education, University of Tasmania.

Caldwell, B. J. and Misko, J. (1984)
'School-based Budgeting: a Financial Strategy for Meeting the Needs of Students'. *Educational Administration Review.* Vol. 2. No. 1.

Caldwell, B. J. and Spinks, J. M. (1986)
Policy-Making and Planning for School Effectiveness. Hobart, Tasmania: Education Department.

Caldwell, B. J. and Spinks, J. M. (1988)
The Self-Managing School. Lewes, Sussex: Falmer Press.

Callahan, R. (1962)
Education and the Cult of Efficiency. Chicago: University of Chicago Press.

Campbell, R. F. (1977)
'Educational Administration: A Personal View of Its Future' in Cunningham, L. L., Hack, W. G. and Nystrand, R. O. (Eds) *Educational Administration: the Developing Decades.* Berkeley, Ca.: McCutchan Publishing.

Carnegie Task Force on Teaching as a Profession (1986)
A Nation Prepared: Teachers for the 21st Century. New York: Carnegie Forum on Education and the Economy.

Carper, W. B. and Snizek, W. E. (1980)
'The Nature and Types of Organizational Taxonomies: An Overview'. *Academy of Management Review.* No. 5.

Chapman, J. D. (1984)
A Descriptive Profile of Australian School Principals. Canberra, ACT: Commonwealth Schools Commission.

Chapman, J. D. (1984)
The Selection and Appointment of Australian School Principals. Canberra, ACT: Commonwealth Schools Commission.

Chapman, J. D. (1987)
The Victorian Primary School Principal: The Way Forward. Melbourne: Victorian Primary Principals Association.

Clark, B. (1975)
'The Organizational Saga in Higher Education' in Baldridge, V. J. and Deal, T. E. (Eds) *Managing Change in Educational Organizations*. Berkeley, Ca.: McCutchan Publishing.

Cohen, M. (1981)
'Effective Schools: What the Research Says'. *Today's Education*. April/May.

Coleman, J. S., Campbell, E. Q., Hobson, C. J., McPartland, J., Mood, A. M., Weinfold, F. D., and York, R. L. (Eds) (1966)
Equality of Educational Opportunity (the Coleman Report). Washington, DC: US Government Printing Office.

Committee on Higher Education (1963)
Higher Education: Report of the Committee appointed by the Prime Minister under the Chairmanship of Lord Robbins 1961-63. London: (Robbins Report), HMSO.

Connell, R. W., Ashenden, D. J., Kessler, S., and Dowsett, G. W. (1982)
Making the Difference: Schools, Families and Social Division. Sydney: George Allen & Unwin.

Cooley, W. W. and Bickel, W. E. (1986)
Decision-oriented educational research. Boston: Kluwer-Nijhoff.

Cuban, L. (1983)
'Effective Schools: A Friendly but Cautionary Note'. *Phi Delta Kappan*. June.

Culbertson, J. (1980)
'Educational Administration: Where we are and where we are going' in Farquhar, R. and Housego, I. (Eds) *Canadian and Comparative Administration*. Vancouver: Education Extension: University of British Colombia.

Cunningham, L. L., Hack, W. G., and Nystrand, R. O. (1977)
Educational Administration: the Developing Decades. Berkeley, Ca.: McCutchan Publishing.

D'Amico, J. (1982)
'Each Effective School may be One of a Kind' and 'Using Effective Schools Studies to Create Effective Schools'. *Educational Leadership*. December.

Deal, T. E. (1987)
'The Culture of Schools' in Sheive, L. T. and Schoenheit, M. B. (Eds) *Leadership: Examining the Elusive. 1987 Yearbook of the Association for Supervision and Curriculum Development*. Arlington, Va.: ASCA.

Deal, T. E. and Kennedy, A. A.   (1982)
Corporate Cultures: The Rites and Rituals of Corporate Life.
Reading, Mass.: Addison-Wesley.

Dror, Y.   (1973)
Public Policymaking Re-examined. Bedfordshire, England: Leonard Hill Books.

Dubin, R.   (1968)
Human Relations in Administration (Second Edition). Englewood Cliffs, NJ: Prentice-Hall.

Duignan, P., Harrold, R., Lane, T., Marshall, A., Phillips, D., and Thomas, B.   (1985)
The Australian School Principle: A Summary Report. Canberra, ACT: Commonwealth Schools Commission.

Duke, D. L.   (1986)
'The Aesthetics of Leadership'. *Educational Administration Quarterly.* Vol. 22. No. 1.

Duke, D. L.   (1987)
School Leadership and Instructional Improvement. New York: Random House.

Dye, T. R.   (1978)
Understanding Public Policy. Englewood Cliffs, NJ: Prentice-Hall.

Edmonds, R. R.   (1979)
'Effective Schools for the Urban Poor'. *Educational Leadership.* October.

Edmonds, R. R.   (1980)
'Schools Count: New York City's School Improvement Project'. *Harvard Graduate School of Education Association Bulletin.* Vol. 25. No. 1.

Edmonds, R. R.   (1982)
'Programs for School Improvement: an Overview'. *Educational Leadership.* December.

Erickson, D. A.   (1977)
'An Overdue Paradigm Shift in Educational Administration, Or, How Can We Get That Idiot Off the Freeway?' in Cunningham, L. L., Hack, W. G. and Nystrand, R. O. (Eds) *Educational Administration: the Developing Decades.* Berkeley, Ca.: McCutchan Publishing.

Fantini, M. D.   (1986)
Regaining Excellence in Education. Columbus: Merrill Publishing.

Farquhar, R. and Housego, I. (Eds) (1980)
Canadian and Comparative Educational Administration. Vancouver: Education-Extension, University of British Columbia.

Fiedler, F. E. (1967)
A Theory of Leadership Effectiveness. New York: McGraw Hill.

Fiedler, F. E., Chemers, M. M., and Mahar, L. (1977)
Improving Leadership Effectiveness: The Leader Match Concept. New York: John Wiley & Sons.

Freire, P. (1972)
Pedagogy of the Oppressed. Harmondsworth, Middlesex: Penguin.

Friesen, D. A., Farine, A., and Meek, J. C. (Eds) (1980)
Educational Administration: A Comparative Review. Edmonton, Alberta: Department of Educational Administration, University of Alberta.

Getzels, J. W. (1977)
'Educational Administration Twenty Years Later, 1954-1974' in Cunningham, L. L., Hack, W. G. and Nystrand, R. O. (Eds) *Educational Administration: the Developing Decades.* Berkeley, Ca.: McCutchan Publishing.

Getzels, J. W. and Guba, E. G. (1957)
'Social Behaviour and the Administrative Process'. *School Review.* No. 65.

Getzels, J. W. and Thelen, H. A. (1960)
'The Classroom Group as a Unique Social System'. *The Dynamics of Instructional Groups.* Chicago: University of Chicago Press.

Giroux, H. A. (1981)
Ideology, Culture and the Process of Schooling. London: Falmer Press.

Glassman, R. B. (1973)
'Persistence and Loose Coupling in Living Systems'. *Behavioural Science.* Vol. 18.

Goldhaber, G. M. (1974)
Organizational Communication. Duberque, Iowa: W. C. Brown.

Good, T. L. and Brophy, J. E. (1984)
Looking in Classrooms (Third Edition). New York: Harper & Row.

Goodlad, J. I. (1984)
A Place Called School. New York: McGraw-Hill.

Greenfield, T. B.   (1973)
'Organizations as Social Inventions: Re-thinking Assumptions about Change'. *Journal of Behavioural Science*. Vol. 9. No. 5.

Greenfield, T. B.   (1975)
'Theory about Organizations: A New Perspective and its Implications for Schools' in Hughes, M. G. (Ed.) *Administering Education: International Challenge*. London: Athlone Press.

Greenfield, T. B.   (1979)
'Organization Theory as Ideology'. *Curriculum Inquiry*. Vol. 9. No. 2.

Greenfield, T. B.   (1985)
'Theories of Educational Organizations: A Critical Perspective' in *International Encyclopaedia of Education: Research and Studies*. Oxford: Pergamon.

Greenfield, T. B.   (1986)
'Leaders and Schools: Willfulness and Non-natural Order in Organizations' in Sergiovanni, T. J. and Corbally, J. E. (Eds) *Leadership and Organizational Culture: New Perspectives on Administrative Theory and Practice*. Urbana and Chicago: University of Chicago Press.

Griffiths, D. E.   (1959)
Administrative Theory. New York: Appleton-Century-Crofts.

Griffiths, D. E. (Ed.)   (1964)
Behavioral Science and Educational Administration. Chicago: University of Chicago Press.

Griffiths, D. E.   (1975)
'Some Thoughts about Theory in Educational Administration'. *UCEA Review*. No. 17. October.

Griffiths, D. E.   (1979)
'Intellectual Turmoil in Educational Administration'. *Educational Administration Quarterly*. No. 15.

Gronn, P. C.   (1983)
'Accomplishing the Doing of School Administration: Talk as Work'. *Administrative Science Quarterly*. Vol. 28. No. 1. March.

Guskey, T. R. and Gates, S. L.   (1985)
'A Synthesis of Research on Group-based Mastery Learning Programs'. Paper presented at the annual meeting of the American Educational Research Association. Chicago: AERA. April.

Guskey, T. R. and Gates, S. L. (1986)
'Synthesis of Research on the Effects of Mastery Learning in Elementary and Secondary Classrooms'. *Educational Leadership*. Vol. 43. No. 8.

Hage, J. (1965)
'An Axiomatic Theory of Organizations'. *Administrative Science Quarterly*. No. 10.

Halpin, A. W. (1973)
'A Foggy View from Olympus' in Walker, W. G., Crane, A. R. and Thomas, A. R. (Eds) *Explorations in Educational Administration*. Brisbane: University of Queensland Press.

Halpin, A. W. and Hayes, A. E. (1977)
'The Broken Icon: or, What Ever Happened to Theory?' in Cunningham, L. L., Hack, W. G. and Nystrand, R. O. (Eds) *Educational Administration: the Developing Decades*. Berkeley, Ca.: McCutchan Publishing.

Handy, C. (1978)
Gods of Management. London: Pan Books.

Handy, C. (1985)
Understanding Organizations. Harmondsworth, Middlesex: Penguin.

Handy, C. (1987)
Understanding Schools as Organizations. Harmondsworth, Middlesex: Penguin.

Hanson, M. (1976-77)
'Beyond the Bureaucratic Model: A Study of Power and Autonomy in Educational Decision-Making'. *Interchange*. Vol. 7. No. 2.

Harlen, W. (1973)
'Formulating Objectives - Problems and Approaches'. *British Journal of Educational Technology*. Vol. 3. No. 3. October.

Harman, G. (1980)
'Policy-Making and the Policy Process in Education' in Farquhar, R. and Housego, I. (Eds) *Canadian and Comparative Educational Administration*. Vancouver: Educational Extension: University of British Columbia.

Hedberg, B. L. T., Nystrom, P. C., and Starbuck, W. H. (1976)
'Camping on Seesaws - Prescriptions for a Self-Designing Organization'. *Administrative Science Quarterly*. No. 21.

Hersey, P. and Blanchard, K. (1982)
Management of Organizational Behavior: Utilizing Human Resources (Fourth Edition). Englewood Cliffs, NJ: Prentice-Hall.

Hill and Knowlton Executives (1975)
Critical Issues in Public Relations. London: Prentice-Hall.

Hills, R. J. (1977)
'A Perspective on Perspectives'. *UCEA Review.* No. 19. October.

Hills, R. J. (1980)
'A Critique of Greenfield's New Perspective'. *Educational Administration Quarterly.* No. 16. Winter.

Hodgkinson, C. (1978)
Towards a Philosophy of Administration. Oxford: Blackwell.

Hodgkinson, C. (1983)
The Philosophy of Leadership. Oxford: Blackwell.

Hough, M. (1984)
'Curriculum: A Necessary Integrator for Educational Administration'. *Educational Administration Review.* Vol. 2. No. 1. Autumn.

Hovey, S. (1986)
'Teachers at the Center'. *American Educator.* Fall.

Hoy, W. K. and Miskel, C. G. (1987)
Educational Administration: Theory, Research, and Practice (Third Edition). New York: Random House.

Hughes, M. G. (Ed.) (1975)
Administering Education: International Challenge. London: Athlone Press.

Hunter, M. (1985)
'What's Wrong with Madeline Hunter?' *Educational Leadership.* Vol. 42. No. 5. February.

Hüfner, K. (1987)
'The Role of Performance Indicators in Higher Education: the Case of Germany'. *International Journal of Institutional Management in Higher Education.* Vol. 11. No. 2. July.

Iannaccone, L. (1973)
'Interdisciplinary Theory Guided Research in Educational Administration: A Smoggy View from the Valley'. *Teachers College Record.* No. 75.

Jelinek, M., Smircich, L., and Hirsch, P. (1983)
'A Code of Many Colours'. *Administrative Science Quarterly.* No. 28.

Jencks, C.   (1972)
Inequality: An Assessment of the Effect of Family and Schooling in America. New York: Basic Books.

Johnson, L. R.   (1979)
The Cultural Critics: From Matthew Arnold to Raymond Williams. London: Routledge & Kegan Paul.

Joyce, B. and Weil, M.   (1980)
Models of Teaching. Englewood Cliffs, NJ: Prentice-Hall International.

Kelley, B. E. and Bredeson, P. V.   (1987)
'Principals as Symbol Managers: Measures of Meaning in Schools'. Paper presented at the annual meeting of the American Educational Research Association. Washington, DC: AERA. April.

Kerensky, V. M.   (1975)
'The Educative Community'. *National Elementary Principal.* Vol. 54. No. 3. January/February.

Klitgaard, R. E. and Hall, G. R.   (1973)
'Are There Unusually Effective Schools?' *Journal of Human Resources.* Vol. X. No. 1. Winter.

Kouzes, J. M. and Mico, P. R.   (1979)
'Domain Theory: An Introduction to Organizational Behaviour in Human Service Organizations'. *Journal of Applied Behavioural Science.* Vol. 15. No. 4.

Kuhn, T.   (1970)
The Structure of Scientific Revolution. Chicago: University of Chicago Press.

Kulik, C. L., Kulik, J. A., and Bangert-Drowns, R. L.   (1987)
'Effects of Testing for Mastery on Student Learning'. Paper presented at the annual meeting of the American Educational Research Association. San Francisco: AERA.

Lezotte, L. W.   (1982)
'A Response to D'Amico: Not a Recipe but a Framework'. *Educational Leadership.* December.

Lightfoot, S. L.   (1983)
The Good High School. New York: Basic Books.

Lipham, J.   (1964)
'Leadership and Administration' in Griffiths, E. E. (Ed.) *Behavioral Science and Educational Administration.* Chicago: University of Chicago Press.

Lopate, C., Flaxman, E., Bynum, E., and Gordon, E. (1969)
'Decentralization and Community Participation in Public Education'. *Review of Educational Research*. Vol. 40. No. 1.

March, J. G. and Olsen, J. P. (1976)
Ambiguity and Choice in Organization. Bergen, Norway: Universitetsforlaget.

Maughan, B. and Ouston, J. (1979)
'Fifteen Thousand Hours: Findings and Implications'. *Trends*. No. 4.

McCall, M. W. Jr. and Lombardo, M. M. (Eds) (1978)
Leadership: Where Else Can We Go?. Durham, NC: Duke University Press.

McGregor, D. (1960)
The Human Side of Enterprise. New York: McGraw-Hill.

Mellor, W. and Chapman, J. D. (1984)
'Organizational Effectiveness in Schools'. *Educational Administration Review*. Vol. 2. No. 2.

Meyer, J. W. and Rowan, B. (1977)
'Institutionalized Organizations: Formal Structure as Myth and Ceremony'. *American Journal of Sociology*. Vol. 83. No. 2.

Meyer, J. W., Scott, R., and Deal, T. E. (1979)
Institutional and Technical Sources of Organizational Structure Explaining the Structure of Education Organizations (unpublished paper). Stanford University School of Education.

Meyer, M. W. (Ed.) (1978)
Environments and Organizations. San Francisco: Jossey-Bass.

Miles, M. B. (1987)
'Practical guidelines for school administrators: How to get there'. Paper read at a symposium of Effective Schools Programs and the Urban High School. Washington, DC: Annual Meeting of the American Educational Research Association. April.

Millikan, R. H. (1984)
'New Paradigms in Catholic Schools'. *Nurturing Growth*. Melbourne, Victoria: Spectrum Publications.

Millikan, R. H. (1984)
'Axiology, Leadership, and the Development of School Culture'. *Axiology and Catholic Education: You the Leader*. Melbourne, Victoria: Spectrum Publications.

Millikan, R. H.   (1984)
'Culture and Imagery in Education: What is it, and What Can it do for My School?' *The Secondary Administrator*. Vol. 2. No. 1. February.

Millikan, R. H.   (1985)
'School Community'. *Conference Journal*. Melbourne, Victoria: Catholic Education Office.

Millikan, R. H.   (1985)
'A Conceptual Model for the Development and Maintenance of School Culture'. *Conference Papers*. Perth, Western Australia: Primary Principals Association of Western Australia, Department of Education.

Millikan, R. H.   (1986)
'The Changing Role of the School'. *The Western Australian Primary Principal*. Vol. 2. No. 2. July.

Millikan, R. H.   (1986)
'Marketing Schools to Their Constituencies'. *The Western Australian Primary Principal*. Vol. 2. No. 2. July.

Millikan, R. H.   (1987)
'The Politically-Expedient Model of Policy-Making'. *Unicorn*. Vol. 13. No. 1.

Millikan, R. H.   (1987)
'School Culture: A Conceptual Framework'. *Educational Administration Review*. Vol. 5. No. 2. Spring.

Mills, P. K. and Margulies, N.   (1980)
'Towards a Core Typology of Service Organizations'. *Academy of Management Review*. No. 5.

Ministry of Education, Victoria (1987)
Implementation of School Level Program Budgeting (Progress Report). Melbourne: Policy and Planning Unit.

Miskel, C. G., Fevurly, R., and Stewart, J.   (1979)
'Organizational Structures and Processes, Perceived School Effectiveness, Loyalty, and Job Satisfaction'. *Educational Administration Quarterly*. Fall.

Moore, W. E.   (1974)
In Loco Parentis: A Research Report from the Generation Study of Secondary School Students. Sydney, NSW: NSW Education Department.

Morgan, G.   (1980)
'Paradigms, Metaphors, and Puzzle Solving in Organizational Theory'. *Administrative Science Quarterly*. Vol. 25. No. 4.

Bibliography

Mulford, W. R. (1986)
'Indicators of School Effectiveness: A Practical Approach'. *ACEA Monograph Series*. No. 2. Perth, Western Australia: Australian Council for Educational Administration.

Murphy, J. T. (1980)
'School Administrators Besieged: A Look at Australian and American Education'. *American Journal of Education*. Vol. 89. No. 1.

Naisbitt, J. (1982)
Megatrends: Ten New Directions Transforming Our Lives. New York: Warner Books.

Naisbitt, J. and Aburdene, P. (1986)
Re-Inventing the Corporation: Transforming your Job and your Company for the New Information Society. London: Macdonald & Co.

National Commission on Excellence in Education (1983)
A Nation at Risk. Washington, DC: Government Printing Office.

National Commission on Excellence in Educational Administration (1987)
'Leaders for America's Schools'. Report of the National Commission on Excellence in Educational Administration. D. E. Griffiths (Chairman). The University Council for Educational Administration.

National Education Association - National Association of Secondary School Principals (1986)
'Ventures in Good Schooling'. Joint report. Washington, DC and Reston, Va.: NEA - NASSP.

National Governors' Association (1986)
'Time for Results'. *A Report on Education*. Lamar Alexander (Chairman). Washington, DC: National Governors' Association.

Norman, M. (1982)
Woodleigh: An Alternative Design for Secondary Schooling. Blackburn, Victoria: Dove Communications.

Olins, W. (1978)
The Corporate Personality: An Inquiry into the Nature of Corporate Identity. New York: Mayflower Books.

Ouchi, W. (1981)
Theory Z: How American Business can meet the Japanese Challenge. New York: Avon Books.

Pascale, R. J. and Athos, A. G. (1981)
The Art of Japanese Management. New York: Simon & Schuster.

Peters, T. J. and Waterman, R. H. (1982)
In Search of Excellence. New York: Harper and Row.

Pondy, L. R. (1978)
'Leadership is a Language Game' in McCall, M. W. Jr. and Lombardo, M. M. (Eds) *Leadership: Where Else Can We Go?.* Durham, NC: Duke University Press.

Purkey, S. C. and Smith, M. S. (1985)
'School Reform: The District Policy Implications of the Effective Schools Literature'. *The Elementary School Journal.* Vol. 85.

Purkey, W. W. and Novak, J. M. (1984)
Inviting School Success (Second Edition). Belmont, Ca.: Wadsworth.

Ralph, J. H. and Fennessey, J. (1983)
'Science or Reform: Some Questions about the Effective Schools Model'. *Phi Delta Kappan.* June.

Riffel, J. A. (1978)
'The Theory Problem in Educational Administration'. *Journal of Educational Administration.* Vol. XVI. No. 2. October.

Roueche, J. E. and Baker, G. A. (1986)
Profiling Excellence in America's Schools. Arlington, Va.: American Association of School Administrators.

Rutter, M., Maughan, M., Mortimore, P., and Ouston, J. (1979)
Fifteen Thousand Hours: Secondary Schools and Their Effects on Children. London: Open Books.

Sallis, J. (1988)
Schools, Parents and Governors: A New Approach to Accountability. London: Routledge.

Sathe, V. (1985)
Culture and Related Corporate Realities. Homewood, Il.: Richard D. Irwin.

Schumacher, E. F. (1973)
Small is Beautiful. London: Blond & Briggs.

Sergiovanni, T. J. (1984)
'Leadership and Excellence in Schooling'. *Educational Leadership.* February.

Sergiovanni, T. J. (1987)
'The Theoretical Basis for Cultural Leadership' in Sheive, L. T. and Schoenheit, M. B. (Eds) *1987 Yearbook of the Association for Supervision and Curriculum Development.* Alexandria, Va.: ASCA.

Sergiovanni, T. J., Burlingame, M., Coombs, F. S., and Thurston, P. W.   (1987)
Educational Governance and Administration (Second Edition). Englewood Cliffs, NJ: Prentice-Hall.

Sergiovanni, T. J. and Corbally, J. E. (Eds) (1986)
Leadership and Organizational Culture: New Perspectives on Administrative Theory and Practice. Urbana and Chicago: University of Chicago Press.

Sergiovanni, T. J. and Starratt, R. J.   (1983)
Supervision: Human Perspectives (Third Edition). New York: McGraw-Hill.

Shakeshaft, C. and Nowell, I.   (1984)
'Research on Theories, Concepts, and Models of Organizational Behavior: the Influence of Gender'. *Issues in Education*. No. 2.

Sheive, L. T. and Schoenheit, M. B. (Eds) (1987)
'Leadership: Examining the Elusive' in *1987 Yearbook of the Association for Supervision and Curriculum Development.* Arlington, Va.: ASCD.

Shoemaker, J. and Fraser, H. W.   (1981)
'What Principals Can Do: Some Implications from Studies of Effective Schooling'. *Phi Delta Kappan.* November.

Simpkins, W. S.   (1982)
'Images of State School System Administration in the Literature on Educational Administration: An Australian Perspective'. *The Journal of Educational Administration.* Vol. XX. No. 1. Winter.

Sizer, T. R.   (1986)
'Rebuilding: First Steps by the Coalition of Essential Schools'. *Phi Delta Kappan.* September.

Slavin, R. E.   (1987)
'Mastery Learning Reconsidered'. *Review of Educational Research.* Vol. 57. No. 2. Summer.

Smilanich, R.   (1988)
Requirements of a Responsive Central Support Service in a Decentralised System of Education (unpublished paper). Hobart: The University of Tasmania.

Smircich, L.   (1983)
'Concept of Culture and Organisational Analysis'. *Administrative Science Quarterly.* Vol. 28. No. 3.

Smyth, W. J.   (1984)
Clinical Supervision: Collaborative Learning about Teaching. Geelong, Victoria: Deakin University.

Sowell, T. (1987)
A Conflict of Visions. New York: William Morrow & Co.
Starratt, R. J. (1986)
'Excellence in Education and Quality of Leadership'. Occasional Paper No. 1. Southern Tasmanian Council for Educational Administration.
Sterne, M. (1979)
'What Makes a Good School?' *Education (UK)*. August.
Stogdill, R. M. (1950)
'Leadership, Membership and Organization'. *Psychological Bulletin*. No. 47.
Taylor, T. (1977)
'A New Partnership for Our Schools'. Report of the Committee of Enquiry into the Management and Government of Schools. London: HMSO.
Taylor, W. (1975)
'The Contribution of Research to the Study and Practice of Educational Administration' in Hughes, M. G. (Ed.) *Administering Education: International Challenge*. London: Athlone Press.
Toffler, A. (1985)
The Adaptive Corporation. London: Pan Books.
Vaill, P. B. (1986)
'The Purposing of High Performing Systems' in Sergiovanni, T. J. and Corbally, J. E. (Eds) *Leadership and Organizational Culture: New Perspectives on Administrative Theory and Practice*. Urbana and Chicago: University of Chicago Press.
Van Meter, E. L. (1977)
'Theory in Educational Administration: Instructional and Content Considerations'. *Journal of Educational Administration*. Vol. XV. No. 2. October.
Walker, W. G. (1975)
'The Future of Educational Administration as a Field of Study, Teaching and Research' in Hughes, M. G. (Ed.) *Administering Education: International Challenge*. London: Athlone Press.
Walker, W. G., Crane, A. R., and Thomas, A. R. (Eds) (1973)
Explorations in Educational Administration. Brisbane: University of Queensland Press.
Weber, G. (1971)
Inner-City Children Can Be Taught to Read: Four Successful Schools. Washington, DC: Council for Basic Education.

Weick, Karl E.   (1976)
'Educational organizations as Loosely Coupled Systems'. *Administrative Science Quarterly*. Vol. 21. March.

Willie, C. V.   (1983)
'In Memoriam (for Ronald R. Edmonds)'. *Harvard Graduate School of Education Association Bulletin*. Vol. 28. No. 1. Fall.

Willower, D. J.   (1969)
'Schools as Organizations: Some Illustrated Strategies for Educational Research and Practice'. *Journal of Educational Administration*. Vol. VII. October.

Willower, D. J.   (1980)
'Contemporary Issues in Theory in Educational Administration'. *Educational Administration Quarterly*. No. 15. Fall.

Willower, D. J.   (1981)
'Educational Administration: Some Philosophical and Other Considerations'. *Journal of Educational Administration*. Vol. XIX. No. 2. Summer.

Wolcott, H. F.   (1977)
Teachers vs Technocrats: An Educational Innovation in an Anthropological Perspective. Eugene, Oregon: Center for Educational Policy and Management, University of Oregon.

Index

EDUCATIONAL MANAGEMENT SERIES
Edited by Cyril Poster